A Filmmaker's Handbook

How to Act Without Being an Ass

Indie Film Industry Tips

Writing Screenplays that Don't Suck

Proper Set Etiquette

Film School in One Book

A Newbie's Cheat Sheet

For

Filmmakers

How Beginners Can Break In

by

Brent Nautic Von Horn

A NEWBIE'S CHEAT SHEET FOR FILMMAKERS

Copyright © 2020 Brent N. Von Horn

Questions and comments regarding this work may be sent to the author at:

Nautic Publishing

Brent N. Von Horn

www.nauticproductions.com

Cover design by Nautic Productions © 2020 Brent N. Von Horn

ISBN: 978-1-7349239-6-4 (Paperback); 978-1-7349239-7-1 (eBook)

First Edition, 2020

10 9 8 7 6 5 4 3 2 1

To Succeed

in Filmmaking you must:

Know the Entertainment World

Understand yourself

Learn the job

and … Apply yourself to doing the job!

This book is organized accordingly. Parts 1 and 2 help you understand the Entertainment World, and yourself. These parts are short, but very important.

The details of filmmaking begin with Part 3, with a glossary of film industry jargon, and then detailed descriptions of the many varied jobs. Even if you feel sure you know what you are, and what you want to be, you'll be stronger in your field the more you understand the other jobs. Parts 4 and 5 are filled with the details of filmmaking – the meat and potatoes of this book.

After that, Part 6 discusses equipment, Part 7 helps with troubleshooting. and Part 8 has DIY tips for making your equipment, or buying cheap.

Just scan the following Table of Contents and you'll see there is a lot to consider. Filmmaking is not easy. You must apply yourself to being the best "You" that you can be, in whatever position you aspire. If you are not committed to working at it, then stop here.

If and when you are ready to succeed, read on:

In Shakespeare's *The Merry Wives Of Windsor*, one of his characters says "… the world's mine oyster, which I with sword will open." The world is your oyster! Open it. You have to use some force (your sword). Nothing worth doing comes easily.

Table of Contents

ARE YOU A NEWBIE?

Don't take offense or shy away from being labelled a "newbie" – everyone starts somewhere. There are many benefits to being new to any industry because you then don't have the bad habits of everyone else.

Be glad you are new. This is an industry where new blood, new ideas, new life is greatly desired. There is no greater melting pot than the Entertainment World. Come in, and bring everything that makes you the unique person you are.

But, at the same time, learn *quickly* how best to fit in!

There's no reason you can't succeed in the Entertainment World

The mere fact that you are reading this book and trying to improve your knowledge and abilities is proof that you are already much better than many of the people you will encounter in the Entertainment World, sad to say.

Whoever you are, you can do it. Just apply yourself. Woody Allen is supposed to have said, "80% of success is showing up," and I believe that is true. The rest would be having the right attitude when you do show up (10%) and then some knowledge of what you're doing (10%).

You need to resolve right here and now to get out there, apply yourself, show up, and learn. Start here.

Why read this book? I've put in my time – thousands and thousands of hours – from which you can benefit in minutes.

Are you looking for short cuts? Don't want to volunteer, or spend the time slogging in the trenches as I have? Well … I have good news, and bad. If you don't want to spend all that time, you can learn what you can from me. That's the good news. Why not start with reading this book? Since I have collected all of this information for you, you can benefit from this short cut. A "Cheat Sheet", as it's titled. Bad news: you still have to work hard and apply yourself.

Creative types are always busy, running around, spinning plates and frantically trying to not drop any, right? Does that sound like you? Read this book. Let me help you spin your plates.

Brent Nautic Von Horn
Tampa, Florida 2020

PART I: KNOW THE ENTERTAINMENT WORLD

Knowing proper behavior gets you accepted – and hired

What is "proper" in the Entertainment World? Acting according to established norms, within any group or society, shows that you belong there. Even when we are talking about the wild and artistic personalities that gravitate toward and tend to succeed in the Entertainment World, if you stand out as someone who doesn't know what's going in the Entertainment World, then you're not going to match the people already "in". No, you don't have to be like everyone else – in fact, it's best if you have a unique voice and stand out – but unique as in special, not ignorant.

People who have broken in already had to scramble to make it happen. This is not a world easily entered. Whether a top producer or a lowly production assistant, those people are not going to blindly trade on their friendships by recommending you, or sponsoring you, or even letting you near their contacts. It is frequently said about the Entertainment World that "It's not what you know, but who you know." Personal relationships are the true currency, more valuable by far than gold, rubies or diamonds. IF (and note, that is a "big if") you are able to meet someone and convince them to help you up, they will do so only if confident you're not going to embarrass them. Opportunity may knock, but you need to do your part. You need to show you know your stuff. You need to be able to assure any potential angel you won't embarrass them by being stupid or ignorant.

Form counts, too, not just style. In addition to fitting in and impressing people, by knowing what to do you are able to work safely and efficiently. Fiscal responsibility, in other words. The film business is … wait for it … a *business*. You may find some fun along the way, but no one's going to bet millions on you unless they're confident you'll do the right thing.

Knowing how to do the job right gets you hired, and rehired

Almost anyone can get hired, once. At least for a short time, until it becomes evident that you don't know what you're doing or how to act. There are, for just about any job in the Entertainment World, dozens of people standing in line, ready to step into your position the moment you're gone. Studios, production companies, producers, directors – they all know this. You need to constantly prove your value, or that revolving door will shove you right back outside.

If you want to get paid as a professional, you should look and act like a professional. You do want to be taken seriously at your job, don't you? Well, then do the research. Now, and every day you have left. Find out how to do the job, and don't stop there but continuously search for better and smarter ways. Reading this book is only a beginning; but it's a good beginning.

Sources of Information

So, you want in? You want to break into the Entertainment World. Be careful what you wish for. This business can be nasty. To put it bluntly, this business is not for ignorant morons.

There is a simple word for many of the newbies who want to get into show business: Bait. Unscrupulous producers, agents, managers, and all other sorts of con artists feed on innocents.

Don't be bait. Don't be ignorant. And try hard not to be a moron! The more you can learn about the Entertainment World, the less likely it is that anyone can take advantage of you, and correspondingly the more likely you are to succeed.

Learn everything you can, from every source available.

Film Schools

Director Quentin Tarantino is quoted as saying, "When people ask me if I went to film school, I tell them, 'No, I went to films'."

USC's film school tuition is $70,000/year. Just saying.

This book is all about learning what you can, as fast as you can, so that you can quickly get out there and make movies. Going to a film school is not necessary. There's no requirement. And once you graduate from a film school with a piece of paper (your diploma), that's what you have – a piece of paper that gets you nothing in and of itself. It would still be up to you yourself to prove that you can use what you know.

One of my favorite sites for soaking up invaluable free knowledge is www.nofilmschool.com. If you hadn't found it yet, you're welcome. But as the site's founder Ryan Koo says, No Film School is not *anti*-film school; the site's purpose is to make filmmaking information open to everyone, even people who don't have the ability to go to film school.

Go to film school if you want. You'll meet great people there and learn your trade fast. But with the growth of free information on the Internet, coupled with digital photography equipment becoming more available at cheaper prices, you can just start making films now, without investing your time and money in tuition.

IMDb ("Internet Movie Database")

Practically the single best thing you can do for yourself, whoever you are and whatever you want to become: get yourself an IMDb account. Go to www.imdb.com and sign up; it's free. You will be able to search any actor and any film, usually finding an amazing amount of information. For example, you can learn what a film's budget was, and how much revenue it brought in. Entire histories of well-known (and lesser-known) actors are available, thanks to this site which has quickly become a vital industry standard. It's hard, now, to take anyone seriously if they don't have an IMDb account.

Put yourself out there. Add to your profile, and make sure you are added onto the pages for film or television projects you work on. Some low budget (or no budget) projects advertise that they will "pay" for your work in the form of giving you an IMDb credit – but you often have to hound them, to make sure they do so, and make sure they get your name right.

Do you need the paid upgrade, the "IMDb Pro" account? I highly recommend upgrading to pro. By doing so, you have more control over what your profile looks like, and that can be an invaluable advantage for you, at any level. Fortunately, it doesn't cost that much.

Get in the habit of doing research on IMDb. I have the IMDb app installed on my smartphone, so I can literally look people up the moment I meet them. Time and time again, I'll be sitting in a meeting and someone across the table will refer to my IMDb page. Yes, it happens, a lot.

You need to learn, and keep learning. IMDb is a fantastic resource. Use it!

Internet Videos
We live in a glorious age of readily-available information! Use it to your advantage. At your fingertips, literally, are thousands of videos and websites where people have spent hundreds of thousands of hours of their time to provide you with how-to videos that you can watch, often for free. Go back in time and tell someone that one day so much information will be at our fingertips, and no one would ever believe you. But it's true.

My favorite YouTube sources for filmmaking tips, hints and wisdom are (in no particular order):

- No Film School
- D4Darious
- Film Riot
- Potato Jet
- CineChimp
- DSLR Video Shooter
- On Set Lighting
- FilmIsNow
- Film Jams
- StudioBinder
- Aputure
- Film Courage
- RocketJump

- Filmmaker IQ
- Indy Mogul
- In Love with the Process

The Film Business

Business = Money

Productions are expensive. Have you any idea how much money it costs to make a film, or even a single episode of a tv show? Search for yourself and you might be shocked at how high the numbers are. A single episode of *Game of Thrones* cost HBO up to $15 Million to produce! Granted, *Games of Thrones* is among the best television shows ever created, and I mention it as the most expensive example I know of, but even "typical" tv shows cost a Million dollars or more to make each episode.

For an idea of why productions cost as much as they do, just pay attention to the length of credits on even smaller, simpler shows. So many names! Imagine, every person making a living in the Entertainment World is getting … well, at least minimum wage. And, in the case of most production crew and cast, a lot more than minimum wage. If you see a hundred names on the credits of a feature film, and you figure say $35,000 for each person (on average) – that's $3,500,000 just in labor. Now, figure in a named star or two for another $10 Million, or maybe a couple A-Lister stars for another $70 Million. We haven't even begun to talk about the costs of equipment, transportation, catering, administration, permits, set dressing, costumes, props, editing, marketing, legal, insurance ….

Never lose sight of the fact that this is a business, and you are an asset in the business. Nothing more, nothing less. An asset, meaning that you are a valuable and helpful part of the production, worth more to the production company than what you cost them in salary, perks, risks or nuisance.

You are an asset, aren't you? As soon as you become a liability, you will be let go. The moment you aren't worth it, the production company will boot you out faster than you can say "Wait, I'll get better!" Get better, now, before they even think about axing you.

Budget

This being business, let's talk money.

Small projects, independent films, student films and the like are almost impossible to put into budget categories, since costs can vary wildly. Many people volunteer time, materials, equipment, locations and skills at this level. Realistically, a short film may cost you $6,000 to produce, which *might* breakdown approximately:

- 20% $1,200 pre-production (writing, planning)
- 50% $3,000 production (mainly food, transportation, locations)
- 30% $1,800 post-production. (editing, sound, music, festival fees)

Many short films are made for nothing at all, or practically nothing. My first short cost me about $30 in tomato juice and red food coloring for fake blood. But many short films are made for much more than $6,000. Two of my friends in film school (Loyola-Marymount in Los Angeles) each spent over $50,000 on their senior project films.

At the other extreme, consider the budget of a big $200 Million Hollywood blockbuster. That's a lot of money … and, of course, it takes a lot of people to make such a movie. *Monsters University*, for example, created 1,117 jobs; *The Hobbit: The Desolation of Smaug* created 1,153. Most of the big bucks go, as one would expect, to "above the line" positions, but even the names at the bottom of the credits are getting good pay, and it all adds up for the studio bean counters.

Here's how the cost of a typical blockbuster breaks down, looking at the example of 2004's *Spider-Man 2* which cost $200 Million to make:

- 10% $20M rights
- 5% $10M writers
- 7.5% $15M producers
- 5% $10M director
- 15% $30M cast ($17M Tobey Maguire + $7M Kirsten Dunst)
- 55% $110M production (including $65M visual effects)
- 2.5% $5M music

An average feature film costs about $30 Million to make. Here's a breakdown of the costs to make 2014's reboot of *Annie*, starring Cameron Diaz and Jamie Foxx, with a budget of $73 Million:

- 23% $17M Cast
- 11% $8M writers & rights
- 3.5% $2.5M producers
- 3.5% $2.5M director
- 47% $34M production (biggest pieces were location expenses ($4.5M) and transportation ($3.9M))
- 12% $9M post-production

You likely think of yourself as a creative person, an artist, even. Yes, good for you. But you also need to think in terms of the value you can bring to a project, because clearly – if there is any point to be gleaned from looking at budgets – movies are expensive to make. If you want people to hire you, you must convince them that you will be an asset, not a liability (i.e. worth more to them than you cost them).

Entertainment World

Read everything you can. Research everything. There is really no excuse in today's world of instant Internet access.

When I first went to Los Angeles, I couldn't afford a subscription to the *Variety* newspaper, but I bought it every day I could, even when it meant driving way out of my way to find a newsstand that carried it. *Variety* is THE source for insider film industry news. It was then, and still is. Oh, I hear you Millennials screaming that you can get free entertainment world news from multitudes of sites and apps on your cell phones. Yes, you can, but for in depth coverage of the soundbites you get for free, you still need *Variety*. Go to www.variety.com and subscribe if you don't want or can't get the paper version.

You'll find many opportunities to purchase classes on acting, directing, filmmaking, and what-have-you. For any given topic, it seems there are hundreds of people holding their hands out for your money, promising you the world if you only take their "Master Class" or whatever they call it. Don't do it! Well, maybe you should, because some of those classes are amazing … but my point here is simply this: Don't do it, until you first learn what you can for free. I find it stupendously amazing that there is so much free information on YouTube, just waiting for your fingertips to search. Do that!

Probably the best way to learn about the Entertainment World is to *actively* watch movies and tv. By this I mean, pay attention to how the show was put together. Look at shots, angles, lighting, good and bad acting, good and bad writing. Recognize the craft. Think about why you like what you like, and just as importantly why you hate what you hate.

Look for your niche. What interests you? How can you help others succeed? Talk with people about what *they* love to talk about, themselves. Listen to them. Find a common thread with something that resonates with you.

When you talk with industry people, you will at some point ask yourself, What is the difference between "Professionals" and "Independents"? Sheesh. Good question. There is no true certification or licensing process, so actors, filmmakers, directors, and so on can all self-identify. I am a writer because I say I am a writer! I'm an actor, I'm a director … because I say I am. Anyone can say these things. I can't tell you that you are *not* an actor, can I? Some people say the word "professional" can be used only after you've been paid for your services – okay, but paid how much? Likewise, some people say "independent" means not having had a certain amount of success, or getting a certain amount of money – but where are those lines? How do you track such things? Are we talking annual revenue, or lifetime earnings, gross or net, or what? Is professional good, and independent amateurish? Are you a professional if you use certain equipment brands? Better, says I, to just forget the whole thing. Don't even try to define professional or independent.

There is a much more meaningful distinction between the terms "Legit Theatre" and "Film". Films can be shown in theatres which also have stages for real life performances, and live stage performances can be recorded on film, so these terms overlap. But generally, legit theatre means the live performance by actors on stage, whereas film means the capturing of actors' images in a camera for later showing. In each medium, someone (producers) spends money to put together a show, for others (audiences) to pay for – but the cultures are totally different. Stage actors have a hard time going to a film set, and vice versa. Film crew are lost behind a stage. You need to learn the specific world you want to join.

In a small way, there is a 3rd world. Performing in corporate meetings is not the same as legit theatre, but not like film, either. Multi-media is common, with actors mixing live performance with pre-recorded work. If that world appeals to you, learn its foibles.

The trouble with teamwork is … finding the right team

Most newbie meetings are full of used kitty litter. Not to sound like a snob, but 99% of the people going to those entry-level meetings are not likely to succeed or move onto anything better. And the single largest reason for that is simply that they fail to push themselves to do anything!

99% of the people you meet in meetings are there to talk and not do anything else, regardless of what they say.

"Ah," you're thinking, "but there is the chance of meeting the other 1%!" Yes, and that's what you have to look for. That's why you need to push yourself to get out there, show up, listen, meet people, and learn new things. Go to meetings, even when you know you'll find 99% BS.

It's a Small World

Thanks to technology, today's world is small, and getting smaller constantly.

This is important to creative, sensitive people because … cameras are everywhere. Media outlets for disclosure of candid pictures and video exists everywhere. Everything gets posted. Nothing posted ever gets truly deleted. Whatever you do in public, you must assume will be documented forever. The lesson: Be nice to all, or live to regret your words like no generation before has ever had to worry about.

The "black balling" of the 1950's Communists scare is history … but I'm sorry to say the same thing happens still, today, through the pressures of social media. People may be "canceled" for the smallest slights. I'm also sorry to say that some of the pressure is, regrettably, a justified reaction to slimy behavior.

I'm not defending McCarthyism or any other system of black balling writers, actors, or anyone else. But … I'm also not saying that bad behavior should be swept under the rug. The #metoo movement of recent years has worked hard to bring to light certain patterns of abuse against women, and I agree wholeheartedly with calling foul on the hurtful behavior of rude, abusive, stupid, or even just ignorant persons.

"Good people" should work with "good people".

Always, please, take the high road. You may have to count to ten, swallow your bile now and then, but in the long run you will be much better off keeping any and all negative thoughts to yourself. Before you post or react to anything, stop to consider whether it is something you will want to see revived 10 years from now.

Put Yourself into the Entertainment Community

Be visible. Put your "brand" out in social media. Making Facebook and Instagram pages is free. Take advantage of those sites, plus whatever else becomes popular by the time this book reaches its readers.

There are "brand managers" you can hire – agents, personal managers, life coaches, etc., by any like name. Once you reach a high level, you will likely hire someone to take care of your image for you, and it can be a full-time job. I suspect, for example, that Robert Downey Jr. does not create his own Facebook posts, and there's nothing wrong with that; whoever does his posts has done a good job consistently presenting him to the world – and he can afford it. Meanwhile, until you hit it big, do it yourself.

One big rule: Be responsive. Check your email and voicemail regularly, and get back to people promptly. Don't ignore posts. Set up your pages such that they require your approval, and make sure you monitor regularly – at least daily. Respond to everything positively, with a comment or at least an emoji (thumbs up or smile). Don't approve negative posts – delete them.

The world moves fast, and it won't stop to wait for you. You need to jump on if you want to go for a ride.

Be Careful of Scams

Many of us first got into the Entertainment World as children in school plays, with a sense that the theatre and film worlds are magical, fantasy places where everyone is happy and the only bad people are the villains who always get their come-uppance in the third act. Well, sorry. Like anything and everything else in the world, the Entertainment World is full of PEOPLE, and that means all types. Even baddies.

Human trafficking is still a thing; it happens. Millions of people are trafficked every year. Put bluntly, the young human body is a commodity for which many people will pay dearly. There are people who snare girls, rape them, drug them, sell them; boys, too. This is especially true in the Entertainment World, because it's relatively easy for unscrupulous asshats to lure young newbies with enticing stories that they can be stars. You will see "casting" ads for distant places, and once they get on a bus, or in an airplane, they have little to no chance to escape. Some scams are semi-legit (where the victims at least get paid). It's gone on for years, stories as old as the bible, and probably will always be a risk.

Is this a warning to stay away from the Entertainment World? No. Have fun, be the light and magic in the world, and celebrate the light and magic in others. Channel all that is sweet, pure, good, wholesome. But for goodness sake! Do so with your eyes open. Pay attention to your surroundings. Don't become an easy victim. Don't be the next kid off the bus that falls into prostitution, drug addiction or human trafficking.

In Ronald Reagan's famous words, "Trust, but verify." Check up on people. We're all tied into social media, where help can be just a few posts away.

Some common scams:

- Modeling, acting classes, dance classes and pictures for children. Are they all scams? Of course not. Whether a school, teacher or program is a scam is probably determined most fairly by what expectations they express to the children, and the parents. If you hear "Oh my god, your kid could be a star! Just sign up, pay these fees, pay for these pictures, pay for these classes" … run. (By the way, these scams are usually aimed at parents. How do you say "No" to your child, after they've been told they can be the next Miley Cyrus?)

- Writers are common targets, too. "Script consultants", "Project Developers" and others with similarly vague titles promise, for a fee, to get the writer's scripts in front of producers.

- Headshots are another common scam, although perhaps "shoddy" is a better word than scam. Headshot photographs are much more than just a picture of one's head, but there are many photographers offering to shoot headshots who know nothing about industry standards and what casting directors need headshots to look like.

- With the advent of digital film files, and the ease with which they can be sent around the world, we've also seen the sad rise of scam film festivals. Most festivals charge an entry fee. Dozens of fake festivals have come to light recently, where festival organizers take the entry fees, but there is never any actual festival. Some fake festivals notify filmmakers that they've won, and then ask for a fee.

- Agents and managers can be scam artists, too. Don't sign up on long contracts! Always make sure you can back out, if and when the relationship is no longer making you happy.

There is never a "last chance opportunity", despite the hucksters' words. Take your time, evaluate opportunities carefully. Never jump quickly into anything. If it's legit, you won't need to blindly rush in.

Keep this is mind at all times: a true opportunity is one in which you are being considered for a job -- that's where they *pay* you. As soon as they ask you to pay for anything … run.

A final word about Entertainment Communities: Porn

If you want to do porn, fine. I'm not here to be a prude or pass judgment on your sexual openness.

But please do realize that porn is its own world. Once you do porn, you are likely closing doors to every other aspect of the Entertainment World.

Please proceed in life with your eyes wide open, at all times. Too many scams are aimed at getting young women (and men) into porn; young bodies are a commodity that people will pay to see. Be assured that you NEVER have to do anything you are uncomfortable doing, and anyone asking you to do so is likely someone you should run from.

Casting Couch

The term "casting couch" refers literally to the idea that a prospective actor (usually female) would be required first to have sex in the casting director's office, on the handy couch right there. But it refers more broadly to the concept that sex is traded for a role, however, wherever and upon whatever.

This has been going on forever.

In this, as in all things culturally, the pendulum of concern swings back and forth. For the last 20 years, relationships among co-workers in corporate settings have been discouraged, or even prohibited. As a corporate attorney, I've been involved in dozens of investigations into allegations of "sexual harassment" among employees, and I've presented training sessions for thousands of employees. I'm glad to say that, in what I've seen, most men understand. With the recent *#metoo* movement, and the fall of several Entertainment World giants who apparently were abusive monsters, things are very different now. Men I've spoken with recently are scared that even the smallest things can now be blown up and used against them.

But are things really different? Ultimately, it's impossible to know what's in another person's mind, and one person might be operating on a perfectly legitimate basis, while the other is secretly using sex to get what they want. I think it would be naïve to think that will ever not be the case.

So … my advice. If you are a casting director, director, producer, filmmaker, or anyone else able to influence the choice of casting, do NOT ever use the casting couch. Do not, in any way, directly or indirectly, require physical intimacies of any sort in exchange for being considered for a role. It's a bad idea, because: (1) it's nasty; (2) it may be illegal (depending on various factors); (3) it opens you up to the risk of blackmail; (4) it's very likely against the policies of anyone you work for – producers, production company, partners' operating agreement, money lenders, etc. -- or should be; (5) in today's cultural climate, you will likely end up looking really bad; (6) your significant other will hate you; and (7) you're totally pathetic, if you have to resort to getting sex in this manner. It's such a bad idea, that you should avoid even the perception of a casting couch. Don't date cast or crew, before or after casting.

However, if you are on the other side of the equation, and you are a functioning adult, then maybe. I still say it's nasty and pathetic, but these are only my own personal feelings. I understand why many people choose to trade what is (honestly) a simple biological function that you're probably doing with others, anyway, for something special that you really want.

But, in any event, the casting couch cannot be forced upon anyone. If you know or suspect something along those lines, please speak up to bring it to light and, hopefully, end it.

PART II: KNOW YOURSELF

"To thine own self, be true" says Polonius in *Hamlet*. Before you can decide what you want to do in life, first figure out who you are and make your decisions accordingly.

"The unexamined life is not worth living," said Socrates as he was on trial for his life (circa 399 B.C.E.). I don't go so far as to say your life is worthless if you don't do some introspection … but I am quite positive that you will make decisions that are bad *for you* if you don't.

You Yourself

Ask yourself, *why* do you want to be in the Entertainment World? Do some deep soul searching. This is not an easy path, despite the American urban legend of "being discovered" just sitting at a soda fountain, and instantly becoming a star. Every "overnight success" has a background story of hard work leading up to that night.

Why are you reading this book? What appealed to you, what is driving you, right now? Do you have a dream? No one can determine your life, but you. Don't follow anyone else's dream.

Meditate, take care of yourself, eat right, sleep right, think things through. Be a good person. Before you can hope for others to like you, you need to turn yourself into someone likeable. Honestly examine your faults and work at fixing them. (No one's perfect, and we all have faults.)

If you have a particular fear, you can either run from it, embrace it, or challenge it. Case in point, my fear of heights: I well recall that day in college when a theatre lighting instructor asked for volunteers to take lighting instruments up a tall A-frame ladder. No one wanted to go up that ladder! If you haven't seen an A-frame ladder used in larger theatres, picture two ladders propped together to form a triangle, each over 20' long, meeting at a point about 18' high. Going up from that center point is another ladder, another 20' or so straight up. The whole thing is mounted on a large, wheeled platform. The worse part, when one gets up on the straight ladder portion, it sways like a dandelion in wind. I raised my hand. I did it. I did it all year, and grew to love it. Sometimes, we have to push ourselves beyond our fears.

Perhaps your fear is one of speaking before groups? Me, too. I got over that (mostly) when I taught 8th grade science for a year in Watts, CA. You think you've faced tough audiences? Just do it, face your fears, challenge them, and you'll see they can't control you.

You should just as honestly recognize your strengths, and be prepared to constantly find new strengths in you. Tell yourself, You are a great person! But control your ego. Succeed without becoming a monster. Go for long-term success.

Attitude

Woody Allen said that life is 80% just showing up. If so, the rest is having the right attitude (and knowing your stuff, which we'll get into in Parts III and IV).

I can't say enough about the importance of presenting a good, positive attitude. Have fun. Smiles are contagious. No one wants to work with a downer; people pull away from frowns. Be positive. Always. Be the person on set with that "Can do!" jump-to-it always-up-for-the-challenge ready-when-you-are approach, no matter how difficult a challenge appears, or how negative others are.

Support others. (Not with money!) Give them props. Praise them. Encourage them. This is the surest and quickest way to turn negative people around and get them on your side – much more effective than telling them their attitude sucks.

Work ethic

"I'm a Midwest boy" was all I had to say to get a job, when I lived in Southern California; people pretty much accepted the idea that Midwesterners have good work ethics. Who am I to argue?

What about your own work ethics? Work hard. Commit to doing your best, at everything you do – or shut this book now. Make sure whatever you do today is the best that you can do today, and then try to do better tomorrow. There's no "easy" button. You learn tricks as you go along to make things easier, but you learn those tricks only through hard effort. Stop looking for formulas and other magic beans. If someone claims to have a formula for success, take a hard look at their own level of success, you know what I'm saying?

Be a decent human being

The biggest problem in the Entertainment industry is simply that a huge percentage of people are outright flakes. Everyone knows it, everyone hates it, everyone is soooo tired of dealing with it – even the flakes – but too many people just accept the situation. When a truly decent person pops up, Wow. It is incredibly refreshing to find someone *real*.

Be real. Say what you mean, mean what you say, and do what you say. Be honest, with everyone. Have integrity (that means doing the right thing, even when no one is watching!) and hold yourself to a higher standard than anyone around you.

One of my favorite bits of advice: Under Promise and Over Perform. You want people to want you around. They will want you if you are helpful. Worry less about what you want, and instead try to figure out what other people want – then try to help them get what they want. They will love you for it.

Be punctual. Don't make people wait on you. Recognize that every time you make someone wait, you are telling them that they don't matter, that you are more important. Maybe you don't mean to be saying that, but that is what they will perceive.

The Entertainment World is a small one, and people talk. People have long memories. Don't burn bridges by being a jerk.

A quick example of jerky behavior and my long memory: After running into a guy at a number of meetings, we decided to meet just the two of us to discuss teaming up on a sitcom idea I had. We agreed on a time and place. A couple days later, I arrived at the time and place. Since I was a few minutes early, I got a table, ordered a glass of cabernet, and spread out my written materials as I waited. 10 – 15 minutes past the appointed time, I start to squirm, and at 25 minutes past I called him, only to be told "Something came up." Oh! Like hell, it did. He probably forgot. If so, I wish he had just owned up to it. If he had said "Sorry, I spaced" I would have forgiven him; shit happens, right? But literally "something came up" means he found something *better* and didn't even bother to call me off. His response came across to me as a big middle finger. Since then, I've run into this same guy many times, and he's asked me again to get together. But, while I can and have worked with him on the sets of others, I will never hire him or team up with him on my own projects. Once burned, shame on you; twice burned, shame on me.

Be the kind of person you would want to hire. The person you would want to spend long hours working alongside. No one wants to hire a douchebag.

Stress

Projects cause stress. Film sets can dissolve into chaos. Relationships can die. Budgets get blown. Equipment breaks. People flake out. Everything takes longer than you expect. You're way behind on your shotlist. Locations prove wrong. Blocking is impossible. Actors haven't learned their lines. And so forth, on and on. It's easy to let it get to you. In fact, it's the rare person who can ride above all of this stress.

Having a clear mind, and being able to keep your head in the midst of chaos, is incredibly important. Prove yourself to be that kind of person, and others will want to work with you.

People appreciate a good "badass"

It isn't easy to take the high road and live by moral principles. It takes courage.

One of my filmmaker friends, Chuck Terzian, recently praised the producer of a film he worked on. He called her a "badass in all the good ways!" Then he went on to share his thoughts on why she was so wonderful to work with. Chuck says it comes down to hitting 2 rules, and 4 guiding principles.

First, the rules, two things that are a must-have:

- Be fair-minded – listen to all ideas, consider all
- Follow through – do what you say you'll do, with tenacity

And then four guiding principles:

- Be creative
- Be kind
- Be open
- Be authentic

Chuck urges us all to be this type of badass. He says, "It is most definitely noticed by those of us who are trying to embody those things ourselves. I love working with people like this and I seek out opportunities for them to work with me or others because I know how much magic these qualities bring to any project or relational dynamic. I love when others seek me out because of these qualities as well."

As someone who once sought out Chuck for these reasons, I highly concur. If only we all could be badass like this.

How to present your best "professional" self

Be professional, whatever that means in any given situation. Do we all just "know" what professional means? I suppose it's easier to say what it does not mean:

- Don't goof off
- Don't rough house
- Don't harass, intimidate, bully, or tell off color jokes
- Don't be noisy on set – of course not after "Quiet on set!" is called, but also before then, because the people who are working need to hear themselves think
- Don't talk politics, religion, or money
- Don't talk about drug or alcohol use – and don't use on set
- Don't smoke on set
- Don't talk on your cell phone in front of others; excuse yourself, to find a private area, or tell the party you will call them back
- Don't ignore people – not even to text others, or play video games on your phone, or even to read a book

This is all common-sense stuff, right? Man, I wish everyone thought so! A makeup artist I've worked with, who I think is superb at her craft, is sometimes not given the job for the simple reason that she talks way too much. You'd think she would realize the damage she does to her own prospects, right? But I don't think she does.

Be professional. You'll be on the right track if you simply pay attention to the mission. There are, on set, almost always one or more persons who are diligently working to get the film made, and at the same time there are others just goofing off, not paying attention, and often impeding the filming (whether they realize it or not). Pay attention, at all times. You can easily spot those that are working vs. those that are playing. Make sure you are helping, not impeding.

Use only professional email addresses. Avoid email addresses like partier@ steadydrinking.com, no matter how funny you think it is.

Be professional on your social media sites, and everywhere else you may represent yourself. Consider having separate sites, to keep your social activities apart from your career. You should keep in mind with every post that it may be shared with the entire world, and nothing ever truly disappears – make sure what you say to the world (in text or picture format) is exactly what you would say to your boss, your clients, your significant other, your parents, your kids, and the Judge, because they will all someday see it

Respond to emails and telephone calls as promptly as you can. Don't "play hard to get". Entertainment people are busy, and they will move on quickly to hire someone else if you fail to respond.

Present yourself in the best light possible, at all times. I mean this (1) literally, in that you need the best headshots; (2) figuratively, that you need a good resume, and you must make sure you're proud of your social media posts and anything else you put out to the world; and (3) associatively, by being involved only with good people whose work and ethics you admire.

Get clear, easy to read business cards that contain a minimum of information. Don't load them up with catchy slogans or anything else that distracts from your name, email, phone #, and what you do.

Example business card (one I used generally, for filmmaking, acting, photography, whatever, so there is nothing about what I do other than the film edge design):

Brent Nautic Von Horn

nauticproductions@yahoo.com
813.505.0435

Plain and simple, but in the film industry I never want to limit myself to one job!

Make sure you get cards with a blank reverse, in plain card stock with no glossy finish, so that you and others can write notes on the back. Sure, this is Old School advice, but it works.

When you've made it big
PLEASE be nice, even after you become a big wig! No one is above behaving like a decent human being. (Even you, Mr. Trump.)

Don't let fame and fortune go to your head, or you'll eventually lose fame, fortune, and your head!

Give credit to your crew and cast. Give credit to others, always, whenever you can. It costs you nothing. Crediting others actually (in an odd backwards way) makes people credit you even more. And come on, you know you didn't succeed without the help of just about every damn person around you!

Be humble.

Recognize your success was due, at least in some degree, to luck. No matter how good you are, your luck could have been different. Many people who haven't succeeded are just short of luck.

Be thankful for all of the support you've had, from even the smallest sources.

On Guard
Per Shakespearean wisdom, "To thine own self be true" (*Hamlet*).

Know yourself. Know your limits. Know your weaknesses, your triggers, and be on guard so things don't surprise you. You are the only one who can truly know the inner you, and it follows therefore you are the only one to control your actions.

Various movies (like *The Last Samurai*, for example) would have us believe that personal honor was the single most important thing in feudal Japanese life. I'd like to think the filmmakers got that right, and that honor is just as important, now. Not that I'm in favor of ritual suicide for lapses, but I wish we Americans placed more value on personal responsibility and honor.

Know yourself – not only the bad things, but your good points, too. Look up the book *Strengths Finder 2.0* by Tom Rath, which makes the case that too often we worry about our negatives, and would do better to focus on our positives. The book contains a test that helps you identify your top five strengths, and what those strengths mean. My own top five strengths, per such test, are Ideation, Empathy, Developer, Connectedness and Strategic … all of which dovetail nicely with filmmaking, thank you very much.

Substances

I'm trying not to preach in this book. My advice is offered in the spirit of constructive criticism, to enable us all to be powerfully effective filmmakers. You've probably met people, as I have, who tell you they are more creative, more free, even more intelligent, when under the influence of particular drugs or alcohol. There are examples of comedians who credit their on-stage mania to cocaine. Robin Williams is a good example of someone who was just as sharp witted and funny even after cleaning up, and I believe he would have been just as awesome if he had never used. You do not need mind-altering substances to be good.

I personally believe all drugs should be legalized, for reasons I won't go into here. But that said, there is a time and place for everything, and mind-altering substances do NOT belong on the set. It is not safe for anyone to be on set, if even only one person is under the influence – there are far too many risks.

Never use drugs or alcohol while working. And I mean "working" in the broadest sense. On set, for sure. But also at any other time and place when you are involved with Entertainment people. For instance, at an awards' show, or an industry party. You are WORKING every moment when you attend such events. You need to keep your head about you.

You may think you are able to act better under certain influences, but I'm sorry to tell you that you are mistaken. Every alcoholic sees themselves as the life of the party. They are (almost) always wrong. Having divorced an alcoholic wife, I know this well from firsthand experience.

Did Robin Williams snort cocaine before going on stage, early in his career? Have other performers benefitted from a "bit of something" to take off the edge of stage fright? Have famous authors found inspiration while using opium? OK, maybe, yes … but for every example of substances helping in a limited circumstance, we all know dozens or hundreds of examples otherwise. My own personal examples: I failed a chemistry test in college, after using caffeine pills to pull an all-nighter and then crashing during the exam; I also wrote what I thought was the best humanities paper ever, while smoking with a friend – and the next day had to rewrite completely, when I saw how horrible it was.

Working with people requires that you interact with their minds. Whatever you *think* about your own performance under drugs, you are not able to fully interact with others. Being high on set is a rude slap in the face to all your co-actors and crew, since they will not be able to count on you to behave / act / perform in a dependable way.

Simply put, avoid becoming your own worst enemy. There are already enough hurdles to leap.

Let other people fuck up

Does it sound like cold advice to allow others to F up? Look, face it, you are not your brother's keeper, you can't change the way other people act, it's not your problem. These are, as immortalized by the great Douglas Adams in his *Hitchhiker's Guide to the Galaxy* series, classic SEPs (Somebody Else's Problems). Don't make them your own.

I don't mean you shouldn't be helpful and offer advice to others. Of course, you should. Filmmaking requires teamwork! What I mean is, if they insist on doing crap, then you have to let them.

Honestly, people learn better by suffering the consequences of their actions.

Praise people, and they will praise you. Even if (maybe, especially if) they don't know they don't deserve praise.

Obviously, the opposite is just as true. If you complain about someone, they will likely complain defensively about you, even if you've done nothing wrong. We see this all day long, right? So why shouldn't it work both ways?

In the Entertainment World, you will see films that you can't stand, actors that you think are clueless, scripts with a stench that repulses you. Take the high road. Do NOT trash talk these productions! If and when you do talk trash, you better make sure you are talking privately with your bestie, who you can trust explicitly to never disclose your ugly words. I bet your Momma said to you what mine always said to me, "If you can't say anything nice, don't say anything at all."

"It's a small world, after all," goes the Disney song. The Entertainment World is sooooo small. You can count on anything you say negative getting out to the people you talk about. It always happens. Bad mouth a cast, a studio, or even just a piece of equipment, and you are almost guaranteed to regret it at some point in time later.

Resumés

HA! Maybe you thought in the creative world you wouldn't have to worry about businesslike things such as resumés? Correct! You should not worry about them. But you should make yourself one, and keep it updated with everything you do.

Best thing, do some research on Google to find the resumés of people doing what you hope to do. Search in the archived materials of industry-related Facebook groups. You'll find different resumés recommended, depending upon whether you want to act, or make films.

Frequently, newbies are uncertain what to put on their resumé. Easy answer: put everything on that in any way makes you look good. You've never done a film, but you took a class? List the class. You've never been the lead, but you were a background extra? List it! And then, as you do more in your pursuit of a career, drop off the weaker things as you get better things to add.

Your resumé should not exceed 1 page. If you've done 155 films, like my friend David Vogel, and they can't all be listed on 1 page, then don't list them all; list only the most recent, the ones you feel show you off the best, or the ones you most want people to ask you about.

Resumés in the Entertainment World are fairly straight forward, and a certain format has become accepted as the standard for actors. It can be and is used generally by all.

Industry resumé format:

NAME

AEA, SAG-AFTRA, SAG-e (if non-union, then delete this line; do not write "non-union")

your website (if you have one)

ph. # (call / text) • email

FILM

Title	Lead	Director / Studio
Title	Supporting	Director / Studio

TV / NEW MEDIA

Title	Recurring	Producer / Network
Title	Guest Star	Producer / Network
Title	Series Regular	Producer / (dir. Joe Famous)

THEATER

Famous Play Title	Character Name	Director / Theater

TRAINING

Class	Acting Teacher	School or Studio

SPECIAL SKILLS

Your special skills go here, anything and everything that you feel might be marketable to a Casting Director. For example, horseback riding, scuba diving, ballroom dancing.

If you're interested more in theatre than film, then put the THEATRE section on top.

Can you be flexible? Sure. We are all "creatives" and creativity is recognized and rewarded, usually. Add your own touches to your resume. Just know when you do that the further you get away from the above sample format, the less professional and seasoned you will appear.

Print your resumé on 8x10 paper, so you can staple it to the back of your headshot. (Amazon has the paper, for about $10 / 100 sheets.)

Your "Other Job"

Something we all have to face: newbies can't make a living in the Entertainment World. You may have dreams of being instantly discovered. I doubt that ever happened to anyone, despite certain myths. Every overnight success story is the product of a long, tortuous, tedious path to get there.

So, how do you make a living in the meantime?

And more importantly, how do you keep your dream alive, while also working to pay bills? Once you start the rat race, it's damn hard to lift your head up for air.

Answer 1: Don't give up. Don't let go of your dream, ever. That said, yes, you should approach your dream however you can, from sensible and reasonable perspectives. If your dream is to get an Oscar, you can't realistically expect to jump right up onto the Academy stage – you have to start somewhere small and work your way up. Your dream needs to be fed. Give it what it needs to grow big and strong.

Answer 2: The secret of life is Balance. Find balance in everything you do. If your dream is to act, then pursue it, and pursue it with gusto … but also pursue other dreams and desires. You are not a one-dimensional dot, or even a two-dimensional plane. As Shrek says, you have layers. Many layers. As much as you love one dream, if you are starving the other sides of your being you will not be happy.

Answer 3: Get a J O B. That's read as the letters "J" "O" and "B", to emphasize the difference between a job and a career. Getting into a career is more akin to following your dream; it's making money at what you want to do for the rest of your life. My daughter wants to be medical doctor. She's well on her way, having completed her undergraduate pre-med degree and now setting her sights on med schools. Along the way she has had employment opportunities that fit into her plan (like scribing for hospital doctors) and those that didn't (like bartending). The jobs that fit her desired overall career path were important to her, and she's been careful to make and keep connections with people she's met. The other times she found employment were just J O B's that she could start and stop whenever, because they were not important.

You want to make it, somehow, in the Entertainment World. That is one of your dreams, or you wouldn't have read this far. So, as you work hard at bettering yourself and moving up into your dream, you need to find ways to live. You need a J O B.

Typically, newbies work in service industry jobs. Those jobs have high turnover rates and it's easy to jump into a new spot. Jobs like:

- Retail store sales. Simple skills are picked up easily, like running a cash register or stocking shelves.
- Food server. Waiting tables or pouring coffee is easy and restaurants are everywhere.
- Food cooker. Not as easy, but still simple enough to learn, and always in demand.

- Office jobs. Basic computer skills (Word, Excel, and PowerPoint) are all you need.

There are some things that make a day job cool for those wanting to get into the industry. First, look for jobs that allow you flexibility to make an audition, or take a few days off to shoot a film. Your J O B may not be so flexible, in which case you will have to quit and find another J O B each time you pursue your dream. You may be able to find a J O B that begins early and gets you out with much of your day available. For instance, a coffee shop's morning shift from 4am to Noon. That way you can hit afternoon auditions without quitting. Or you may find that you can take on a J O B such as night watchman or toll-road attendant, and spend a great amount of time on the job actually writing your screenplay, learning lines, or reading this book.

Second, just as my daughter has found jobs that feed into her chosen career path, you can also get J O B's that help with your dream. I don't mean work the receptionist desk at Sony Pictures, but instead look for ways to build the elements you need to succeed. You want to act? Waiting tables is acting – damn right it is! You walk up to a table and you have about 2 seconds to make a good impression, and earn a good tip. Every table is a different performance. You must think on your feet and adapt quickly, while at the same time taking care of the logistics of the scene (i.e. getting food and drink). This is truly no different than being in front of a camera or on stage.

Or, if you're a writer, look for J O B's that help you understand the human condition, that help you see the stories all around us. Social workers see humanity at its foulest, providing unlimited fodder for scripts.

Whatever your dream, figure out what elements can make you stronger, and find a J O B that helps you build those elements. Helping people find the right shirt allows you to work on your people skills. Balancing accounts helps you get ready to budget your production.

Answer 4: Make money as you go. If you keep learning, keep pursuing your dream, keep making yourself better, there will come a time when you are still a newbie but not at the rank bottom clueless level. You will start to pick up real skills. Perhaps your acting improves, your writing becomes more polished, and/or your technical filming knowledge makes you more valuable on set. Recognize your value!

You may be able to start making a little money in the Entertainment World, while still keeping that J O B. It's rare that a person can just cold-turkey move from one to the other. You are more likely to transition.

For instance, if you are an actor, sign up with a commercial agent and start getting a gig now and then. Chump change, to begin. But it's money. And as you go, you can hope to make more.

As you learn how, you can help others. Camera work. Sound. PA. Directing. Editing. Creating trailers and promo pieces. Makeup. Effects. Freelance production jobs can bring in some cash. After creating films and running sound and camera myself, I found that others were willing to hire me for their productions. To begin with, I helped others for free. I volunteered my time. I even drove great distances to do so, if I thought there was a chance I could learn something. Then after a while, I charged $50/day and then $100. Still chump change, and the hours were long so I rarely even hit minimum wage, but this is how you start to make a name for yourself and work your way up to something that actually pays a living wage.

Know your value

Speaking of learning your craft and the amount you can charge for your services, let me stress that you do so.

One of the mistakes made by me and pretty much every other newbie I've known is the failure to recognize our value and charge accordingly. Sure, when you're just getting your feet wet it makes sense to give away your time, because in exchange you're getting an education. You're learning as you go. But after a project or two, you have learned enough to be of value. Giving freebies after that does nothing to help you.

If you feel you must give something away, to make a connection or get into a certain position or gig, do it … but trade that for something clear and meaningful. Perhaps you give a discounted rate, instead of free, and if you do so be sure to let them know that you have given them a benefit. Perhaps you trade to get others to work free on your projects. Perhaps it's connections you pay for, an introduction, a good word.

Beware Success

When you make it big, don't go immediately to the Lambo dealership. Be smart.

Keep in mind that this is an industry where you will be unemployed frequently. Regularly. At the end of every project, you're unemployed and sometimes you will have large gaps between projects. Don't celebrate success by spending so much that you jeopardize your ability to weather the down times.

You've heard John Travolta's story? Supposedly, when he first hit it big he got some advice from old "blue blood" families on how to build and maintain wealth. The advice was simply, "Don't spend the principal. Live on interest." Travolta is said to have continued sleeping on his friend's couch long after he had decent pay checks coming in, and didn't spend ANY of his pay, but instead invested it, and learned to live on the interest. He supposedly still has every penny from every film he's ever been in! Of course, once you've made millions it's easier to live on interest, but you can believe it took a huge amount of will power for him to make it that far, without giving in to the temptation to buy stuff.

Start With Low Expectations

Only a few top stars make a real living from film, and something like 98% of SAG-AFTRA members do not. Directors, even good ones, may get a nice penny from a film, but rarely enough to make a living, especially when the next project may be months or years away. Don't expect to become wealthy any time soon.

This industry rewards creation. Creating a project and steering to success leads to big returns. The many people (1,000's) hired along the way by the production will make money, but crew and cast struggle to make a living. Get good, and you can make a decent living. Then become or join in with the top-level creators. Writers, producers, and directors – people "above the line" who can put a project together and earn a percentage cut.

PART III: KNOW THE INDUSTRY JOBS

You must know what you're doing

The first two parts of this book lay the framework, stressing how important it is for you to really know the Entertainment World and yourself. The answers are only hinted at, because ultimately you have to go out and learn the business, just as you must discover yourself. Read and study what you can, and then get out there and learn by doing.

In this Part III, let's start examining the real reason you got this book – real industry knowledge. Watch the credits at the end of any show or movie, and other than the main cast and some top positions (like "director"), the eyes of most people glaze over quickly as hundreds of names and weird titles scroll by. Gaffer? Key Grip? Colorists? Foley Artists? 2nd Unit? What the hell are all these things?

You may already be working in the industry, or perhaps you are brand new, or looking to switch from one division to another; either way, understanding the industry lingo and job descriptions is crucial to being able to jump in and work.

And don't worry. The next section (Part IV – Know How To Do Your Thing) expands further, going deeper into details on techniques and equipment, and how the jobs are done.

They say, "The devil is in the details." How true. You might go to film school, or jump into making films, or get on the stage, or rent film gear, or write screenplays, or … maybe your "big break" will come as you wait tables on that influential producer who just happens to be looking for someone just like you. Opportunity does knock. But whatever doors you manage to open and walk through, when you get inside you better be able to do what it is that you're expected to do, no matter how difficult, how complex, or how detailed.

The smarter you are about it, the better your chances of success.

Lingo

Fans of John Malkovich in 1988's *Dangerous Liaisons* will remember that delicious moment when he says to a very young Uma Thurman, "Now, I think we might begin with one or two Latin terms."

Secret Language

So, imagine this. You've made a number of short films, which have garnered awards and praise. You feel pretty good about your filmmaking abilities, and yet remind yourself to be humble, too. Now, at long last, you're part of a major production, a true Hollywood blockbuster, with A-Lister actors and a two-hundred-million-dollar budget. You've arrived for your first day on set, and the director of photography says to you, "Get a grip and Hollywood a flag on the key. You might need to Texas an apple box."

Huh?

It's not Latin, but filmmaking jargon can be like a foreign language.

When you are on a set, not knowing the slang will mark you as a rank newbie. Embarrassment is the least of your troubles. You could slow the production, waste money, put lives in danger, and get fired.

To complicate matters for you, not all film people talk like this, and jargon varies in different places. You won't hear much of it on the sets of small indie films, or student films, not until you get to sets staffed by full-time roadies. Also, like all slang, jargon changes with time and is continuously evolving. So learn this stuff, but be prepared to find different uses out there. Keep your ears open.

There are some things which you are more likely to hear, like "he's 10-1" (meaning he went to the bathroom). Other jargon, like an Abby Singer, is rarely heard. I've gathered here in the next several pages the most useful (and fun) idioms to know:

- 10-1: leaving the set to go to the bathroom
- 20: your location
- 86 That: get rid of it (also, Strike)
- 100: when an actor has been through everything (HMU / wardrobe / any other check) and is ready for filming
- Abby Singer / Abby Shot: the 2nd to last shot of the day; calling out Abby Singer lets the crew know to start packing up and cleaning (see Martini Shot)
- Above the line: that part of the budget associated with major creative talent, including stars, director, producer(s), writer(s)
- ADR: Automated Dialogue Replacement (aka Additional Dialogue Recording), i.e. re-recording dialogue when the initial dialogue was bad for some reason
- Alan Smithee film: the pseudonym used by directors who don't want their name on a film, usually because it's that bad
- A-List or A Level: the top actors (usually getting paid millions)
- Ambient Light: the light that is naturally in your scene, without any discernible source
- Andy Gump: portable toilet

- Apple box: a box, usually wooden, for standing on or placing equipment on. It's 20" x 12" wide and 8" tall. A "Half Apple Box" is 4" high, and a "Quarter Apple Box" is 2" high. A 1" high box is called a "pancake".
- Atmosphere / Atmos: BG
- Autopilot: an actor Invited to go to the set when the actor is ready (for example, after the actor is done in HMU)
- Baby: small tripod
- Baby Pin: a 5/8" metal rod for attaching lights and other equipment
- Baby Plate: metal plate with a baby pin
- Barn Doors: black metal folding flaps on the sides of a light or camera that can be folded in or out, blocking light
- BG (Background): everything visible in frame behind the main action, usually blurred to some degree
- Background: 2nd meaning, the extras who populate the rear of the scene
- Barney: blanket placed over the camera to reduce the noise coming from the camera
- Beaver Board: a baby pin plate (baby plate) screwed onto a pancake apple box
- Below the line: budget production expenses that are not above the line, including costs of materials, music rights, marketing, publicity
- Best Boy: any technical assistant, apprentice or aide for the gaffer or grip, male or female
- Blimp: a blimp-shaped case covering a microphone, used to minimize noise from air currents as the microphone is moved around (and covered with a Dead Cat if windy)
- Blocking (a shot): running through a scene prior to filming, to determine the placement and movement of actors, cameras, lights and crew
- Bogey: a person, vehicle, animal, etc. invading into the set, and especially into the camera frame
- Bokeh: (pronounced both bo-ka and bo-kay, depending upon who you ask) this is the blurring of a background behind a sharply in focus subject
- Boom: a counter-balance pole used to hold a camera, mic or light
- Boom: camera movement, raising or lowering the camera (also Jib)
- Bounce: light that has been reflected (bounced) into a scene
- Break a Leg: means "good luck with your performance" though the origin is unknown. Possibilities: (1) ancient Greeks stomped their feet instead of clapping, so a really good show was one that hurt your leg stomping; (2) the edge of a defined stage area is the "leg" or "leg line", and performers were only paid if they crossed that line; (3) bowing is also breaking a leg, and an actor only gets to bow in curtain calls; (4) understudies wish the principal actors to get hurt, so they can go on; (5) saying "good luck" tempts bad luck, so instead one wishes evil; or maybe just because (6) you are in the "cast".

- <u>B-Roll</u>: footage of locations, background, scenery, extras, etc. that does not include shots of the principal cast
- <u>Brick Box</u>: storage area (and likely recharging area) for walkie talkie bricks (batteries)
- <u>Brooklyn Reflector</u>: foam board with tin foil glued to one side, for a cheap light reflector
- <u>BTS</u>: Behind the Scenes, usually referring to photographs or video taken on the set other than as part of the production's main show footage
- <u>Butt Plug</u>: Junior to Baby Pin Adapter
- <u>C-47</u>: a clothespin, which makes a very handy clamp for gels and other light items (I've heard two possible origins (1) supposedly grips had to come up with the name when studio accountants rejected their request to pay for clothespins; and (2) the shape of a clothespin looks somewhat like a military plane by that name, I guess if you squint hard enough)
- <u>C Stand</u>: aka Century Stand – a 3-legged telescoping stand with distinctive "turtle base" legs, usually steel or aluminum, used typically for holding lights, booms, and reflectors. (Developed originally to hold 100" square reflectors which were known as "Centuries", hence the name.)
- <u>Call Sheet</u>: a notice put out to all who need to show up on set, with names, times and locations
- <u>Cans</u>: headphones
- <u>Catchlight</u>: reflection(s) of light in a person's eye
- <u>CGI</u>: computer generated imagery
- <u>Cheat It</u>: when an object or person is temporarily moved out of place, in order to get a shot (without revealing such movement in the footage); also, when separate things, people or places are made to look as if they were together, when they weren't
- <u>Choker</u>: ECU, usually just on the actor's eyes
- <u>Clapper</u>: the slate board or clapboard, for "slating" "marking" or "clapping" a scene at the beginning of a take, to identify the take; also, the person doing the slating
- <u>Clipping</u>: (1) the top of a sound wave that exceeds the limits of the recorder and therefore does not get recorded – sounds horrible! (2) speaking into a walkie before pressing the broadcast button
- <u>Cold Brick</u>: depleted battery (usually walkie talkie battery)
- <u>Commando Cloth</u>: Duvetyne
- <u>Combo Stand</u>: a C Stand with a light stand (tripod) base, usually
- <u>Condor</u>: aka Cherry Picker, a crane meant to lift people in a basket
- <u>Continuity</u>: the process of attempting to assure that shots filmed out of sequence match well, for example that an actor is wearing the same shirt
- <u>Copy</u>: "I understand"

- Courtesy: a blanket, flag or other item that protects something or someone from intense light
- Covered Wagon: a soft-light bar, covered in chicken wire to support a diffusion cover
- Cowboy: a camera shot of an actor from the waist up, as if riding a horse (but not showing the horse, of course)
- Craft Services: food table / catering / snacks and the people in charge of such
- Crafty: the workers in craft services
- Crane: a counter-balance arm (like a boom or jib, but beefier) used to lift cameras for aerial shots, anywhere from 8 to 200 feet up; the cameras are usually remote-controlled, though some larger cranes are manned
- Crane Shot: a camera shot taken from a crane; frequently replaced now with drone shots
- Crew: everyone other than performers (cast)
- Crew Up: the hiring of the crew
- Crossing : said as a courtesy before walking in front of the camera
- CTO and CTB: Color Temperature Orange (3200K tungsten) and Color Temperature Blue (5600K daylight).
- Cutter: a small Scrim, used to block light (it "cuts into" the light)
- Day Playing / Day Player: working on a set for a day (or two); applies to both cast and crew
- DCP: Digital Cinema Package -- the collection of computer files (visual, audio and data) formatted to enable theaters around the world to show a film on their digital projectors
- Dead Cat : the fuzzy thing on the end of a microphone, meant to stop (or diminish) the sound of wind
- Dolly: platform on wheels, usually for a camera
- Dolly: camera movement, moving the camera toward or away from the action
- Dolly shot: a moving shot, taken from a camera mounted on a moving platform
- Dolly Track: the rail or pipe that the wheels of the dolly ride upon
- Donut: a soft donut-shaped fabric connection between lens and matte box
- Double: the person who temporarily takes the place of a leading actor, for a dangerous or difficult stunt, or for tedious activities such as preparation of the shot for focus and lighting, or for body shots (nude scenes, and close ups of hands, feet, etc.)
- Double System: set up where sound is recorded separately from the camera (see Single System)
- Dub (or Dubbing): the act of adding a new replacement soundtrack; often referring to replacing dialogue
- Dunning: the process of adding studio-shot foreground action to background action shot elsewhere

- Duvetyne: aka Commando Cloth: thick black cloth used to black out light
- Dynamic Range: the range of lighting situations where a camera can capture both over and under exposed subjects in the same shot (i.e. without changing settings)
- ECU: extreme close up
- Ensemble: a large cast with no true leading roles
- Ergorig: a body brace worn by a cameraman to help alleviate the stress of carrying a camera
- Establishing Shot: long or wide shot at the beginning of a scene, to make the location clear
- Exposure Bucks: jokingly, what you get paid when you volunteer for free
- Extras: actors who have no lines and are generally in the background; Featured Extras are extras who are singled out for a close up, or particular action, or even a short line or two of dialogue.
- Eyebrow: the top shutter on a matte box
- Filmlock: the point at which the takes have been selected and pieced together for the final film
- First Team: actors with speaking lines, and their stunt players (see Second Team)
- Fix it in Post: fix it during post-production, in the editing process. Often said in jest, as the best practice is always to do it right in the first place.
- Flags: Barn Doors. Also, Scrims / Cutters used to block some or all light
- Floppy: a flag with one or more sides loose (i.e. not stretched in a frame)
- Floppy Cutter: a cutter with an additional hanging piece of fabric
- Flying In/Out: bringing something into the set, or taking it out of the set
- Flyswatter: a large, framed fabric diffuser held aloft on a Condor
- Focus Pull: changing focus during a take
- Foley (Foley Artist): adding incidental sounds (such as footsteps, raindrops, the turn of a doorknob) in post (named after Jack D. Foley, 1967 American sound technician)
- Football: the accordion file containing all paperwork for the day, passed off from the AD department at the end of shooting to Transpo, who takes it to the office
- Frame: everything visible to the camera
- Frame Up: getting to that point in a take where you know what the frame is (i.e. what is visible in that take)
- FX: Effects, sometimes delineated as SFX (sound effects) or VFX (visual effects) – and sometimes people use SFX meaning special effects
- G & E: gaffers and electricians
- Gaffer: the chief or head electrician, responsible for the design and execution of the lighting plan
- Gag: a double Knuckle (Grip Head)

- <u>Gel</u>: colored plastic film, used to change the color of light leaving a lighting instrument or entering a camera lens; most common are CTO (to make a cool light warmer) and CTB (to make a warm light cooler)
- <u>Generals</u>: the meetings you *hope* your agent can get you into, industry networking meetings
- <u>Giraffe</u>: a mechanical boom mic
- <u>GOBO</u>: Grip Head
- <u>Golden Hour</u>: the hour or so right before sunset, when the sky colors are beautiful and the lighting is perfect for the look many cinematographers love
- <u>Greens Dept.</u>: people on set responsible for placing foliage and other landscaping pieces, like making fake rocks
- <u>Grip</u>: crew member responsible for setting up dolly track and camera cranes, moving props and equipment, etc.
- <u>Grip Arm</u>: a Grip Head with 5/8" straight rod extending from the C Stand
- <u>Grip Head</u>: aka Knuckle or GOBO, this is the joint by which reflectors, lights, or anything else can be held by a C Stand
- <u>Guerrilla film</u>: low-budget non-union film shot without seeking location permits, often with a minimal cast and crew
- <u>Gun Mic</u>: shotgun mic, typically on a boom
- <u>Hand Pats</u>: sounds, usually added in post by Foley, of such things as a hand patting someone's back, but also broadly meaning all such contact sounds, like picking up a coffee cup
- <u>Haze</u>: smoke or fog, often added (even indoors) for a soft lighting effect
- <u>Head Room</u>: capacity above the sound level selected on a recorder, for recording of a sudden outburst before Clipping
- <u>High Pass / Low Pass Mic Filter</u>: a high pass option on your mic reduces the level of low (bass) frequencies. Think of it as allowing high (treble) frequencies to pass. Conversely, a low pass will filter out high frequencies.
- <u>Hip-pocketed</u>: represented by an agent without signing a contract with that agent; an unofficial arrangement
- <u>Hitting a mark</u>: actor's term for getting to the correct place on time, often marked on set with gaffer's tape or with a weighted "T marker"
- <u>HMU</u>: hair and make-up
- <u>Holding</u>: where actors wait to be called to set
- <u>Hollywood it</u>: hold something in place by hand (rather than clamping it to a stand)
- <u>Honey wagon</u>: portable toilet
- <u>Hoofer</u>: dancer
- <u>Hot Bricks</u>: fresh batteries for walkie talkies (usually carried by PA's)
- <u>Hot Set</u> : a set ready for filming (in other words, this means do not touch or move anything!)
- <u>IMDb</u>: Internet Movie Database, found at www.imdb.com

- IMDb Rating: an actor's rating on IMDb
- In the Can: footage
- Inviting / Invite to Set: the set is ready for the named actors (see Self-Motivated)
- Jib or Jib Arm: a boom-like arm which raises and lowers the camera while keeping the angle of the camera fixed on target – often counter-weighted (essentially, a small Crane)
- Jib: camera movement, raising or lowering the camera (also Boom)
- Juicer: electrician
- Junior to Baby Pin Adapter: a pin which fits into the Turtle base of a C Stand, to mount a light very low (aka Butt Plug)
- Key Light: the main or primary light on a subject
- Keying: accidently pressing the broadcast button on a walkie
- Knuckle: Grip Head
- Last Looks: notice to HMU / Wardrobe to check / touch up an actor right before filming
- Lavalier (or Lav): a small mic, usually clipped to an actor's lapel or otherwise hidden in clothing (aka Wire)
- Legs: legs of a tripod
- Library Shot: stock footage, usually unimaginative or commonplace
- Lock It Up (or Lock Up): just about ready to shoot, so stop people from entering into the filming area and make sure everything is quiet
- Logline: a short, introductory summary of a film; a film's premise
- Long Shot: a shot taken from far away, often using a wide angle lens, so the subject appears small in the frame
- LUT: Look Up Table; a series of edit selections that can be packaged together, and marketed, so that one may apply a certain "look" to video in editing
- M&E: Music & Effects soundtrack (in other words, all sounds except for dialogue, which is on its own track)
- Martini Shot: the final shot for the day – a heads up for the crew, so they can start packing -- after the Martini, it's a Wrap
- Mask: covering or blocking a portion of the frame
- Master Shot: a continuous shot showing the entire scene
- Match Cut: a transition between scenes that focuses on the same or similar item
- McGuffin: the object, person or place being sought (obsessively, urgently) by a character
- Medium Shot: a shot from medium distance, which roughly speaking generally means a shot of the actors from the waist up (or knees)
- Meet Cute: the scene where two characters who will later get together first meet
- Method Acting: a style of acting taught by Stanislavsky (early 1900s) and then by Strasberg (1899-1982), where the actor gives realistic performances based on personal experience

- M.O.S.: shots without audio
- Moppet: child or pre-teen actor
- Online Editing: after picture lock, the editor can send the film out to others for refinement, for example for addition of the musical score, or to a sound editor for ADR
- Opal: a white or cream colored Scrim
- OTS (Over the Shoulder): a shot focused on one actor, from the perspective of just behind and adjacent to another actor, showing a minimal portion of the 2nd actor
- PA (Production Assistant): assistants helping with almost every aspect of filming on set
- P.A.: a personal appearance, often contractually required of lead actors
- Pan: camera movement, aiming the lens left or right (also, "pan" is what most amateurs say when the want the camera to move in any old direction – but see Boom, Dolly, Jib, Roll, Tilt and Truck)
- Parfocal: a lens that can be zoomed in and out while keeping its focus
- Park (Channel): the channel a production selects that everyone with a walkie talkie should stay on, by default (as in "Park on 12")
- Pick Ups: shots taken after the main shooting is wrapped, usually shots of close up items, background, or extras; also applies to re-shoots or additional shots determined to be necessary during editing
- Picture Lock: the stage of editing where the order and choice of scene takes is finalized and approved. Stage just prior to online editing.
- Pin Mic: a lavalier mic
- Planted: an item, such as a mic or light, hidden on set
- Plosive: the popping audio sound from words beginning with "P" "B" and sometimes "C" and "G"
- Points / Points coming through: something sharp (i.e. pointy), big, awkward and/or dangerous being carried through
- Pop: drawing the eye, as in a subject that pops out of the frame
- POV: point of view
- Practical: a light source visible in the frame, such as a floor lamp or candle
- Prebiz: pre-production planning
- Preditor: a person who is an all-in-one filmmaker, able to produce, shoot and edit.
- Pull Pull: a meet cute, where both characters are pulled to each other (love at first sight)
- Pulling Focus: changing the focus of the lens during a shot
- Pumpkin: counterweight which clamps to an arm or leg of a C Stand
- Push Push: a meet cute where the characters begin as adversaries
- Push Pull: a meet cute where only one character is hooked at the beginning, and the other is turned off
- Q Rating: an ad research rating of how easily a celebrity is recognized

- Rack Focusing: technique that blurs the frame from one focus point to another, used to draw attention from one item to another
- Reaction Shot: a quick shot that records an actor's reaction
- Red Eye: aka Wig-wag
- Reel: a short video (2-5 minutes, generally) showing a collection of an actor's or director's (or other person's) best work
- Reflector: any surface which bounces light back toward the subject
- Rhubarb: background conversation (usually mute or muttered) by extras (who can literally mouth "rhubarb" quietly for a convincing look)
- Riding the Levels: a sound engineer adjusting the recording levels up and down for varying sound volumes during a take, for example to record the sound of a quiet argument that becomes a loud fight
- Rig: the camera in a cage, and all equipment mounted to it
- Roll: camera movement, laying the camera over to one side or the other
- Room Tone: audio recording of the set with no action (i.e. all actors and crew holding absolutely still and quiet), used to record background noise
- Run and Gun: filming with little or nothing more than a camera (common in documentary-style filmmaking)
- Scratch Dialogue: dialogue recorded just to hold place, for example when a grip reads the lines of an off-screen character
- Scratch Recording / aka Sync Recording: the sound recorded by the camera, used mostly to help the editor sync to the sound recorded by outside recorders
- Screen Test: a filmed audition
- Screening: the showing of a film
- Scrim: fabric or other material held within a wire frame which is used to block some or all light
- Second Team: Stand Ins
- Self-Motivated: actor leaving Holding to go to set, before being Invited to do so
- Sides: the page(s) of the script being shot that day
- Single System: recording both visual and sound on a camera
- Slate / Slating: The clapper board, and the act of marking each take
- Slider: a shot where the camera moves perpendicular to the action; also, the equipment used for such take, often rail(s) with a camera dolly
- Snipe: any footage shown before a film, other than trailers (for example, the turn-off-your-cellphone bit)
- Soft Sticks: called for when the slating is to be done quietly
- Special Effects (SFX): effects done on set (contrast with visual effects)
- Spotting Session: meeting with Director and the Music Supervisor, during which the Director points out where in the film s/he wants music, and why.
- Sprinter: a person or vehicle used to run for things

- <u>Squib</u>: small explosive effects package, like the fake blood that simulates a bullet strike
- <u>Stand Ins / SI</u>: people who stand in for key actors, as camera and lighting set up (aka Second Team)
- <u>Steppage</u>: when 2 people talk at the same time on the same walkie channel
- <u>Stepping on/off</u>: actor coming onto or leaving the set
- <u>Sticks</u>: tripod
- <u>Stinger</u>: extension cord
- <u>Storyboard</u>: a sequential series of drawings, photographs or computer graphics used to indicate the desired shots
- <u>Strike (or 86)</u>: remove from set
- <u>Striking</u> called out by Gaffers before turning on (or off) bright lights
- <u>Swing Gang</u>: workers who move props and equipment to and from set
- <u>Tail Slate</u>: called when slating is to be done at the end of a take
- <u>Take</u>: one run of the camera, a single shot
- <u>Technocrane</u>: camera crane with telescoping arm, on a wheeled dolly
- <u>Texas</u>: placed on its end (usually referring to an apple box)
- <u>TFP</u>: trade for prints
- <u>Tight On</u>: close up
- <u>Tilt</u>: camera movement, aiming the lens up and down without any sideways motion
- <u>Topper</u>: the head of a company or organization
- <u>Trailer</u>: a short film used to promote a longer film
- <u>Transpo</u>: runners, transporting people and things
- <u>Trickline</u>: black 1/8" cord (sash cord)
- <u>Truck</u>: camera movement, sliding the camera left and right
- <u>Turtle Base</u>: the 3-legged base of a C Stand
- <u>Vampire Pin</u>: a lav holder with two sharp pins (fangs) for holding in clothing
- <u>Video City</u>: the monitor viewing area set up for the director and VIP's to watch what is being filmed as it's filmed
- <u>Visual Effects (VFX)</u>: effects created in post (contrast with special effects)
- <u>Walkie</u>: walkie-talkie, a 2-way radio
- <u>White balance</u>: a process (and button) that tells your camera what "white" looks like in the lighting of any given location
- <u>Whoop-whoops</u>: extra sounds added to sound effects, to make them more interesting and appealing (for example, adding horns or bells to an explosion)
- <u>Wig-wag</u>: the red warning light over a stage door, designed to flash during shooting. AKA "Red Eye". Usually one buzzer at start, and two buzzers at conclusion of shooting.
- <u>Wild Lines</u>: recording audio of an actor's line(s) on set (as opposed to later, in a sound stage, which would be ADR)
- <u>Wild Sound</u>: recording audio on set of sounds which can be used for Foley effects

- <u>Wire</u>: lav mic
- <u>Wombat</u>: another name for a Dead Cat
- <u>Woof</u> or <u>Walk Away</u>: indicates a good take
- <u>Wrap</u>: end of shooting (for the day, for an actor's last shooting day, or Final Wrap for the film)

Working with Creative People

If I were walking down a dark street late at night toward an unknown group of people, I'd feel better knowing that they were "theatre people" or "artists" rather than any non-creative types. Sure, I admit stereotyping and bias. But, in general, I find creative people have empathy and are more likely to accept me.

BUT … oh, boy. Creative people can be "divas", too. Feelings can be hurt so easily, especially when people open themselves up, emotionally, with the expression of their passion projects. A filmmaker spending months (or years!) developing a project is likely hypersensitive to any criticism. An actor digging deep for inspiration, the same. It is sometimes very difficult working with people in the industry. Understand the pressures, to help you understand and help the persons.

Acting is a tough job

Everyone can act. We all do. Your friend asks if she looks pretty, what are you going to say? We pretend and tell "little white lies" every day, all day long. We act, we put on a persona, we create roles for ourselves, every day. Because of this, some people think acting is easy. After all, they say, little kids are born practically acting from day one. But if you think it's easy to act in a film, on stage, or for tv, just try it and I bet you'll change your mind immediately. Hell, just go to one audition. Acting is a tough job. It's the process of seeming natural, when what you're doing (essentially, living in someone else's skin) is anything but natural. Not everyone can do it, and only a very few can do it well.

Nerves? Stage fright? Poor memory? Fear of rejection? Shy? Untrained? Low self-esteem? Bad breath? Lack of confidence? Two left feet? Dyslexic? Active bladder? Bad eyes? Twitch? Stutter? Lisp? … we all face these very human challenges. Actors work hard to overcome them.

Give, to get

You may be reading this book because you are (or want to be) an actor. It's just as important for you to read even if you are not, because you (as any other type of filmmaker) will be working closely with actors … and you better understand the needy beasts.

Actors must be able to focus, to "get into character" – whatever that means to the actor, and however they learn to accomplish it. Each actor is unique, so the approaches will always differ. But whatever they must do, let them do it. Do not interfere, do not joke, do not belittle. Don't do anything to take them out of their process.

Don't make eye contact while they are rehearsing or performing (unless, of course, you are the other actor in the scene, in which case you absolutely must make eye contact).

Don't laugh and kid around, even if you think you're far enough away from them.

After a take, good or bad, don't applaud. You might mean well, but it is a distraction that takes them out of the scene, and ruins their preparation. It will be harder for them to do the next take. There will likely be another take, and another, and while they are on set they are still working.

Perhaps you've been around a seeing eye dog, trained to help blind people? If so, you know not to pet the animal while it is working. There will come a time later, after the dog's handler has given a command to release it from duty, when you can pet and play with it. It's important not to distract the dog, however, when it has an important job to do. Give actors at least the same respect.

Even the best intentioned applause or other praise takes the actor "out", because you are commenting on the actor's abilities, and not on the character's traits. It makes them think about themselves and their acting, instead of thinking about character and story.

If you are the director or one of the limited few crew members whose input is welcome (AD, producer, writer, possibly) then make sure you comment on the *character* and not the *actor*. For example, you can say, "She (the character) is obviously upset at that line, but when do you feel she becomes upset? Is it back here when so-and-so says ….?" Talk about character motivation, character background, action justification, and interpretation of the script. Talk about what you think the writer intended for the character, to see if you and the actor are on the same page. And LISTEN to what the actor has to say, because that tells you how they are interpreting and internalizing the character. If the actor says "This is how I would feel" turn them back to instead determining how the character would feel, since the story is about the character not the actor. But do listen to the actor: once in a while they may say something helpful.

The more the writer gives the actor, the better the actor can bring the character to life. Look for clues in the script. Look between the lines. Figure out subtext. Consider how the character fits into the whole storyline, and how other characters relate or feed off of what they say and do. These are part of what actors should do to prepare, prior even to rehearsal, but they don't always. Many times you (if you are the director or 1AD) will need to prod them along.

Now, a warning about the beast. Don't say to your actors things like, "Do it this way" or "No, that's all wrong" or "You don't understand the character." If you are an actor, then you already know better not to say such things to other actors. These things are likely to set off the delicate nature that barely hides beneath the actor's thin skin. Psychology, people.

Remember, making the film is our mission. It is our *only* mission. As fun as it may be to gather to tell jokes, or discuss the latest movies, or compare new cellphones … when on set, one must at all times constantly remember that there is a job to be done, and never enough time to do it. To succeed (defined as ultimately making the best film possible), everyone must work together, cheerfully.

Shared purpose

Ultimately, you (filmmaker, producer, writer, actor, director, editor, PA, designer, costumer, artist, grip, cameraman, crafty, DIT, or *whatever*) look good only if and when everyone else does.

Results speak for themselves. Make a crappy film, and no one cares about your abilities. Make a great film, and everyone loves you for being part of it.

When you develop a project and meet with people to form your cast and crew, do so with the intent of building a cohesive team. Work to avoid splinter groups, secret promises, backroom deals that favor one group or the other. Things that divide and set your people against each other will backfire on you, in the long run.

You (everyone!) must work hard on the mission at hand, namely the bringing to life of a particular story. Make sure EVERYONE is on board with the mission. Everything else is secondary. From top to bottom, this needs to be the guiding principle of everyone in your production, so that the loftiest actor won't hesitate to lend a hand, and the lowest member of the crew likewise commits to moving the project forward. For example, the other morning I was driving to a set on which I was working as 1AD, when one of the lead actors called me. His car had broken down. He was stranded, stuck somewhere in a parking lot an hour away. I asked him what he wanted to do, and I was very gratified to hear him say he wanted to get to the set ASAP, without delaying the production, and we could worry about the car later. Good man! I would not have brow beat him if he had, instead, wanted to fix his car situation (because forcing an actor to get onto set when his mind is elsewhere is likely to be a waste of time, anyway), but I admired his dedication to the mission.

When actors accepting their Academy Awards thank every possible person they can think of, there's a good reason for that. It takes a village, working together, to make a good film.

Finding Actors

One of my favorite scenes from *Shakespeare in Love* involves auditions for what ultimately becomes the play "Romeo and Juliet" – though, at the time, I think they were calling it "Romeo and Ethel, the Pirate's Daughter." In the movie, we see a number of poor actors delivering the same monologue horribly, until one of the worst is selected for a role! The director character explains that the actor is his tailor, and giving him the role pays a debt. That's one way to get your actors, I suppose. (Actually, not far from the truth. I once struggled with what I saw as a really bad casting choice before my director let me in on a little secret: that actor was also an investor in the film!)

You can cast yourself, your friends and family. That might even be a must, for newbie filmmakers who may not be able to attract other actors. As you grow, however, you will eventually expand to other actors. So, how do you find actors?

A casting notice is the simple answer. Facebook is an easy (free!) way to get a notice out. Make sure to put a few key things in your casting notice: whether you offer pay or not, a short description of the character(s) you need, your location (generally), the date and time of when you will hold auditions, and any specific instructions (like, prepare a 1 minute monologue, or send a headshot). If you already look at Facebook acting and casting groups, you know how frequently people fail to include these basics. Many casting notices don't even tell you if the auditions are to be held in Los Angeles or Miami, or even the U.S. The most common question in the comments is "Where is this?" It's maddening. It makes no sense to excite people out of your geographical range – you'll only exasperate them into leaving snippy comments about wasting their time.

When you hold your auditions, be kind. You will be under a mountain of stress, yourself, but consider how uneasy, afraid, and worried are the people coming in to audition in front of you. Points on holding an audition:

- Put out a clear notice. Headline your notice with where you are, something like "Tampa Actors! Excellent roles available!"

- Include the items above in your casting notice. Make sure you are very clear about how people should respond, where they should go, what they should do to prepare, and what they should bring with them. Put yourself in their shoes, and give them the information you would want.

- Hold your audition in a large enough place that people can spread out, comfortably. Some productions get a ballroom or conference room at a hotel. Some hold them outside in a park. Choose a place where there are plenty of shady spots to sit down.

- Have a room for the actual audition, or at least a spot that is out of sight, and hearing, of everyone else waiting to audition. That room needs to be large enough for you and your crew, with space for the actor to perform in front of you.

- Use clear signage. Where to park, where to wait, where to go, and when.

- Put at least one person in charge of the actors waiting. That person controls when actors go into the room for their audition. Use a cell phone, or walkie talkie, to coordinate, so that the door to your inner sanctum never opens in mid audition.

- If you video your audition, have that set up and run by someone who can do it without calling attention to the process. It's a tool. Don't let that tail wag the dog.

- Talk to your actor when they come in. Talk first, to say "Hello, come on in." They are nervous. Disarm them. Be personable, but brief, and have them begin quickly.

- Then, just as quickly, thank them for coming in and say goodbye.

- Not all (in fact, few) follow this, but my preference is to follow up with every actor, even those not selected. You will see these people again, the next time you need actors, so … treat them humanely. Keep in mind that these actors talk to other actors.

Filmmaking ain't easy

Anyone can act, but not everyone can act well. It is not an easy job, at any level or stage. It's hard to get up in front of strangers to audition, hard to break apart a script to discover the subtext, and hard to perform on set with all the constant distractions. Have some sympathy.

Similarly, anyone can make a movie, but not everyone can make a good movie. You know how hard it is to make even a short film! Realize that it's just as hard for everyone else, cast and crew, though they each have their own challenges.

Learning to work well with others, to "play nice" and encourage rather than browbeat, is the key to getting your film done, and done well. No one watches a crappy film; they watch happy films.

Working with Stars & VIPS

Six Degrees of Kevin Bacon or "Bacon's Law" isn't just a parlor game. In the game, the point is to connect everyone to Kevin Bacon in the least number of steps. For example, Ian McKellen was in *X-Men: Days of Future Past* (2014) with Michael Fassbender and James McAvoy. Fassbender and

McAvoy were in *X-Men: First Class* (2011) with Kevin Bacon. Therefore Ian McKellen has a Bacon number of 2 degrees.

OK, enough about Mr. Bacon. Point is people are interconnected. And the point of that is to caution you. What you say and do can get back to people – in fact, it WILL get back to them.

Keep this in mind, no matter your level or the level of your co-workers. It's true on the playground, and it's just as true in Hollywood power circles. That good-for-nothing actor you gripe about today may well be tomorrow's "best actor" to whom everybody listens. Be smart, and don't give anyone a reason to fire back at you.

Stars are People, too
Today's "star" was yesterday's nobody. Even after becoming a "star", they still put their pants on one leg at a time, just like everyone else. They are human, still.

Don't get star-struck. They will accept you most easily if you just treat them like ordinary people, especially like ordinary people who want to be left alone.

As a young man I had a job in a huge bookstore in Texas, where everything is huge. Charles Bronson used to come in to get books – unfortunately, this was a time in his life when his wife Jill was dying of cancer. They read a lot of books to each other. Bronson would ask for my help, because I never once stared at him, asked for an autograph, made movie references, talked to him about anything other than the books he wanted, or in any other way made him feel uncomfortable. I helped him, when he needed help, without trying to get anything from him for my own benefit.

I once sat in the back of the La Jolla Playhouse next to Bob Byrne, lead singer of the band Talking Heads, and at the intermission I whispered, "Aren't you Bob Byrne?" He whispered back, "Yes, but keep it quiet, please."

Follow Bob's advice: when you meet stars, be cool. Keep it quiet. That's what they want, and they will appreciate you for it. Honestly, they're sick and tired of being recognized – even though they must, of course, put a game face on when they are spotted. They just want to do normal things, like normal people. They want to go bowling! I'm sure you've heard stories of the outrageous disguises worn by stars such as Elvis and Michael Jackson, just so they could slip out for some fast food.

You will meet famous people – cool, huh? If you're fortunate, you'll get to work with them. Don't ask for autographs, or pictures. And don't sneak a shot of them, either! Don't drop their names in your social media posts, to make yourself look cool – because it will do the opposite when they and their friends see it.

Just be cool. Someday – you hope – you will be at that star level, so you can practice now by behaving as you would want to be treated.

VIPs on set

Not every important person is a "star" or otherwise recognizable household name actor.

VIPs on a set may be studio execs, or power industry people, or just the director's family. Whoever they are, make sure you treat them with courtesy. You may not know who they are, but imagine how pleased the producer will be to find out how well you greeted his second cousin from Des Moines.

Have you ever seen a person on a set who seemed totally clueless and out of place, and yet they are there? They might even have a title, like "associate producer" (AP). Warning bells, warning bells! If they're on set and not running from security, they are obviously friends of someone important. Don't insert foot by commenting on how clueless they seem. Instead, greet them and offer to help them with whatever they need.

Until you discover that they truly are hiding from security, this is the safest approach: assume they are someone very important.

Your friends on set

Are you allowed to invite your friends to visit you on set? Never presume. Never invite anyone on set, without being certain that it's approved. And, if you do bring your friends on set, make sure they know how to behave. They should treat people just as you would. Don't bring anyone you don't fully trust because whatever they do will reflect upon you.

Working with Crew

Don't think deference is due only for actors. It's perhaps even more important that you take care of the crew, since they are the people who can – more than any other actor – help you look good … or not.

Don't touch equipment, unless and until you speak with the department head. Even if you are super knowledgeable (or think you are), until you go through the right channels you don't know what rules are in place, or if any equipment requires particular care.

Again, since this bears repeating, even if you are the Executive Producer and can afford to replace what you break, don't touch anything without first checking with the right people. This is pet peeve #1 with crew members. You will get onto Santa's "naughty" list if you touch their stuff, even with the best intentions.

A close second peeve is getting in the way. They have a job to do. Don't block them.

Positions

You may not care much about titles and positions. I know I personally do not. I've handed out too many titles, in the corporate world, and held too many myself, to be impressed.

HOWEVER, some people feel very proud of their accomplishments and the recognition they've obtained. A title can be super important to some people. Respect that. Go through channels. Make sure it is OK for you to work with person A or person B. Clarify with the department head. Hold department meeting(s). It makes them feel good. It also helps you create an efficient, productive, and loyal team.

The Shock of Coming from Theatre

There are two different worlds: film and theatre. Perhaps I should say three worlds, because television is its own thing, but usually one lumps tv and film together – they both present stories through recorded media, rather than the live world of theatre. (For this discussion, I'm saying "film" when I really mean "film and television.")

Many differences between film and theatre are obvious. For instance, a theatre play runs start to finish, with few if any stops. But in filming, probably the most frequent thing heard on set is "Cut!" after which filming stops. Film actors can, and often do, literally film one line at a time, whereas stage actors must memorize pages of dialogue, as well as remembering their complicated blocking cues. Film actors have the luxury of being able to repeat their lines, until the director is happy with just the right inflection and delivery; stage actors rehearse, and when the curtain goes up they better get it right! Probably the biggest difference for actors is the idea that on stage an actor is required to deliver a performance that can be seen and heard by the audience, but film actors are told to forget the camera exists at all; film actors are minimalists, compared to stage actors – they use small movements, small facial changes, small vocal inflections. Film actors don't worry about projecting out to an audience; they rely on the ability of the camera and sound crew to catch their performances.

For a writer, the difference is most pronounced; film writers are treated nothing like theatre writers, at least when it comes to their reputation and standing within their communities. In the theatre, writers are treated like gods whose words are sacrosanct; directors and actors alike bend over backwards to discern the writer's intent, in order to bring the writer's precise language alive. But in film, writers are seen as necessary evils, and just about everybody feels entitled to change dialogue without any qualms about it. Writers moving from theatre to film must swallow their pride, along with their tongues, and suffer the most galling changes to the words they crafted ever so carefully. Newbie screenwriters are often shocked to learn how little they are paid, and how little (or no) control they have over how their work is filmed. I don't know why the difference.

Making films is expensive and one can argue that the money people insist on the right to change the script, but making theatre productions is also very expensive.

Theatre actors study the script, break it down to discern every teeny tiny bit of meaning, and then they carefully memorize and rehearse so that they can give a true performance. But film actors will frequently change lines, simply because they have trouble with a consonant, or think something else would "sound better". Or maybe just because they were too lazy to learn the lines. That actor doesn't stop to think that the writer no doubt anguished over every line and every choice of word, to make sure it fit properly in the script; most film actors don't worry about such – they are only focused on themselves and the moment. Right or wrong, this is the commonly accepted culture in the film world.

Of course, it is possible that an actor may on the spot come up with a better line than the writer. It does happen. In my opinion as a writer, it happens rarely.

People – "Job Descriptions" in Filmmaking

People on the set – so many! Even for a short film, the number of names in the credits can be daunting. I've seen 8 minute films with over 50 names in the credits! Fifty people involved?! And, of course, that's a mere drop in the bucket, compared to the casts and crew of large blockbuster movies. There are too many names to even count in the credits of a typical Hollywood feature.

So, how can you hope to make sense of everything when you get onto one of these big sets? Like everything else, prepare ahead of time.

Disclaimer – job descriptions vary

I'm hesitant to get into discussing what various people do on set, without first acknowledging that you will find different job descriptions in just about every film company and on every set. I'm writing this book primarily from the perspective of newbies getting into the Entertainment World, which means a lot of student films, and indie films, rather than blockbuster Hollywood. There are job descriptions in SAG and WGA, and the other unions, although even there you will find much variety in the actual practice of the jobs.

Flexibility, in other words. "Creatives" frequently don't fit labels or stay in well-defined categories. Small (student/independent/low budget) films require people to wear many hats; only big productions have strictly stated job descriptions.

Creativity requires flexibility. This is probably one reason why big budget films can fail, if the production company is too rigid in its organization and operations, and too likely to squash the creative juices that flow best with human interaction.

What follows are descriptions of positions that I have found to be generally true on sets. (You're free to quibble.)

Common Positions:

Executive Producer (EP)

The true boss. The admiral. The money source, or the one connected to the money. Perhaps one person on a smaller production, or many as the project size increases. A company (for example, a product brand like Chevy, or Coke) may serve as the EP, instead of a real person. The EP hires everyone else.

Director

Captain of the ship. People generally forget the money people, and attribute the creation of films to directors. The Director is the creative face of the film, even more so than its stars, because the Director, like the captain of a ship, is in charge of getting the film made. The Director guides everything from the actors' performances to the operations of the crew. Of course, s/he must delegate many functions.

Director of Photography (DP)

The DP is the camera pro who determines the lighting and framing of each shot, to get the Director's intended look and feel. Often operates the camera, especially on smaller crews.

Production Designer

A Production Designer helps the Director and DP create particular looks – for example, to get 1870's London just right – with appropriate sets, props, and costumes.

Producers

Coordinators for the EP. There is a world of difference between the EP and the other various types of producers. And there are lots of other types of producers. But think of them all as junior officers, tasked with oversight of separate parts of the production. For example, you'll see Marketing Producers or Financial Producers. These people have authority over their section only.

Line Producer

The purse strings. The Line Producer creates the film's budget, keeps track of all costs below the line, and doles out the money as needed. On a small production, likely the same person as the UPM.

Unit Production Manager (UPM)

Reporting to the Line Producer, the UPM oversees the logistics of daily operations, like scheduling and staffing.

Production Coordinator	Reporting to the UPM, the Production Coordinator handles logistics, such as shipping and set-up of equipment.
Production Assistant (PA)	*Magical Elves.* The more the better. Production Assistants are helpers hired to be handy – to run for replacement batteries, send out call sheets, pick up crew, even get donuts and coffee. Often maligned as the lowest rank, they are one of the most necessary and helpful positions.
1st Assistant Director (AD)	The 1st AD, or 1AD, runs the film set on the day of shooting, as the Director's right hand, which allows the Director to concentrate on the creative process. Duties vary, depending upon what the Director wishes to do personally. The Director will often focus on getting the best possible performances from the actors, while the 1AD manages the logistics of the set. Pre-production, the 1AD storyboards the shots (often with the DP), works with the Director to determine shot order, and drafts a shooting schedule. It is the 1AD's job, ultimately, to make sure the Director gets as much footage as possible "in the can".
2nd AD	The 2nd AD, or 2AD, is the 1AD's right hand. The 2AD prepares call sheets, and manages the movement of cast on set.
3rd AD	On larger productions, a 3AD or multiple 3ADs may be necessary. These are assistants, helping the 1AD and/or 2AD. Typically, they manage movement of large casts and extras.
Script Supervisor ("Scripty")	The Script Supervisor "lines the script" during shooting, noting the coverage of each take. They also keep track of continuity. Aka "Continuity Clerk" (or fka "Continuity Girl", since the position was traditionally held by a woman).
Location Manager	A Location Manager finds locations, and (often with 2AD) gets any required permits.
Camera Operator	The person actually operating the camera. Sometimes the DP, or even the Director.
1st Assistant Camera (AC)	1st AC helps set up the camera and lenses, and pulls focus.
2nd Assistant Camera	2nd ACs are key members of the camera crew, setting up, moving gear, slating, and recording shot information.

Production Sound Mixer   The Production Sound Mixer is responsible for getting the best possible sound on set.

Boom Operator   A Boom Operator holds the boom mic near the actors, just out of frame. In smaller crews, this is often the Production Sound Mixer.

Key Grip   A Key Grip is the person responsible for all equipment (such as lights, dollies, cranes, platforms).

Gaffer
or Chief Lighting Technician   The Gaffer is the head of the Electrical Department. Designs and implements the set's lighting plan on set.

Best Boy   Best Boy is the best electrician in the Gaffer's team. They assist the Key Grip and the Gaffer. They order and oversee delivery of lighting equipment.

Special Effects Supervisor   The Special Effects Supervisor is responsible for creating the film's visual effects. May also be in charge of audio FX and CGI.

Music Supervisor   The Music Supervisor chooses the music, and obtains necessary licensing.

Art Director   Art Directors help the Director create an overall feel for the film.

Props Master & Stylist   The Props Master is in charge of finding and managing all props. The Stylist is on set, making sure the props look good. Often the same person.

Make-up Artist   The Make-up Artist makes sure the actors look correct for the script, which includes regular street looks and such visual effects as bloody cuts and bruises.

Hairdresser   The Hairdresser makes sure the actors' hair looks correct for the script – hair styles, loose bangs, etc.

Costume Designer   The Costume Designer is responsible for designing and creating the wardrobe that fits the script.

Seamstress / Costumer   Seamstress(es) work with the Costume Designer to get the costumes looking right, and keep them in appropriate condition.

Additional Job Descriptions (somewhat alphabetical, or else by department or function):

Filmmaker	A general, vague term for anyone involved in film making. Most often used for those at the top, who forge the identity of the work – writers, producers, directors.
Associate Producer (AP)	Often considered not to be a "real" credit, because this title is frequently handed out to someone the production owes a favor to, or friend assigned to take care of specific aspects of the production, or as a bone thrown to the writer or other production executive. They may be hands-on, below the line, involved with a particular task; such as, for example, editing the script, or coordinating set construction.
Assistant Producer	These are probably people really involved in the hard work of making the production, because celebs and money people don't want to be called "assistant" anything.
Co-Producer	Someone who shares producer responsibilities with other producers. Duh. This is a title frequently used for someone who handled a specific (and important) aspect of the production. Such as, for example, getting the main star to sign, or bringing the script.
Supervising Producer	Oversee other producer(s), which is basically the job of the EP. This person might be assisting the EP.
Coordinating Producer	Coordinate other producers. This is done, for example, when a studio (or multiple studios working together) produce several related films (think Marvel), or two related films at the same time (for example, the two sequels to *The Pirates of the Caribbean*) and it's important to make sure the films are consistent.
Consulting Producer	Assisting writers or Producers. Often former executive or co-producer on the show.
Development Producer	Frequently the first person involved in a project. They take ideas, or select screenplays, to come up with the premise of the show, and convince others to get involved to turn the ideas into shows. They secure rights, if necessary.

Post Producer	In charge of post-production (primarily editing and dubbing)
TV Producers	Assist the EP, to develop, fund, budget, hire, and guide production of network tv shows. TV Producers are creative decision makers, above the line, not usually involved in the daily grind.
ADR Recordist	Records replacement dialogue in a sound studio.
Audio Recordist	Member of the sound crew, responsible for audio recording equipment on set.
Aerial Specialists	Pilots who fly aircraft carrying the aerial camera crew.
Animal Trainer	The person responsible for an animal's performance and care on set.
Animators	People who use a variety of techniques to make images appear to come to life on screen, including 2D drawn animation, 2D computer animation, stop frame animation, and 3D computer animation.
Art Department	The biggest department on a film, responsible for executing the Director's and DP's vision for the look and feel of the film.
Art Dept. -- Coordinator	Oversees the Art Department, which is tasked with the visual artistry of the set.
Art Directors	Project managers within the Art Department, responsible for Art Dept. budget and schedule of work.
Art Dept. -- Leadman	The lead person of the Art Department, in charge of swing gangs and set dressers. Reports to the Set Decorator.
Art Dept. -- Swing	Set dressers who dress (set up) and strike (take down) sets.
Assistant Script Supervisor / Coordinator	Point person between writers and production. Responsible for distributing script changes, and taking care of clearance issues.
Assistant to Producer	An administrator working with the Producers. Tasks may include coverage on scripts ("readers"), drafting letters, making phone calls, etc.

Assistant Stereographer	Helps the Lead Stereographer assess the relationship between convergence, interaxial and focal length, which are all vital parameters in 3D modeling.
Broadcast Engineer	Electrical engineer for radio and television broadcasting.
Cable Puller	Looks after cables. Often follows roaming cameras, to care for trailing cables.
Casting Director (CD)	Organize the casting of actors, working with Director and Producers. Also negotiates fees and contracts.
Casting Director Assistant	Assist with casting process.
Casting Recruiter	Reaches out to talent agencies, to get talent to audition.
Celebrity Booker	Reaches out to and contracts with star performers.
Caterer	Tables or catering trucks set up with meals and/or snacks. Also called "Craft Services".
Clapper	Person slating each take. Sometimes the Loader. Often the 2AC.
Craft Service ("Crafty")	Caterer. May refer only to snacks, if differentiated from catering meals. May also be tasked with cleaning the set.
Cinematographer	The DP.
Colorist	Skilled in editing, specifically in altering color.
Commercial Director	Director specializing in audio visual advertising.
Composer	Writes original music.
Compositor	Creates visual FX by layering images.
Concept Artist	A graphic artist position, working with the Art Directors to produce images – usually quick sketches to reflect the concepts discussed.
Construction Coordinator	Construction manager, in charge of constructing sets.
Creature Designers	Artists who create masks, body parts, and entire creatures.
Dialect Coach	Person who trains actors to speak in diction or with particular inflections.

Digital Imaging Technician (DIT) aka "HD Technicians" – person on set who assures quality control of digital image collection.

Data Wrangler Person on set responsible for collecting the raw footage digital storage media (usually cards or hard drives) from cameras, and transferring the data to the editors. They keep track of who has the footage, too.

Director of Programming In television, responsible for selecting, planning and scheduling programs.

Director's Assistant Administrator, assisting the Director. Duties may include coverage of scripts ("reader"), drafting letters, and making phone calls.

Distributor Coordinates the distribution of a finished film to theaters and other exhibitors.

Drone Operator Person qualified (and licensed, as necessary) to fly drone aircraft.

Dubbing Mixer Sound re-recording mixers.

Editor Film editors organize footage, select takes, and assemble shots together to create a seamless film. They also add sound, music, effects and graphics.

Field Director Oversees the direction of the story, while the crew is in the field.

Field Producer Oversees the direction of the story, while the crew is in the field. Liaison between crew and news media – sets up interviews. Often will shoot the video and write the story for a reporter.

Fixer A person paving the way for a production to film abroad.

Foley Artist Person who creates incidental sounds meant to bring images to life (for example, the scrape of a boot on a wood floor).

Food Stylist Person who makes food look yummy, before photography.

Graphics Operator During tv broadcast, runs graphics over the bottom 1/3 (typically) of the screen, for insertion of names, scores, news, etc.

Grip	Responsible for building and maintaining all of the equipment in the Camera Department (for example: tripods, cranes, jibs, camera rigs, dollies, dolly track)
Dolly Grip	A Grip that moves a dolly.
Jimmy Jib Operator	Crane operator, for cranes and jibs holding cameras (with and without camera operators) as high as 100' above the set.
Lighting Designer (LD)	Works with Producers, Directors and other designers to create the look of the project through appropriate lighting.
Lighting Supervisor	The most senior role in tv lighting departments.
Lighting Technical Director	designs the lighting for multi-camera tv productions.
Loader	The person who loads the film into the camera. Frequently also the Clapper.
Location Scout	Searches for locations.
Marine Specialist	Underwater DP, or other consultant, assisting with underwater shots and stunts.
Marketing Director	Develops marketing campaigns.
Marketing Assistant	Assists the Marketing Director. Duties include demographic reports, researching markets, and coordinating meetings.
Master Control Operator	In tv, responsible for monitoring the quality of on-air broadcast.
Matter Painter	Person who creates the artwork used (typically) as background.
Mechanical Effects	aka "Practical Effects" or "Physical Effects" – FX usually done during live performance, such as break-away set pieces, pyrotechnics, and mechanized props.
Motion Graphics Designer	Graphic design for motion pictures, such as credits or company logos.
Music Editor	Responsible for piecing together the show's music.
Music Supervisor	Mediators between composers and the production. They oversee spotting sessions with the Director.
Music Truck A2	Assistant on set responsible for audio equipment and cables.

Musical Arranger	Person who adapts a musical piece for new voice or instrument.
News Director	Controls the news gallery during newscast. Selects camera angles, graphics, and guest shots.
News Editor	Person who edits for newscasts.
News Producer	Person who selects the daily news elements for broadcast.
Personal Assistant	Usually administrative, but can include almost anything.
Postproduction Coordinator	Works to facilitate a smooth post-production process, coordinating editing with ADR, colorization, CGI FX, and other post-production processes.
Postproduction Supervisor	Maintain good communication between the different parties involved in post-production.
PR Assistant	Entry-level public relations position.
PR Executive	Interprets opinions, and advises top management, to create and bolster the goodwill of a project.
Production Executive	Oversees the production of a project.
Production Designers	Heads of departments, such as the Art Dept. They help Directors achieve the desired look, and provide schedules and budgets to Producers.
Production Managers	Organize business, finance, and employment matters.
Production Accountant	Responsible for managing finances for the production.
Production Assistant	aka "Production Runners" – duties vary widely, including administrative, PR, crowd control, and cleaning.
Production Coordinator	Supports the Production Managers, especially in working with different companies or departments.
Production Secretary	Administrative assistance for the Prod. Manager and Prod. Coordinator.
Production Supervisor	aka "Postproduction Supervisor" – oversees the entire post-production.
Project Manager	The lead in planning and managing a specific project.

Promotions Producer	In tv, person responsible for creating and editing news, public service announcements, and commercials.
Rigging (electric)	aka "Rigging Grips" -- Persons responsible for setting, hanging and focusing lighting instruments. Also sets up scaffolding.
Rights and Clearances	Person who gets the rights to use music, tv and movie footage.
Rotoscope Artist	Creates mattes, for compositing.
Second Unit Director	Director of a second filming unit, usually small and subordinate. Tasked with filming less-important shots and B-Roll.
Segment Producer	Producer of individual segment(s) in a multi-segmented production.
Series Producer	aka "Show Runner" – responsible for day-to-day operation of a tv series.
Show Runner	Series Producer
Set Decorator	Person who provides anything on the set, other than the set's structural components.
Set Dresser	Responsible for making the set look realistic and lived in, as opposed to looking like a brand new set.
Set Painter / Scenic Painter	Scenic Artists who create backdrops, primarily.
Sign Writer	Responsible for writing and making signs used in the production.
Social Media Specialist	Manages interactions of social media with the production.
Sound Designer	Provides sounds required by the script.
Sound Engineer	Operates and maintains sound equipment.
Sound Assistant	Assists with recording sound on set.
Sound Editor	Creates the film's soundtrack by synchronizing sound elements to visual shots.
Special Effects Supervisor	Chief of the production's on set special effects crew.

Stage Manager	In theatre, the Director's right hand. During performance, they are in charge of the stage and backstage.
Steadicam Operator	Camera operators able to film using stabilization equipment while moving.
Stereographer	Member of a 3D production.
Still Photographer	Takes photographs on set for marketing purposes.
Story Producer	In reality tv, the person who creates story lines when editing the footage.
Storyboard Artist	An artist assisting the Director or 1AD in interpreting the script visually, shot by shot.
Stunt Coordinator	Arranges and plans stunts.
Stunt Driver	Performs vehicle stunts.
Tape Logger	Reviews footage, and makes notes regarding content and quality of each take
Technical Director (TD) or Technical Producer (TP)	Usually the top technical person in a production company or theatre.
Teleprompter Operator	Transcribes scripts or recordings into files readable on teleprompter machines.
Transcriptionist	The person who transcribes spoken language.
Travel Coordinator	Schedules travel for each department.
Unit Publicist (UP)	Generates publicity, which helps sales agents sell the film, by serving as a liaison between media and the production's producers, cast and crew.
Voiceover Artist	Actors providing voice recordings in sound studio.
Webcaster	Essentially, broadcasting over the Internet; develops and implements ways to integrate the production with streaming media.
Writer(s)	The author of the original script, plus all others who added to or altered the script.

Film Festivals

The Circuit

When you've made a film (short or long), you can submit it to be shown in festivals around the world. Festivals are literally everywhere, and most don't require that you be present in person. Some festivals are themed (for example, only showing films by women directors, or only films made in Detroit, or only science fiction), and some are general. You can easily find the festivals by going to www.Filmfreeway.com and making yourself an account.

It is easy to set your film up on FilmFreeway. The site is very user friendly. Most festivals charge an administrative fee for entering your film -- perhaps $20, perhaps $95; the more prestigious the festival, the more expensive usually. Luckily for us newbies, there are many festivals which are free (though they do tend to be those that are themed, like for only high school students). Me, I submit my films to all the free festivals. Why not?

Getting your film accepted by a festival is a rush, especially the first time. Going to a festival, seeing your film for the first time on a big screen! This is a fun game. It's captivating. When your film is accepted, you get "laurels" (badges) that you can use in your advertising and for other bragging purposes. Then, if you win an award, you get more laurels! Some people add such laurels to movie posters, in some cases so may laurels that it's hard to see the poster.

Laurels look like these:

Go to festivals for the fun of it. Don't go, thinking that you are close to fame and fortune. It's like an actor hoping to be discovered while enjoying a milkshake; might happen now and then, but you better not hold your breath waiting for it to happen to you. There could be agents, producers, distributors, and the like at the festivals … could be. Some festivals, like Sundance, are more likely to be full of true industry movers and shakers, than others.

Games, Cons & Frauds

Because it is fairly easy to start a festival, many people have. And that, unfortunately, opens the door for fraud. I've heard stories of outright fake festivals. This has been such a problem that

FilmFreeway now requires a festival organizer to provide proof that they have an actual real life theater in which to show films, but the scammers can get around that requirement.

Cash prizes, or any prizes of value at all, are rare. Don't enter festivals to get rich because it's just the opposite. Getting selected, and even winning, is just good for bragging rights. And the slim chance that the recognition could lead to further acclaim, and even a distributorship, for your film.

Beware the request for a "DCP" file format. A DCP is a Digital Cinema Package computer file that is actually a collection of digital files which store and convey digital cinema (DC) audio, image, and data information. Theaters need a DCP to show films on their digital projectors. If you have your film in DCP format, it can be shown at movie theaters anywhere in the world. Downside? It takes a very expensive computer to make a DCP, and the cost to have others convert your film to DCP runs about $1,000 - $3,000. A typical feature-length film in DCP will fill up a 1TB hard drive. If you plan to show your film around the world, get a DCP. But I mention it here because film festivals almost always show films in the more common formats (MP4 for example). Film festivals usually just hook up a laptop and play films, which is not the best quality – nothing like the quality of a DCP – and prone to bugs, but cheap and easy. Some festivals require a DCP, perhaps because they are big time and present only show quality films in major theaters (Cannes, or Sundance, for example) … or, perhaps because they sell DCP conversion services? Yes, I fell for this when I was putting my first short film into festivals. The Marina del Rey Film Festival was happy to take $400 to convert my little 8 minute film into a DCP. A fool is born every minute, right?

Beware any festival charging more than a modest entry fee. Some hit you with multiple fees, not just file conversion but also fees for attending, fees for not attending, and so on.

Media

Your best friend

Quick to love you, and just as quick to turn on you, it's smart to think of the media as that friend who secretly wants to see you fail. Keep your wits about you, at all times. Don't be a deer in the headlights.

Ever notice how big celebrities always look good in photographs? Sometimes the young ones are caught unaware. For example, you can find one of Brad Pitt's early paparazzi shots online, where he looks totally clueless. But not now. In pictures of Brad now, he always looks like he has a secret to share, like he's onto something and could say something clever any moment. That isn't by accident. Brad has learned to look savvy whenever anyone can see him.

Peter Hurley (the BEST headshot photographer – look him up) tells actors to "squinch" their eyes, because it makes you look clever. Not squint like you can't see, or as if you're tired or stoned. It's more half-squint, just enough to avoid the deer-in-the-headlight vapid look. Once you're onto this, you'll see that celebrities always squinch. They always look like they have something important to say.

If and when you find yourself speaking with media, do the squinch.

Use the media, with your eyes open
Squinch, but for Holy sake, keep your eyes open – as in keep your wits about you! The successful performer is the one who knows how to market themselves (examples, Madonna and Lady Gaga). Never lose sight, even for a moment, that you are part of a business (the business of "you") and the media is also in business (the business of "it").

Whatever you want to say to the media, say less, if even that. Be polite and warm, but move on to speak with others (non-media) quickly. Reporters are pushy, and they have numerous tricks to prevent you from moving on, but you must learn to do so. Be George Clooney – super warm and friendly, AND aloof at the same time. You've heard the showbiz advice "Always leave them wanting more" and that holds true especially for reporters.

I don't mean that the media is always a nest of vipers. Not always. Use them for your benefit, not theirs. Stage theatres almost always reserve prime seats for critics because you never want a critic to see you from a bad angle, or to not see you at all. You can control your own image through social media today – use it, embrace it. When you are out at festivals, be prepared to steer reporters to your social media; give them a postcard "press kit" that says only what you want said, and then politely say, "Thank you. I must move on. Have a wonderful night!"

Did I mention press kits yet? You should have a "media kit" for yourself, with three biographies: a short bio (1 or 2 sentences), a medium (100 – 200 words), and a long (300 – 500 words). Your media kit should have contact information, including representation if you have any; a filmography; awards; and a short pitch about your current project. Each of your projects should have its own media kit, which includes your bio and contact info, plus logline, synopsis, cast information, reviews, and a sample (script pages, trailer, behind the scenes pictures, etc.) of the project. Always be prepared to hand out a business card or post card that steers media and other people to a designated website where they can download the entire media kit.

Casting Directors
Why So Important
CD's (casting directors) are invaluable to producers and directors, and therefore to you, too.

Film is big business, and no one knows that more than producers and directors trying to cast a project. The audition process can be long and tiring, expensive and frustrating, but so important because making a bad casting decision can sink the entire project. CD's are money protectors. It's risky to commit money on unknown, untried, untested, unproven actors. A production would love to use only top-tier actors whose talents are already proven, but that means maximum salary for each role. There's never enough money, and corners must be cut … but then we're back to the risk of lesser actors. That's where a CD comes in. Producers don't have to worry about casting if they can trust a good casting director. CD's work with actors, pay attention to actors, follow their careers. It's a CD's job to be able to say to a producer, "Let's try this actor. They can do it and they won't break your bank."

That's your agent's job, too. The difference being that your agent is supposed to say that about you, regardless of whether it's actually true. Agents pimp you out. Casting directors will speak truth about you.

So … always treat CD's with the utmost respect, kindness, and care. They can be your friends, much more than media will ever be. Get on the CD's good side, and they will open doors for you.

Representation

It's tough to go alone in this world. In any world. Having friends can be a big boost to everything you want to do. The trick is, finding the right friends. And not friends who will cause you to ask, "With friends like that, who needs enemies?"

Representation is sometimes necessary, but not necessary at all times. Don't feel like you must immediately jump at the first (or the 10th) opportunity to sign with someone. Take a step back and think about each choice; talk it over with your real friends, do some research, sleep on it. It's a common misconception to think that you *need* these people. Afterall, look how far you've come without them! You may be able to continue without representation. "Cream rises to the top!" Or you may find that having representation opens doors, and gets you into the meetings you are unable to get into by yourself.

In the Entertainment World, there is always a plethora of people nearby with their hand out, ready to represent you. All, of course, at a cost. These are primarily: agents, managers, attorneys, and unions.

Agents

Agents work at talent agencies. An agent may be the only agent in an agency, or one of thousands.

What they do

Making a deal to get you cast. That's it. That's what they do. I mean, they do other things, too, that are all related to making the deal, like negotiating contracts, setting up meetings and helping you network. But it's all aimed at getting you cast. They are not there to teach you how to act, hold your hand after a bad audition, or give you pep talks (although many do). An agent works as much for the production companies as for you.

Here's how it works. Production company ABC is filming and needs three supporting actors, but ABC long ago realized what a pain it is to hold mass "cattle call" auditions to find bit players or tap dance carefully around the egos of big star. ABC may get directly involved to find its stars, but they are way too busy to go through that hassle for supporting roles, day players, or background extras. And not just the auditions, but also all of the other administrative junk that goes along with hiring actors. Keeping track of them, complying with payroll laws and regulations, paying them …. ABC just wants to make a movie!

So ABC contracts with the Yippy talent agency. Now, Yippy needs to find the actors and handle all of the payroll obligations. Yippy turns to its files and calls in a number of actors, and perhaps Yippy holds the cattle call auditions, until such time as Yippy can deliver suitable actors to ABC. And not just any actors. Yippy's reputation is on the line, because ABC will not hire Yippy next time, if any of the actors fall short of expectations. So Yippy figured out long ago that it's very hard to find good actors on short notice, especially through the process of open auditions. It's much better to have actors already signed up, so all Yippy has to do is open their files and assign people. But signing up actors, and vetting them to make sure they are good enough that Yippy can rely upon them, is not an easy task; it takes a lot of time and energy. Here's where individual agents come into play. At Yippy, let's say there are ten agents, Yip1, Yip2, and so on. Yip6 signed you up, after seeing you and becoming impressed with your abilities. She has your resume and headshot. Every day, Yip6 looks at the casting notices that come into Yippy and she struggles to find roles that match the people she has signed up. If she thinks you fit, she puts you forward, and probably has to argue for you over the other Yips who have done exactly the same thing. A good Yip fights for you. If successful, Yip6 tells you to go to ABC. If you are called into ABC for any purpose, no matter why, it is an "audition" and you must WOW them. Your agent Yip6 doesn't get you the job, she just opens that door. ABC will toss you back and ask Yippy for someone else if you don't prove yourself immediately. And there's always someone else.

Many companies won't bother to get into the mess of hiring actors at all. They rely 100% on talent agencies for all of their talent needs. These companies are golden geese for the talent agencies because they need many actors. Do you think Yip6 represents you? or the golden goose? From you, she might earn a few pennies, but through Yippy's relationship with ABC she expects to earn big bucks. Of course, she says represents you ….

Payment

And of course, this is all about money. ABC saves time and hassle (money) by not doing auditions. Instead ABC hires Yippy (money). Now Yippy hires agents (money) to find actors. Yippy and Yip6 get paid only when they find acceptable actors AND those actors follow through with ABC.

Agents take a cut out of the money paid to you. They take their cut right off the top because ABC usually pays Yippy, not you. Typically, agents get 10% if you're union, and 20% if you are non-union. Agents in some states may be able to charge more, depending on that state's laws; however, if you are union, it is 10% across the country, because the agent has *voluntarily* agreed to comply with the union's collective bargaining agreement. Some state laws have limits. For example, 10% is the max in California for all actors, union or not.

Agents can also be paid an extra "signing bonus" by ABC. Let's say ABC pays you $1,000 to perform a part. Yippy gets $100 and you get $900, right? Well, maybe. ABC might have a side deal with Yippy, for example something that says Yippy gets an extra $100 if they get the actor committed within x number of days, or if the actor is hot. So Yippy gets $200. You (the actor) get none of that side deal money. I'm oversimplifying. The point of this is to simply point out that agents are in business for themselves, and while they represent you … keep your eyes open.

What to watch out for

Because talent agencies and agents must be licensed, they are regulated by laws in California (and in some other states). This makes them much more trustworthy than managers who are not regulated by laws (more on this below), but doesn't mean that all agents can be trusted. Keep in mind at all steps along your journey, agents represent you but are really working for the production companies.

Every agent will make you sign a contract. They want you to be available when and if they call you, and not out working for another agent. The agent's contract may be dictated to some degree by legal requirements, but there are still things you should watch for. Chiefly, what is the range of representation? By this I mean, geographically and timewise. Also, type of use. An agent may sign you only for Los Angeles gigs, and only for a year, and only for commercials. Or the agent may sign you exclusively, meaning you can't accept any work other than what comes through the agent. Can you ever terminate the contract? Get an attorney to advise you, before you sign the contract.

The worst thing in my book are the "do nothing" agents. They sign you, and then sit back literally doing nothing for you. These people count on you to go out and find openings, and then when you do luck into something, they demand their 10%.

For example, my friend Doug lucked his way into a couple big movies, and based on such decided to move out to LA and be a star. He got an agent quickly. But then found himself sent by that agent to the general cattle calls open to everyone without agents. He got fed up and switched agents, multiple times – sometimes breaking his agency contract, and living with the risk that they could come after him. Agents caught onto this, making it even less likely that they would send him out. Don't be Doug. Take your time deciding and ask around before you sign with any agent.

An agent makes you money, not vice versa. They should never ask you for money. Your agent may point out the need for quality headshots, or recommend acting classes, but they should not make a racket of it. In other words when your agent insists you only use her photographer … run.

Types of Agents

My examples above are mostly for actors and directors, talking about "Talent Agents". I apologize to the rest of you newbies. There are other types of agents. "Lit Agents" represent film and/or tv writers, and there are agent to help crew find positions.

How to Get an Agent

Here, I have no "easy" button for you. If you're a writer, the best way to get a Lit Agent is to write a really good script that gets attention, and then have several more ready to show them because Lit Agents don't want to sign one hit wonders. You need to generate lots of material. "Writers write!" as they say. Win contests, like the Nicholl (www.oscars.org/nicholl), and network at the larger film festivals and film markets.

If you're an actor or director, put your skills out for the world to see, in festivals, contests, showcases, YouTube, Vimeo, and everywhere else you can. Put your films out on Vimeo and get them presented as "Short of the Week."

Agents rely on word of mouth. Develop a presence. Use social media to your advantage. Befriend casting directors. Get people talking about you.

The Big Agencies

Los Angeles and New York, those are the biggest entertainment cities so that's where the big agencies are. But they have satellite offices elsewhere, and there are plenty of smaller agencies in just about every major city.

The largest talent agencies are:

- Creative Artists Agency (CAA)
- William Morris Endeavor (WME)
- United Talent Agency (UTA)
- International Creative Management Partners (ICM)
- Gersh
- Paradigm
- Agency of the Performing Arts (APA)
- Verve

Bigger agencies get more opportunities in through their doors, but you may have more competition for each spot. Smaller agencies may have fewer opportunities, but more likelihood to focus on getting you out there.

Managers

What they do

Casting is what managers *don't* do; agents do that. Agents negotiate deals, managers do not. Where agents are focused on the business of your acting, managers are focused more on you yourself. You want your agent to be out there hustling for you. You manager will talk you off the bridge, help you through bad days, encourage you to eat right, recommend classes for you, and even argue with your agent for you.

Managers are like life coaches. They help you figure out your life, strategize, plan. They motivate you. They are like your best friend, though one you pay for.

Payment

Most states have laws regulating agents. Agents usually have to be licensed, and bonded. But conversely, most states have no such requirement for managers. No minimum requirements at all.

Where agents are limited by law in most states to 10 or 20%, there is no limit on what a manager can charge. 20 – 30% is common, and I've heard plenty of stories of managers taking 50%! I've read, however, that most legit managers take 10%.

What to watch out for

Because anyone can call themselves a manager and there is no regulatory oversight, there are unfortunately many bad managers. Sleezy types. People who won't hesitate to take advantage of earnest newbies. Listen to your instincts, and run when your inner voice tells you to run.

Unfortunately, many newbies are so eager to make it that they are willing to sign on with the first person who shows them any attention. When I was an entertainment attorney in Los Angeles, I bet a week didn't go by without someone bringing me a contract to review from a manager. I saw contracts so poorly written, and so unfairly biased against the actor, that I almost always recommended against signing.

For example, some contracts never end. Imagine that. You sign, and you are literally committed *for life*. ALL contracts should expire, or at least have some mechanism by which you can get out.

Some contracts failed the "Cut and Paste Test." This is what I call looking at a contract to see if its defined terms track consistently through. If they call you "Actor" on page one, but then

"Performer" or page two, and then something else further on, it tells me the manager copied sections from various other contracts and no one (at least no good attorney) has gone through the whole contract to make sure it's put together correctly. People who cut and paste contract sections like this will invariably create conflicts, where the contract says different conflicting things.

Hell, I've even seen contracts in LA where you could tell the paragraphs had literally been cut and pasted, since the paragraphs were photocopied onto the page at different angles! Font changes, spacing changes, and other format changes are another dead giveaway.

The biggest single thing to watch for is simply this: What will the manager be obligated to do? Here's the sad game that gets replayed over and over in Hollywood: so called "managers" sign up hopeful newbies, and then the manager does absolutely nothing. The contract hooks the actor forever, but there is no clause describing what the manager must do, or the stated duties are so minimal as to amount to the same thing. These scumbag trolls just sit back and wait. They resurface only if and when you hit it big. They know newbies will continue to try to succeed, and while most give up and fade away, a certain percentage will succeed. From the actors POV, they wonder where their manager went, and are shocked when the manager pops back up years later to demand 30% (or more) of the actor's wages.

Get referrals! Talk to those referrals! Do your homework. Watch out for scumbags, and make sure (1) you are dealing with fine, reputable people, and (2) you can extricate yourself from any situation when you are no longer happy with it.

The Big Management Companies

Los Angeles and New York, those are the biggest entertainment cities so that's where the big agencies are. But they have satellite offices elsewhere, and there are plenty of management companies operating in just about every major city.

The largest management companies are:

- 3Arts
- Anonymous Content
- Zero Gravity
- Circle of Confusion
- Bellevue
- Echo Lake
- Kaplan / Perrone
- The Gotham Group
- Untitled Entertainment
- Brillstein
- Management 360

- Madhouse

Entertainment Attorneys

One of Shakespeare's quotes is often thrown at me:

> *"The first thing we do,*
> *Let's kill all the lawyers."*
>
> *~ Henry VI, Part 2*

This line is often misquoted and misunderstood. It sure sounds like lawyers are bad, doesn't it? But in the play, this line is spoken by a dastardly villain who is plotting to cause maximum chaos. In that context, it's quite complimentary that the evil-doer wants to rid himself of the ones who can administer law and order. (At least, I was proud to once wear a t-shirt with this quote!)

So … don't kill the lawyers, okay?

Entertainment is about creativity, which is pretty much the opposite of the practice of law as the legal system relies heavily upon precedent. There is a natural conflict. This is one primary reason why I urge you to seek out an *Entertainment Attorney* and not just any old attorney. Find someone who understands and operates within the Entertainment World.

But let me back up. There is actually no such thing as "entertainment law." There is no study of law specifically known as "entertainment law", and no student ever graduated out of law school as an "entertainment attorney." It is not its own field. Entertainment law is simply the practice of law with entertainment clients, and by that logic we would also have "Plumbing Attorneys" "Animal Control Attorneys" and "Pizza Delivery Attorneys." Entertainment Law includes everything that entertainers need, depending entirely upon who the entertainers are. So, it's primarily contract law, which is a true legal subject.

Value

Like insurance, the value of getting an attorney is often determined best in hindsight. Your project goes bad and you face staggering damages, that's when you realize you should have had the contracts reviewed.

Attorneys seek to protect your interests. It's the core of their job, more than agents, managers, or any other representative.

Entertainment Attorneys are also very much deal makers. Because their value lies largely in their knowledge of the Entertainment World, and their connections within, they are generally expensive. A "good entertainment attorney" is an attorney who knows about the entertainment world, its players, its needs, and its contracts. Don't spend your hard earned money to train an attorney new to the industry. Attorneys with experience are well worth the pound of flesh they charge.

Some Entertainment Attorneys work on an hourly rate basis, or flat rate. Most, however, work on a percentage basis, typically 5 - 10% of the deal.

What attorneys do for you

Entertainment Attorneys negotiate deals, including the contracts, watching out for your best interests. They try to get you the best residuals, for example, or help you retain merchandizing rights, or sequel rights. They protect your ideas against theft. They swim the shark-infested channels of Union forms.

One the best things that entertainment attorneys do for newbies comes about just by hiring them. Here's what I mean. An indie filmmaker in Florida wanted to hire John Travolta's daughter, Ella Bleu, for a supporting role in a feature film. However, he found he couldn't reach the Travoltas; he was told by the family's manager that they would only speak to an agent *or attorney*. So, the director hired me. This is common, especially for A-Listers. You can imagine how many people must try to contact John Travolta, and he can't possibly know which ones are safe and which are the weirdoes. By going only through agents and attorneys, he avoids the constant hassle and risk that the person contacting him doesn't know the proper etiquette and culture of the film world. I'm sorry, but A-Listers don't want to risk talking with newbies!

Going through attorneys is also common for major entertainment companies. Their reason is simple: it protects against the risk that someone surfaces later claiming "they stole my idea" – don't laugh, this happens all the time. Having an attorney involved gives both sides the comfort of knowing that a record of the timing of all meetings and disclosures exists, along with notes (perhaps even copies) of exactly what was discussed. Companies can expect entertainment attorneys to counsel their clients to be reasonable, since the attorneys understand not only the laws but also the entertainment world.

Quick example: I once (long ago, when young and dumb) had an idea for a tv show and I did the most stupid thing imaginable: I telephoned studios to pitch it. This is not how to pitch ideas! People laughed and hung up on me. Until someone at FOX (which was a brand new network at the time, and hungry for content) listened long enough to like the idea. But then they had to stop, and told me they were allowed by company policy only to discuss new concepts with attorneys. "Well, I am an attorney!" I said, and we were able to keep talking.

Of course, I'm biased. But I strongly recommend working with entertainment attorneys.

Unions

Keep track of your hours

You may someday wish to join an entertainment-related union. There are pros and cons of joining, and the timing of when to join if you decide to go union. But even while you are a newbie, even if unsure whether you'll ever join, keep track of your hours on various projects. If you want to join a union, you will one day have to provide evidence of your experience, in order to qualify for admittance.

Keep a log of everything you do, and have the director or producer of each project sign your log whenever possible. Keep the daily call sheets for each day you are on a set. Keep BTS pictures of yourself on set, even selfies. The more "proof" you may someday be able to offer, the better. And even if not for union admittance, you will one day be glad to have a record of your journey to success.

SAG / AFTRA

The main union for actors is SAG-AFTRA. Used to be, not long ago, these were separate unions. The Screen Actors Guild (SAG) for movie and tv actors, and the American Federation of Television and Radio Artists (AFTRA) for many other performers.

Unions still feel the need to fight against the machinery of big business. When SAG and AFTRA were separate, some people felt they did not have enough bargaining power against huge media conglomerates. In 1999 and 2003, merger votes failed. Celebrities like Tom Hanks, Richard Dreyfuss, Alec Baldwin, Nicholas Cage, Billy Crystal, Susan Sarandon, Morgan Fairchild, and Martin Sheen were in favor of merging, but not enough members rallied to the cause.

However, in 2012 the merger was approved. Anti-union sentiments in society generally had made it harder for both unions, and together they are stronger.

To be an actor, you don't have to join SAG-AFTRA. Actors have either non-union or union status. Most newbies are non-union, and the majority stay non-union. Within union membership, there are different categories. Budget categories. Non-voting option (FI-CORE or DPNM Dues Paying Non Member). If you decide you may want to be in the union, you'll need to read up on it because there's too much to list here. This book is for newbies, so I'm just going to barely touch on union matters here.

What does SAG-AFTRA mean for newbies? Well, for one thing, it's important to realize that union members can't work in non-union films. When you cast, union members are not allowed to audition or accept a role. There are exceptions, and sometimes union actors break the rules, and anyway it's the actor that gets into trouble with the union not you ... but in general, it's a bad idea to cross the line. Filmmakers can contact SAG-AFTRA and make their project a union film. But the process is full of landmines. For example, you need insurance, payroll administration, and compliance with various rules (such as providing a meal every 6 hours). It's not impossible … but I'll leave such complexities to the next book.

Modeling

Legit

The modeling world is very hard to break into. "Cream rises to the top" is the most applicable means to describe success in modeling: you either have the looks or not. Legit agencies are very picky. Yet there is variety among the agencies, and newbies can sign on with lower-tier agencies that are more likely to sign up new talent. In any event, the legit agencies will make you money, and they take a percentage, but they never charge you. This is how you know they are legit.

Scams

Sad to say, scam modeling agencies are very common, just about in every town. They prey especially on kids (more specifically, on parents).

You'll hear their pitch: "Oh, you have the look! Yes! Wow! You just need to sign up for photographs from our photographer, and classes from our instructors. We have a package deal that only costs you $2,000 – it's a bargain!"

Run.

Any legit agency will have plenty of models that you can talk to before you sign anything. Those models will tell you that nothing is free, and yes you have to spend money to make yourself look good, but the agency should not in any way be making money off of the process. Remember, agencies are there to make money for you.

Police

You will draw official attention

Almost every set I've been on had some level of police presence. Small, independent and student films are often filmed "guerilla style" – meaning no permits, no location authorizations, just run-and-gun camera work.

In downtown Tampa, I was once standing on a curb with other businesspeople, taking a smoke break (years ago, sad to say I smoked). A motorcycle pulled up next to us. The driver jumped off and aimed his video camera at the beautiful young woman who arrived sitting behind him. She was, even in the Tampa midday heat, wearing a full-length fur coat. As we bystanders gaped with our mouths hanging wide open, she opened her coat to reveal that the coat was all she wore. Wow! She posed for the camera in front of our shocked faces, and then they jumped back on their bike, just as a police car chirped its siren. They zoomed off, through traffic, and all the cop could do was shake his head. I don't know what that video was for, but I'm sure they didn't have a permit, and likely would never have gotten a permit to do what they did. Sometimes, guerilla style is the only way.

On one of my own films, recently, we had a plastic bb gun that looked like a real 9mm. We were filming in public early one morning at a deserted beach – but within sight of some beach houses. When my actor picked up the gun to goof off with it, I quickly had him hide it again, but the damage was done. Within the hour, two police officers approached us, saying that neighbors had reported concerns about a weapon.

On a friend's film which was filming a scene at my house, neighbors called police to complain about the number of cars parked out front. The police came, asking to speak with the property owner – me!

In both these cases which I've brought up as examples, I satisfied the police by cooperating fully. On the beach, I told them as they walked up that we had a plastic toy gun; I didn't try to hide it. After telling them, I asked if they wanted to see it, and then followed their instructions carefully to get it out to show them. I then agreed with their advice that I store the gun in my car, rather than where my actor could reach it. Regarding the parking complaint at my house, the police said the concern expressed by the neighbor was that an emergency vehicle might not have been able to fit down the street. That sounded stupid to me, since large panel trucks were driving through just fine even as the officer and I talked, but I did not argue with the police! Don't ever argue. In fact, the director of that film (a young hothead) wanted to argue, and I pulled him aside so that I could deal with the officers in a more non-confrontational manner. I agreed to move some cars – whoopie – and the police left, satisfied that they did their job.

I've worked on sets where we had permits, but sometimes we greatly overstepped the boundaries of the permit. Do so carefully, and watch diligently for police – be prepared to pull back quickly!

I'm not advising anyone to break laws. If you feel you must enter a "gray area" of law to get your stuff done, that's on you, and you need to be prepared if and when the police show up. Make sure that you identify yourself as the one in charge, if you are the producer or director, or if it was your choice to violate whatever law. Be honest, be open, cooperate with the officers to make sure they understand it's you and not anyone else on your crew. And if you get a ticket or are arrested, well … shit happens. Call a defense attorney.

PART IV: KNOW HOW TO DO YOUR THING

Part IV of this book is intended as a hands-on "help me" section. You already know who you are, what role you wish to play in the Entertainment World, and how you and your role fit into the whole. Now, to succeed, you need to learn how to be *really good* at what you do.

What follows is meant to help you, but by no means should this book be the end of your education. Every subject I touch on here could itself be expanded into a full book, or many books, and in fact already has been: there are dozens of books out there to help you. And there are multiple other sources: teachers, the Internet, master classes, on-the-job training. Never stop learning!

Storytelling

Every person is a storyteller
This section is for you! For everyone. Everyone needs to focus on storytelling because that's what filmmaking is all about. Don't think that this stuff is just for the writers to worry about. So much crap gets filmed that falls flat, because people neglect to tell a good story.

Good films and tv, like good books, are not just jumbles of images. No matter how cool the images may be. You've probably heard already that a long hard day of filming may result in a mere five minutes of finished show! That's not because only five minutes was shot, far from it. That five minutes was likely pulled from hours and hours of raw footage. But the takes recorded by the camera, and the corresponding sound files recorded by the sound recorder, are just raw images that must be sorted, cut and polished so that they come together to effectively bring the script to life.

What are the three most important things necessary for a good film? Alfred Hitchcock answered this question with, "The script, the script, and the script."

Good shows are always good because they tell a good story. GIGO applies. (That's "garbage in, garbage out" in case you don't know.) A good script tells a good story. If there is no good story, then even the best script is destined to result in, at best, a mediocre production. There's really no saving garbage. You can polish a turd, but it's still a turd. You must tell a good story! If you fear your story isn't very good, then stop and re-jigger until you do. Rewrite the entire script, if that's what it takes. Hire a Script Doctor if you like a concept but don't feel up to the task of reworking it yourself.

If you are part of a production, then you are part of the story-telling team. Most obviously, the producer, director and writer have the loudest voices in telling the story. But everyone on set, everyone developing the project before filming, and everyone working in post, contribute to the final product. Whether you are actor, director, producer, writer, designer, PA, gaffer, grip, 2AD, stuntman, foley artist, scripty, craft services, security … and on and on, you are part of the whole, and the whole will not be good without all of its parts being good.

Producing

The primary storyteller is the producer. This is why producers stand up to accept Academy Awards.

Producers produce. (LOL, but it's true. Just like directors direct, writers write, and actors act.) Think of producers as the bosses, because they are. And like all bosses in all industries, they must keep their eye on the big picture items. They don't "do" much (or any) of the actual work – at least, not anything you can point to in the end – and yet, everything is done because of their guidance and pushing.

The whole project starts with the Executive Producer, the person who says "I'm going to do this." A writer or someone else may have come up with the idea, or even the script, but it is the producer who figures out how to share it with the world. Generally, what producers do runs as follows:

- Purchase the rights if someone else came up with the story
- Write the script or hire a writer to do so; then re-write it ("polish" it), and write it again until satisfied it tells a good story
- Hire and manage key players (writers, other producers, director, designers, talent, crew)
- Determine the necessary budget
- Secure funding
- Oversee the project to be sure it stays on budget
- Schedule the production
- "Crew up" i.e. hire the crew
- Get the crew working
- Manage crises during production (i.e. keep the crew working)
- Oversee post-production (editing, music, ADR, credits)
- Market distribution and sales of the project
- Stand up to accept awards

As you see, producers stick with the project from inception to execution, from idea all the way to DVD.

What makes a good producer? Be a people person. Producers connect people. They are deal makers. They dream big, and let others figure out logistics (unless you are the Line Producer that has to figure out the nuts and bolts). Good producers create good work, by connecting good people. They launch careers.

How does one become a producer? By starting at the bottom, generally. Walt Disney started with entry-level "inking" at an art studio. David O. Selznick began as a lowly script reader. Learn everything about everything, and move up. Create a free profile on sites like ProductionBeast, where you can post your availability and search for producer jobs: for you clickers, the site is https://app.productionbeast.com/jobs.

Focus on story

Whoever you are, you need to focus on story. This applies, first and foremost to the writer. But it applies to everyone else, too, and I urge you to read the following pages about the writing process, even if you are not (today) a "writer." You may someday be a writer. Even if not, understanding the elements of story writing will help you in your filmmaking.

Many scripts fail to tell a story; they are instead just descriptions of a situation. For example, I recently worked on a student film which was about a man who lived in Nazi Germany and was able to continue living because his family had learned how to transfer one's consciousness into another person's body. The script was about the creepy old guy who kidnapped homeless men, in order to live in their bodies. Okay … but that's all the script was about. Basically, the script could be summarized as "there was this creepy old man who stole bodies". That is a situation, not a story. For it to be a story, there needs to be a set-up, conflict, and resolution. When I pointed this out to the director, who was also the writer, he said it was too late to change the script. We filmed it anyway. Fortunately, the director fixed his problem by focusing on the plight of what was initially a side character, the detective investigating the series of homeless deaths who ends up a victim of the old man. This happened because the actor playing the detective was so good that the director used more of his cuts, and slowly came to realize that this was the story he should have written in the first place.

Writers need to write stories. Actors need to express the story, through their bodies. Filmmakers need to bring the story alive, through sound, images, editing, set dressing, props construction, wardrobe, makeup, and so on.

Many times, when a production seems bogged down or losing its way, it's because people are stuck on details and forgetting to tell the story. This is true even in million-dollar productions. How many times have you been bored by endless action sequences with characters you don't care much about?

Elmore Leonard said you should just not write the parts that readers skip. Skip the boring parts. Specifically, Elmore advised against long character descriptions, long descriptions of setting, long … well, I think his point was, tell the story quickly. In film terms, this is often said as "Get in late, get out early." Start each scene late -- when action has already begun, in other words. In real life we walk into rooms, say hello, shake hands, find a comfy seat, smell the flowers, get a drink, and so on. Skip this stuff unless it is important to your story. Likewise, move from one scene into the action of the next, without pausing for "goodbyes" and other unnecessary and interrupting elements.

Writing

> *"I'm receiving a lot of questions from writers asking where to submit scripts or how to sell them. Others ask how to sign an agent, attach directors or producers, etc. You won't like the answer, but here it is:*
>
> *You're asking the wrong questions."*
>
> ~ Christopher McQuarrie
> (screenwriter *The Usual Suspects*)

Start Now: Today, not Tomorrow

The above quote is the start of a long Twitter feed from Christopher McQuarrie. It's well worth Googling. The gist of it all is simply that you must stop waiting on others and make your own art happen. McQuarrie won an Academy Award for Best Original Screenplay for 1995's *The Usual Suspects* (one of my favorite movies!), and yet he says he sat around for years after that asking these same questions. Until he realized his career didn't start by submitting scripts to others. He says, "the secret to making movies is making movies – starting with little movies no one will ever see." That's how he started. And that's how you need to start.

"A writer writes" is the truest truism I know. If you write, you are a writer; if you are a writer, you write. Like most writers, I go through long periods of no or minimal writing, whether because I'm "busy" or depressed, which are just excuses. When that happens, I remind myself that "A writer writes" and force myself to sit down to write. There is no good excuse for not writing every day, even if for only 10 minutes.

Got an idea? Write it down, because 10 minutes from now it will be forgotten. There's nothing worse than that horrible realization that the idea you had earlier, which seemed awesome, has now slipped away from your brain.

Keep a dream journal. You'll be amazed at the creativity of your sub-conscious mind.

Writer's block? We all suffer from it, now and then. There are bits of strange advice out there (Google it!), but to me the only way to get past writer's block is to just start writing.

Screenwriter Charles Bukowski said, "Writing about writer's block is better than not writing at all."

Get Educated

Learn! Whether in school or in the "school of hard knocks", the more educated you become, the better. There is nothing wrong with years of academia, theatre or film degrees, bachelors, masters, doctorates … but it's not necessary. When I go to auditions, I wish I could count on being chosen, simply due to the fact that I have a theatre degree; but, no, that doesn't happen. Honestly, no one has ever cared that I have a theatre degree.

Education is never a waste. In order to be a good storyteller, you need to be tuned into the human condition. Observe the world. Open your eyes. Get "woke", as my daughter says. Pay attention to what's around you. At any given moment there are stories unfolding all around you. Funny and sad, inspiring, and depressing … study them. Use them.

Anyone can string words together, and by so doing call themselves a "writer." But do you have anything to write about? Every writer needs to find their voice, to write about their passions. That's why they say, "Write what you know."

What if the doctor you went to had never studied medicine? What if your lawyer skipped law school? To get good, you need to study. If you want to write mysteries, read mysteries. If you want to write screenplays, read screenplays. Fortunately, you can find free screenplays online, often for free.

You should read what you like, and also for comparison purposes some that you don't like. It's just as important to determine what you feel is wrong in some works, in order to avoid that in your own writing.

Ask people for unbiased reviews of your writings, then listen and learn from their comments and reactions. This is amazingly hard because you naturally become attached to your creations. You might not like what they say, and you don't have to change a word, but think hard about what they say. Appreciate any and all constructive criticism. It's all good.

Find writers groups, where works can be reviewed and critiqued. Find groups of writers and actors who get together for cold readings. Participate, both as a writer and as an actor, so you can truly hear the words come to life. Provide helpful comments for other writers because that, more than anything else, will help you recognize and fix problems in your own stuff.

How to Write for Film & TV

I'm not going to attempt to teach you how to write. You only learn that by starting with a decent education, a modicum of talent, and plenty of doing. But I will try to give you some tips on the process, which might hopefully help orient beginning writers, and maybe even provide a nugget or two for advanced writers.

Anyone can be a writer. Or maybe I should say, anyone can call themselves a writer. There is no single certification or licensing board, no standards, and indeed nothing at all to stop you from writing something, right now. Got an idea? Scribble it down before you forget it! It might suck; if so, throw it in a drawer, or the rubbish, and forget about it. But … the good ideas tend to call out to you. They don't like to be ignored. Look at it; add more to it; research some details; think about story twists, plotlines, characters; throw together a rough outline; play with your outline, especially with potential interactions between characters. Got good ideas that don't seem good enough to make into a script? Combine those ideas! Write a rough first draft script. Maybe write a treatment before writing the script or pilot episode. Maybe write a series bible. Maybe have your friends and family give you feedback. Maybe sell the script, or produce it yourself. Maybe make a million dollars. Maybe! And there is truly nothing stopping you.

I started writing fiction stories and screenplays as a young child, and I proudly called myself a "Writer" all through school years and well into my adulthood, even before I ever published anything. Don't let anyone tell you otherwise; if you write, you are a writer. (It's up to you to become a *good* writer, but that's different.)

There is no single way to write, and if you ask 10 writers for advice, I bet you'll get 20 different opinions. There are countless books on writing, for the stage, for tv, for film, for fiction, for documentary, for journalism, and so on. Read what you can get your hands on; reading is never a waste of time.

Writing Good Dialogue

Characters need to have clear goals, but at the same time you (the writer, director, actor) need to hide those goals in the art of your story. It's all about the subtext.

Your audience needs to be able to follow exactly what each character wants, the hurdles they face, and the conflicts between the characters. But you can't just write all that. Character one, "Hey, I need to get that thing!" to which character two responds, "I need it myself, so we have a conflict." No! What a character thinks and feels is *subtext*. If you have your character just plainly say what they want or what they're doing, that is called "on the nose" dialogue. For example, your protagonist leaves the room, saying, "I'm leaving." Well, duh! We can see he's leaving.

Subtext drives all of our daily conversations, in the real world. It should be no different in your work. Although … you need to also at the same time tell your story in a way that the audience can understand. Art. Filmmaking is art, and it's not easy. Find the balance.

Try not to turn your dialogue into plot information. Dialogue is character. Every spoken line should be necessary for your story, or else it needs to be cut. <u>Every line, every word</u>. Dialogue can (if you must) provide information, but even then, it should also tell us about the character's weaknesses and strengths, push another character, add conflict and pressure, wake up (shock) the audience, or foreshadow what's coming.

Quentin Tarantino credits the powerful dialogue in his films on his origins as an actor. He has no "throw away" characters. Actors jump at the chance to be in Tarantino's films because they know every role is fun and important to his stories. Ideally, every character you write should be one an actor would want to play, because that means they are characters an audience wants to see.

Exposition (your story plotlines) is something that should come out through what characters are saying *about something else.* So the kid ready to run away from home because she's tired of her mom's drinking says anything but that. Perhaps they have a fight over the age of the milk in the refrigerator, and the drunk mother's defense of old milk is the final straw.

"Show, don't tell" is the guiding principle. Lots of films have too much chit chat, which gets boring. Cut to the chase. Show what's happening, instead of having a character talk about it. Another principle is "Get in late, get out early." Write your scene, then tighten it up; get in late (past the "Hello") and out early (end with the raised gun, instead of the gory description of the bullet's exit wound).

One of the biggest problems with newbie writers (and directors) is their insistence upon "sounding natural" … the inclusion of what we hear every day, in almost every conversation. Things like "Hey, how's it going?" "Good morning" "Catch the game last night?" "Man, I need a cup of coffee" even just "Hello" and "Goodbye" in telephone calls – yes, this stuff is part of natural conversation. But it's garbage in your script! It's "shooting the breeze" dialogue, where characters are "just talking." Stop it! Every time you write like this, think of it instead as "shooting yourself in the foot" and "just time wasting."

You need meaningful dialogue. Dialogue that is hard for a character to say, and hard for another character to hear. Dialogue that creates tension, and builds it to a breaking point. Cut out the chit-chat. Your script needs to tell an important story (defined simply as a story that people want to see), and you need to carry that thought into each scene. Find ways to make every scene meaningful, or else suck it up and cut the scene – if you don't cut it now, you'll cut it later, or someone else (your editor, say) will cut it for you.

Watch out for clichés that will immediately seem old and hum drum to your audience. Watch lots of films, and you'll see some bits again and again – like starting off your story with characters waking up in bed. Mix it up, find fresh ways of telling your story. Instead of that alarm clock at the beginning of the day, start your story with a search for a lost shoe – or whatever you can imagine even better than that.

Structure – Treatments & Outlines

Many tv and film writers begin with a "**Treatment**", or a "**Pitch**", which is a short summary of your script. It should introduce the main characters, and tell the story quickly; a treatment for an episodic show will summarize the storylines of the pilot and each planned episode, and discuss any story arcs. A Treatment can also reference your intended audience, draw comparisons to other shows, identify any named actors you may have interested in the project, and speak to how you see certain points getting produced. It's rarely purchased, but can be used to get the attention of someone who may want to read your script. A Treatment can be used to help you obtain financing. Most importantly (in my mind), a treatment helps you explore your idea, to see if it has legs (i.e. if it can sustain interest for 90 minutes, or episodically); from the treatment, you can more easily write an outline, and your script.

There are no real rules. Treatments can and do vary wildly. Especially if you are writing a treatment to help you write. Write whatever works, for you.

Beware, however, writing mush. The treatment should help you, and anyone else, understand your story. It should be short, clear, concise. Typically, 4 to 12 pages.

A treatment is not the same as an "**Outline**". Advice on outlines is all over the place because many writers use all sorts of outlines, and many use none at all. I highly advise creating an outline prior to writing. Other writers take the contrary extreme: just start writing to see where it goes. Hey, whatever works for you.

An outline can be shared with others, basically for the same purposes as a treatment. But a treatment is usually written to share your ideas with others, where an outline is usually written only as a tool for you to use to keep your writing focused. I know a very good writer of a fiction series who tells me she never uses outlines; instead, she lets her characters tell her where to go in the next chapter. I personally do the same, in that I am open to seeing how the writing goes, and changing the plot as new ideas get fired in my brain. But I also think outlines are extremely helpful, not only to keep your writing from veering off on tangents, but also to help you pace your writing. For a book like this one, writing an outline first enabled me to list hundreds of ideas in bullet-point format, which could then be reorganized into a workable structure much more easily than one could revise blocks of text. But again, do what works for you.

A "**Bible**" for episodic shows is similar to treatments, in that it contains short summary information of your plot and characters.

[Note: Don't get ticked off at the use of the word "bible", it's not meant as a statement for or against any religion. Merriam-Webster gives as an alternate definition of the word "a publication that is preeminent especially in authoritativeness or wide readership." For example, "The Fisherman's Bible" as title for a fishing guide. Maybe I should call this book the "Filmmaker's Bible" … maybe? (*wink wink*)]

For a sitcom, the show's bible exactly fits the Merriam-Webster definition: the ultimate voice on what goes on in that sitcom's world. Typically, sitcom episodes are written by many different writers. They all need to know the base parameters of the sitcom's world and its characters.

There are "**Pitch Bibles**" and "**Show Bibles**" which are similar, but distinctly different.

Pitch bibles are used to help pitch the series to production companies and networks, and to funding sources. A pitch bible is a treatment or pitch, on steroids. Its purpose, bluntly, is to convince people to greenlight the show. Where a treatment or pitch may be exciting enough to get attention, one may deliver a pitch bible to convince others that the show has enough depth (legs) to sustain interest over many episodes, even many seasons. A pitch bible would typically contain:

- An overview of the series
- Character bios
- A summary of the pilot episode and season 1 episodes (sometimes episode by episode), plus an idea of where future seasons would go to prove the show's longevity
- Comps – comparisons to old and currently existing shows. This is a shortcut way of describing your series. For example, *Game of Thrones* could be described (though poorly) as *Downton Abbey* meets *Lord of the Rings*.
- Tone – is the show mostly upbeat, or down?
- Demographics – what audience does the show aim to reach?
- Why the show is timely or otherwise ripe for production
- Budget – an idea of the costs of production
- Actors – if any famous actors have expressed interest

Pitch bibles are best kept short and concise as possible because you want money lenders and other busy executives to read it.

Show bibles, on the other hand, may be incredibly long. They are used more as internal tools for cast and crew to make the show. They are an overview of the show meant to keep the show on its true course. This is crucial and very helpful to incoming writers, directors, producers, designers, and other creatives who may become involved well after the show's early development, and in some cases even years after a show has been running. Show bibles typically contain:

- An overview of the series
- Synopsis of every show that has aired so far
- Plot lines and character arcs, both existing and planned

- Any must-have rules of the show. For example, in one of my projects there must always be a second death in each episode. Weird, but it fit the title and therefore was a rule that all writers had to obey.
- Discussion of long range plans
- Everything needed to communicate the world of the show to the people producing it: writers, producers, directors, designers, etc.
- Even costume design, with fabric swatches, may be in a show bible

Where pitch bibles may commonly be 10-30 pages, show bibles can be hundreds of pages and multiple volumes.

Visual Writing

Write "cinematically." In other words, write from the point of view of an audience looking at the film frame – and restrict your writing to what is seen within the frame at that time. For example, your writing shouldn't include such things as "He thought about the last time he saw her" because there is no way for the actor to show that thought in the character's head. (If it's important for the audience to know what he's thinking, then you need to show it, perhaps as a flashback.)

Films are visual, and so should be your screenplays. Use words that bring the story to life. Remember, Shakespeare wrote both for the masses and for the elite audience members that wanted poetry. Don't pull out your thesaurus just for the sake of trying to impress anyone. But find words that convey images. For example, instead of saying your character "walks" here and there, find places where he "strolls" or "saunters" or "paces", because each of those give a slightly different feel.

I personally do not like use of such phrases as "We see …" and "Coming into frame …" because they take me out of the story, and because they too closely hint at directions for the producer and director to follow. Plus, such phrases don't add anything. Instead of writing "We see a large school bus, pulling up to the curb" it's better to write "A large school bus pulls up to the curb." (Note, also: active is better than passive.)

Story Elements

Every story is the same, right? Of course not! Every story is different, unique, special, because no human being is just like another and we all go through our own separate lives. But … well, actually, all stories are pretty much the same, when you get right down to the themes and ideas expressed. Humans are human, and as much as we want to think we are each of us sooooo special, we're all part of the species and all dealing with the "human experience."

Look at the Greek and Roman era plays of Sophocles, Aristophanes, Seneca, and other classical writers. Just about everything in our society and technology has changed since those plays were written approximately 2,000 years ago, but it's clear that human nature has not changed much at all. What was funny or tragic back then, still is. "Human nature" is essentially the same, over thousands of years.

Even in Shakespeare's time, it was already recognized that there are only so many plots. Human nature is human nature. Did you know Shakespeare stole plot ideas from earlier writers? You can find books and articles arguing that there are only a limited number of plots, and that all stories ever expressed fit into such short lists. For example, books like *The Seven Basic Plots* by Christopher Booker and *20 Master Plots* by Ronald Tobias, or a 2016 academic study titled "The Emotional Arcs of Stories are Dominated by Six Basic Shapes." The art, however, in filmmaking lies in the mixing and expression of these plotlines.

I'm not telling you this so that you can "find the magic formula" and go write the next *Die Hard*. My point is, you must find the human aspects of your idea, and bring out the story or stories within that context. A story written for a robot to read or watch would be drastically different, I suspect. A robot may value all sorts of information that we humans would gloss over, and the robot would likely slight emotions and feelings. Keep in mind at all times that you are not writing for robots; you're writing for humans. Know your audience. Write for them. Your production doesn't have to follow any formula, but it must connect to our human experience.

Arc

Every character should have an arc. They start somewhere, and end up somewhere else. If your character doesn't change, that character is boring, and doesn't belong in your story. You can get away with this for background characters. However, if a character has a name, then that should be a character the audience is expected to care about, some one important to your storyline, and that character needs to be brought to life in the writing, and in the acting. What ultimately happens to that character should matter to viewers. Likewise, every film or tv show should have an arc. A start, and an end. Take the viewer for a ride. Otherwise, what are you doing? If you're not telling a story, you're just masturbating with camera equipment.

Sitcoms are the exception to the above rule, in that the characters do not change over the course of an episode. You can watch episodes of *Gilligan's Island* (for example) in any order, because no matter what happens at the end of each episode they are still the same seven people stuck on a deserted isle. Other sitcoms follow this pattern, but allow characters to arc over seasons; for example, the guys in *Big Bang Theory* go from date-less geeks to married men.

Your stories can be simple or full of crinkum-crankum. But they must get our attention, and hold it.

While there is no "magic formula", it pays to look for one. There are many good ways of breaking down a story and examining its parts. By doing so, you make sure you have put in enough elements to make the story meaningful and satisfy your readers / viewers.

Conflict

Is there something which MUST be in every story? Yes. Conflict. Without conflict, your story is just a rambling collection of character or setting descriptions. There must be meaning, and that meaning is found through conflict. If there is no conflict, the scene will be flat, boring.

The story really begins only once desire is established. Showing a happy character who wants nothing is no story at all. And once you have a character wanting something, you need to show why that character may fail. Conflict is created by the different and contrasting wants of your characters.

A scene without conflict belongs on the editing floor. A script without conflict should never leave your desk.

Format

Nothing turns industry people off faster than poor formatting that makes a script difficult to read. One could argue that a script can be written however a writer wants, so long as it tells a story well. But the film and television industries have been around for decades, and certain standards in the writing of screenplays have come to be accepted, and expected. Varying from such industry standards results in a script that screams "Amateur!" In the eyes of industry script readers, if a writer cannot follow these standards, then what else don't they know? What else have they done terribly wrong in their script? Busy script readers have no desire to teach you how to write. As busy as even the most junior script readers are, a poorly formatted script probably won't even get read. Personally, when I'm asked to read someone's work (which I am usually happy to do) I'll mentally note the first couple formatting issues and keep reading. But when I get to more than a couple … I stop reading and the discussion then is about formatting. That is NOT the reaction you want from your readers!

Formatting is not hard. Yes, there are many different formats. For example, a Hollywood feature script is formatted very differently than a play written for stage. But you can learn which format to use, for which production areas, quickly and easily with the help of many fine books on the subject, or some Google research. If you write using Final Draft software, there are template format forms built in. You don't need Final Draft because you can (as I did long ago) create your own "styles" in Word, to allow you to format different parts of your script with just a keyboard stroke or two. (But seriously, get Final Draft.)

There are actually many software options, free and otherwise. Here are the ones I recommend:

- Microsoft Word – because most people already have it. Really, any text editor. You can set your own tabs, using examples from scripts, and create "Styles" to allow you to apply formatting wherever you want. Not having dedicated software should never be your excuse for not writing!

- Final Draft – my favorite, and highest recommendation. It is not free. I think I paid a few hundred dollars, and periodically they want more money for updates. Final draft is very easy and helpful to use. It is also the most widely used and accepted software in the film industry. Productions will appreciate getting your script in Final Draft.

- Celtx – free, although I'm not sure if it is intended to be free only to students or only upon a trial basis; there is a paid version, which I haven't tried. I am not a big fan, mostly because I love Final Draft so much. But … free.

Final Draft is broadly accepted as an industry standard. In my humble opinion, it is well worth the cost. I wish I had bought it much earlier in my career. As it was, I paid for Final Draft and used the heck out of it way before ever making any money on selling my writing services.

One tip often given for writing screenplays is that there must be plenty of "white space" on each page. What does this mean? Well, first recognize that it's not a law; it's just a recommendation. By "white space" is meant that a page should not look like a brick wall of solid text. This is because scripts are meant to be visualized, more so than read like one would read a novel. Think with some pity about the poor schmuck hired by production studios to read piles and piles of new scripts; they are paid peanuts, and expected to read an ungodly number of scripts every day (or, as is usually the case, every night after they've put in a full 8 – 10 hours at some other J O B). If you want your script to be recognized as the best of the bunch, you need to write with that poor schmuck in mind. Keep your action paragraphs limited to a line or 2, or say at the most, 4 lines. Break action up into pieces that can be easily visualized, and by doing so keep the reader entertained. Keep the eyeballs moving quickly down the page. Don't make the reader struggle to read your script, no matter how clever you think you're being!

Loglines

Loglines are what you would say your story is about if you had only a few seconds to do so. Shorter even that the classic elevator speech. Another way to think of it: this is what might one day be printed in the television guide to describe your show.

So what, you say? Who cares, why would you need a logline, when you can just let some tv technician type in a summary later?

A well-crafted logline helps you in multiple ways. Of course, it helps to be able to quickly communicate the central concept of your story. If your producers, your director, your writer, and your stars, are all on the same page, then performances and production choices will all conform quickly.

An effective logline is one that tells the essence of your concept, in a way that gets attention and makes people want to see more. For example, *Lethal Weapon's* logline is as simple as they come: suicidal cop.

Another reason to carefully craft your logline is to help you as a writer. Making it forces you to determine the core idea of your work, and once you have that you can finetune your work to really develop that central theme. Some writers figure out their logline after finishing the script, but doing so ahead of writing acts as the spearhead of your outline.

Outlines

Ask 5 writers about whether they do outlines, and what type, and you'll get 10 opinions, at least.

I swear by outlines. But I also swear by the importance of feeling free to vary from your outline, letting your work lead the way, letting your characters speak to you. Your mileage may differ.

Outlining may lead to stories that seem too obvious, with characters following what is obviously the writer's path, and not the path the characters would choose themselves. Pay attention as you write to other options the characters have. You may choose to let a character go where she wants to go – and you should never ignore an option open to a character.

Selling Your Script

Copyright Registration

You've worked hard, maybe for years, to get to the end of your writing project. Many writers never finish. You did. You're excited, you're proud of yourself, and rightfully so. Until you sit back and ask yourself, "Now, what?"

First, before you let your script out the door, you need to protect yourself. Understand copyright law. I'm presuming most of my readers are in the US, and therefore I'm talking about US law; if you are elsewhere, you need to carefully research how things are done in your country.

Briefly, as the author you own the rights to your writings (the "copyright") just by the mere fact that you did the writing. Your copyright means that no one can use your writings without your permission. If you've written something in the course of your employment by someone else, then what you wrote is likely a "work for hire", and in that case the copyright is owned by your employer. Essentially, your employment serves as the assignment of your copyrights to your employer. There are other ways you can transfer your rights, including for example selling your copyright. But if you haven't transferred your rights, then you alone control the use of your writing.

If someone without your permission uses or copies your work, or a significant part thereof, you can send them a "cease and desist letter" which demands that they stop, and even that they pay you a reasonable portion of whatever gains they've received from using your work. Copyright law is full of exceptions, so the use of a small amount of your work is likely not an infringement of your rights. There are exceptions for parody, and for educational purposes. The law is tricky. Any particular situation should be reviewed by an attorney.

If you want to enforce your copyright, you need to first register your work with the US Copyright Office. Fortunately, your rights start on the date you wrote, and not on the date you registered. If you can prove that you created your work on a certain date, then you should be able to object to anyone's use arising after such date.

This is why some people recommend mailing a copy of your script to yourself, in a sealed envelope that you keep sealed after receiving it, and stick it in your files ready to show anyone the postmark. I'm afraid this approach is more urban legend than sound advice because a sealed envelope proves nothing, really. Anyone can mail an empty unsealed envelope and seal it later.

To research more about US copyrights, go to www.copyright.gov. Go to www.eco.copyright.gov to register your work electronically; it costs about $35 - $55. Usually takes a few months (and I find much longer after COVID19). It's a good idea to register for peace of mind, and it's also neat to get a formal piece of paper back from the U S of A with your name on it.

You can also register your screenplay with the Writers Guild of America (WGA) by going to www.wgawregistry.org for $20. This does NOT take the place of registration with the US copyright office, but some potential buyers will only look at your script if you have a WGA registration number, too. So – do both. (To be fair, understand that WGA registration is not legally required, and many people will tell you that it is a waste of time and money – and actually harmful, in that some writers register with WGA and wrongly think they are then protected. Understand, too, that WGA registrations expire in a short amount of time.)

Sell

So, what can you do if you do have a script, and you have protected your rights by filing for a copyright registration? Easy answer: Sell it!

If you are like me, and probably most people, you wrote purely for the fun of it, and you've never ever had any far-fetched fantasies about actually making money with this crazy obsession. Right? Oh. Alright, I admit I've had such fantasies, too. After all, you do hear stories once in a while about someone selling a script. You may be able to sell your script, perhaps, maybe, I don't know … but there are rumors … it happens … maybe.

Be realistic, however. You won't get rich. As a newbie you'll get, at best, a few thousand dollars for your script. That's right, no riches. Not until you earn your place as an established and proven writer. Also, expect that you will need to sell all rights to your script, which means transferring your copyrights. You may try to retain certain rights, such as the right to write sequels using the same characters, but the money people are going to fight you on that. Want to retain the merchandising rights, so that you can make toy versions of your characters? Want to turn your script into a novel? Or a stage play? You guessed it: the money people will not want you to retain any rights – and the Golden Rule ("Whoever has the money, makes the rules") will usually prevail, at least until you're a famous writer. (You will be much happier if you write for the fun of it.)

So, you have a script, it's protected, and you don't have a buyer … what can you do? That pretty much describes the situation that nearly all writers are in, especially newbie writers. Here are some ideas for what you can do to get yourself out of that mire:

Get an agent

Good luck with this one. All agents worth anything are super busy, so most won't even consider taking on unknown writers. You have to first prove yourself, say by selling a script or at least having a viable offer on the table, before they'll bother with you. It's a bit like a bank giving you a loan only if you have collateral: an agent will gladly take you if you already have a buyer!

There are many ways to get an agent, the easiest by far being to let the agent contact you. Once you start winning festival awards, or get exposure online, or produce product, or otherwise become visible to the industry, the agents will swarm. How, then, do you find an agent if you have not otherwise already succeeded?

Query letters

The equivalent of cold calls. A query letter is a letter sent via old-fashioned snail mail, or email, to agents, production companies or prospective buyers. You can find names and addresses through a number of sources: for example, IMDb lists production companies.

Your query letter should:

- Be addressed to a specific person. Don't waste anyone's time sending "to whom it may concern" blanket letters out. Personalize your message.

- Begin immediately with your pitch for your story. Not who you are, or why you're writing – these things can be discussed later. Hook them, as best you can, right away.

- A logline. One or two paragraphs that *sell* your story. Come on, you are a writer, yes? Prove it! Write a compelling pitch, something which makes the reader really want to read more.

- Mention your audience, and any marketing platform you may already have developed. For instance, if you have done a "proof of concept" short film that has garnered awards and/or followers, talk about that!

- Compare your project favorably to existing work, and then describe how yours differs in positive ways.

- List your accolades, if any.

- End by thanking them.

- Keep your letter short, brief, and easy to read. You're not writing to retired literary giants, but tired over-promoted executives.

- Write in a strong voice. You are offering them money, dammit.

- Attach the first 3 - 10 pages of your work, and invite them to ask for more.

Note that many writers would alter the above advice. Everyone has their own style, and writers swear by their own tricks of the trade. For instance, many writers advise against sending pages of your work out. One writer I met believes a query letter should be no more than a quick compliment of someone's project followed by asking them what types of projects they'd like to see.

Film Festivals for Writers

A relatively small number of film festivals have categories for writers to enter screenplays, both shorts and features. Getting recognition for your writing is rarely an immediate boost to your career, but it can't hurt! And there are stories of writers leap-frogging into success after (and because of) getting awards. You may potentially catch the eye of a producer, or you may potentially get an agent – longshots, but worth aiming at.

The festivals recommended for writers are:

- Blacklist (for already established writers)
- Sundance Writers Lab
- Nichols
- Page
- StudioFest
- Austin Filmfest
- Stage 32
- Scripapolooza
- AFF
- Screencraft contests

Submit your script to film festivals that judge scripts. Go to www.filmfreeway.com and you will find many festivals around the world that accept submissions. Getting accepted into festivals is thrilling, and when your film is selected you will earn a "laurel" to show the world how special you are, for example one of mine:

Most film festivals charge an entry fee, anywhere from a few bucks to hundreds of dollars. The choice is yours. As for my recommendations, I'd say if you are a newbie screenwriter, stick to the festivals that you can enter for free – there are some. Beware film festival scams that take your entry fee, or charge you a fee after selecting your film, but never actually hold a festival. FilmFreeway requires festival organizers to have a website, and they must also attest to having a forum theatre in which to show the films – and even a letter or other proof from the theatre – but such things can be faked. Because of the scammers, as I write in 2020 there are calls for regulation of film festivals, but we shall see. What I would recommend is that you carefully check reviews on festivals, prior to sending any money.

Self-Produce

You may choose to keep your script and produce it yourself. There are a few "rags to riches" stories like this, and if you have even a small amount of time and money to invest, why not try? The secret to this approach is being reasonable in your expectations. Don't try to make a $200 Million Hollywood style blockbuster by yourself, even if you have the money! Stick to a much simpler, much easier to film, concept. Kevin Smith wrote, directed and starred in the 1994 film *Clerks* that was made for only $28,000 but got picked up by a major distributor and went on to bring in millions in the box office. These things happen. If you haven't seen it, watch it – it's very funny! But watch it, too, for what it can teach you about independent (cheap and feasible) filmmaking. For example, Kevin filmed in black and white, used his friends for actors, filmed in locations that were available for free, and did just about everything himself (camera, editing, sound, etc.) in order to make the film. The first film from Robert Rodriguez (*El Mariachi*) is another example of a cheaply made independent film that became a big box office success; Robert financed that film with his credit cards, for around $7,000.

Even if you are not up for or willing to film your whole script, you can film a short example of your script. Sound hard? Damn right, it can be. (Even with this book.) But if you film a "proof of concept" project, you will have a much easier time demonstrating the merit of your ideas. You can film the entire script, maybe just as a video of actors sitting around a table and reading your script. Or film just a part of your script, maybe just one scene. Or film something that is not part of your script, but a new scene that introduces your world, your character(s) or your scene(s). For example, if you wrote *John Wick* (and your name is Derek Kolstad) you could have filmed a short scene about hitmen getting paid in gold coins to convey the feel of your script. Whatever you do, keep in mind that the aim is to create something visual that can get attention, go viral even. You need it to be fun, exciting, upbeat … and probably short, since in these "Modern Times" most viewers have the attention spans of a small puppy.

Other (cheaper) options

Want to dip your toes in without spending thousands of dollars? Unsure if your script is good enough? Feel like you need help, before risking your pocketbook?

Look for writers groups in your area, groups that read scripts or portions thereof and give each other useful criticism. If you find no such group, start one and have them read your material. Listen carefully, with an open mind, and you'll find plenty of pointers. This is a great way to grow, as a writer. You don't need to take their advice (and honestly, in my experience very few writers ever do take the advice of other writers), but getting feedback can't hurt. You may learn more by critiquing the work of other writers – because it's always easier to point out others' flaws, rather than acknowledge your own. Joining writing groups is also potentially valuable because you may find the contacts you need in order to find people to buy your script.

Get online reviews of your work. Create a free account on www.zoetrope.com which is a site where writers can post their writings and get reviews by other writers. The reviews, in my experience, range from helpful to meaningless, and the expression "you get what you pay for" comes to mind. However, sometimes the comments from other writers can really help you see a problem and solve it.

Look, too, for groups of actors that like to do cold readings. For a writer, there is really nothing better than that first time you hear your script come to life. Listening critically to the flow, the dialogue, and the readers' reactions, you'll be able to hear what works and what doesn't. As an added benefit, you will meet actors, which may help you in your own casting efforts.

Have your friends and family read your script. This can be helpful, but usually they are too timid or too inexperienced to offer any real feedback. Don't fall into the trap thinking you're a good writer just because your besties like it! But listen to any constructive criticism they may offer, because how your work comes across to them is very likely an indication of how it would be received by audiences, in general, and by literary agents, producers, or other potential buyers, in specific.

Put your film or script online. Put a video on YouTube and/or Vimeo. YouTube is free, although that means you have to put up with ads; Vimeo costs you some amount to post (not much), and then you have the benefit of knowing your audience can watch without annoying ads.

Use Social Media to steer attention to you, your script, and you film. You can create a Facebook page, for example, and use that to spread the link for your YouTube / Vimeo video.

Improve Your Script

You thought you were done, but … nothing is ever perfect. Get an editor. Or story consultant. Or some other assistant, by any other name. Someone with industry experience, who will help you tear your script apart and polish it up nicely.

A producer may become interested in a project because a script already exists. Often, however, producers come up first with an idea, or a theme, that they like, and then hire a writer to create a script. Even if they start with a script, there is a good chance the producers will hire additional writer(s) to re-write, alter, change, or otherwise "polish" it. In the film world, scripts are never final. They are subject to change at all stages in the process, from pre-production, to rehearsal, through filming, and even later in post-production editing.

If you are a screenwriter, you likely need a script editor. Almost every script I've ever read is full of mistakes, even those that got produced. Wait, you say, maybe that means I can make plenty of mistakes and still get my script produced? Granted. Maybe. But then again, don't you want to do everything you can to increase the odds that your script gets accepted? Why turn the readers off, by demonstrating your sloppiness?

There are different levels of editing – with greatly different costs, timing, and scope of review. The simplest form of editing is proofreading, which aims to just find your and correct your typos.

A "developmental editor" examines craft. They focus on plot, character, and structure. They make suggestions; they do NOT do the work for you.

"Line editors" look at paragraphs and sentences. They focus on writing style and big technical problems. They make changes to fix the problems they see. They should work using tracked changes, and you need to review and accept or reject each one. (By no means should you ever just "Accept All.")

Directors and producers are fond of thinking they can rewrite your script. They always think they are great writers. Because of the Golden Rule ("Whoever has the gold, makes the rules") they usually get to change the script however much they want. They may hire a "Script Doctor", i.e. another writer to polish your script, and even rewrite it completely. If you have enough clout as a screenwriter, you may insist on contractual clauses that restrict or prevent changes to your script, absent your approval.

Editors are readily available, online if not locally, although rarely for free. For editing, expect to pay about 1 or 2 cents per word for basic proofreading. Other types of editors will help you with developing your story structure, on a more meaningful level, but of course that will cost you more. Before you hire an editor or consultant, make sure you understand exactly what they will be doing; many good editors will edit your first 1,000 words for free, as a sample of what type of review they do, before you engage them to do the rest.

Funding

I started this section on How To with storytelling. That's first and foremost, because without good storytelling, all else fails. Producers and writers need to keep this in mind, especially, because they are often involved in a project's gestation. They set the tone, and begin the story.

But another key consideration there at the beginning, or almost the beginning, is the question of budget. Newbies really shouldn't plan a production that needs a $100 Million budget to bring to fruition. We can think big, but must find ways to bring big concepts down to manageable logistics. For instance, writers should think about needed locations, and not write something that requires, say, actors floating in the International Space Station, or even a character getting off of an airplane – unless you have access to shooting in an airport or the realistic expectation that your budget can handle the cost!

Getting funding is a primary job of the producer. Or, getting people to work for you at a discount, or even free. It's all about your budget. Find more money, or get more services and product for what money you have. There are various ways you can hope to accomplish this.

Private Equity

Often, in the indie film world, films are produced using private equity, in other words money from key individuals. Often from the producer, in fact. We've all done this. You made a video and put it on YouTube? Well, any cost of doing so was paid by you, I bet.

Films can be made cheaply. The short films I've worked on have had budgets ranging from $300 to $12,000. I've made two short films of my own for under $100, and they were good enough to get accepted into film festivals. It's a mistake to worry about the money. Worry instead about making something good within your budget, whatever that budget is.

There are stories of filmmakers who mortgage their house, max out their credit cards, and borrow from friends to finance a film. I can't recommend that. I think you're much better off doing what you can, and growing so that you can do more next time. Especially if you're new at the game and still learning.

The real trick is using OPM (other people's money). Get others to invest in your projects. The surest way to do that, is to have a good story, good script, and also a good track record of successful prior projects. So, focus on getting there. A true newbie probably won't be able to convince anyone to invest, but that can change (will change!) at some point after you have good work to show people.

If you don't have a solid record to tout, you might consider loans instead of investments. I worked on a feature where the director had borrowed money from his friends, promising them a 25% return. Risky. Fortunately, he kept his costs down reasonably and as of the writing of this book it looks like he will be able to sell his movie for at least what he has in it. But plenty of projects don't make back the costs, and a filmmaker that guaranteed results to investors would be in a world of hurt then.

No money at all …

Filmmakers are good with networking, and trading skills. We work on each other's projects, often for free, because we know it comes full circle; the person you are helping today may be the one helping you tomorrow. You're an actor? Or a camera person? Yeah, but you can also be a grip, a PA, a background extra, too. Help each other out!

If you are in this position, please be sure that anyone volunteering their time for you actually gets some useful education out of the process. And try to keep them in mind for future *paying* positions. Give back your time when they need you. Nothing is lower than a filmmaker taking advantage of the eagerness of newbies.

Exposure Bucks

Sometimes we give our time freely, counting upon the idea that our involvement in the production will lead to riches in the form of connections, praise, audience acclaim, media attention, IMDb and resume padding, and the eventual offer of real payment on future gigs. This working for "exposure bucks" is worth doing, especially when you are new and learning.

Just make sure you do actually get exposure. Make the most of the experience. Keep a log, with the names and contact info of people you meet. Keep notes as you learn different skills, or test different equipment. (That's how this book started!) Add everything you do to your film resume. Post POSITIVE messages about the projects and people on social media; build people up, which encourages them to return the favor.

If you, as a producer, have no money to pay people, then try to convince them of the value of exposure bucks. Follow through, though. Make sure you give them credit on IMDb, and everywhere else you can. Be fair. You can be certain that your next project will fall flat if people are burned by you.

Some Compensation

If you want to be a real filmmaker, try to pay your people at least some amount of compensation. While calling in favors from friends and offering exposure bucks will work for a while, as you grow so will your need for competent people around you.

Whatever your budget, try to pay people. There's nothing wrong with being honest about the limitations of your budget, and giving people a chance to work at less than they would otherwise hope for – it's their choice. Hopefully, though, you can pay enough to at a minimum pay for their gas, parking and any other out-of-pocket costs.

Deferred pay

You can "pay" your actors and crew by not paying them, and instead promising them some amount of future pay contingent upon the success of your production. Yes, you can do this. It's allowed even under SAG/AFTRA rules. Of course, not everyone will work under this condition. The general thought out there is that "deferred pay is no pay."

It's tempting to offer deferred pay, but for both sides there are multiple issues that make this a subject better dealt with in detail in a book for more advanced filmmakers. Be careful with this subject. Get an attorney and put the terms of payment in writing.

Pay to Play

Some productions will offer you a chance to act or work on a film, if and only if you contribute some amount of money to the budget. This "Pay to Play" arrangement is looked down upon quite a bit in the industry, as it smells like taking advantage of newbies desperate to break in.

But don't move on so quickly from this idea. In the right setting, it has merit. If you want to create something, you would do well to find people who share your passion and are willing to put some of their own money in, as you are doing. This is a true collaboration. If you go down such road, make it fair. Everyone contributing should have an ownership interest, to some fair degree. Perhaps everyone gets a "producer" credit for their resume, or each person gets a percentage of an eventual (Hail Mary) sale.

If you are producer on such a venture, the key to making it work is being sure everyone is on the same page. Be transparent. I highly recommend contracts. Spell everything out, clearly, fairly, and follow through.

Big Star

One way to get funding is to first cast a major star. If your project is enticing enough to attract the attention of a star, then you will find major financers willing to back it. Ask the star! S/he probably can connect you with money people from prior productions.

On the flipside, having a star attached who does not have money connections may hurt your chances at getting a major production going, because your money people may have their own ideas about who to cast.

Proof of concept

You may not be able to raise the money needed to do your project justice. Blockbuster scripts are not cheap to film. Consider creating a building block, instead.

A "Proof of Concept" is a small production done on the cheap and used as a calling card to get attention. Its purpose is only to show that the idea has merit. Once people get excited by the idea, then the whole thing can be re-filmed.

Many TV pilots fall into this category. They are filmed with the budget available, and then marketed. If and when the show is "picked up" by a network or other major company with money, it usually gets completely reworked.

Creating on the cheap and selling might not be ultimately satisfying to you, the filmmaker, but if you got it sold then you have succeeded and can move onto your next concept.

Today, with the cost of good cameras so low, and readily available free distribution options (such as Vimeo or YouTube), you can put out your own proof of concept quickly and for relatively little money.

Directing

> *"Pick up a camera. Shoot something. No matter how small, no matter how cheesy, no matter whether your friends and your sister star in it. Put your name on it as director. Now you're a director. Everything after that you're just negotiating your budget and your fee."*
>
> ~ James Cameron

Director

The producer hires the director. Let's get one thing clear up front. The director is not the top boss. Even though a director may lord it over everyone else involved, and we generally refer to films by their director, the director answers to and may be fired by the Producer. (Probably, the "Executive Producer," to be specific.)

Being a director is stressful. Everything and everyone points at the director, the moment anything fails. It is a lonely spot. As with the captain of a ship, be prepared for the loneliness at the top. Decision making is your burden, with an eye on costs and people management. You can't play around.

Not everyone is cut out to be a good director. It's a "Chicken or egg?" question. Some people may say that certain jobs require an innate ability one is born with. While I've never tried, I'm certain I would fail as a car salesman; it's just not in me. My son is a born leader, with people skills I am in awe of. Directing is one of these functions that one is either able to do well, or not. Is it in you? Do you think reading this book will teach you how to direct? How I wish I had such penmanship powers! But I do hope and trust that, if you have the right temperament already, my words may help you fine-tune your talents.

What a Director Does

A director directs. Ha! I bet you saw that coming. But kidding aside, what a director does and does not do is not set ion stone. There is no single way, no formula, no one rule, for how to direct. David Mamet in his book "On Directing Film" says that "the work of the director is the work of constructing the shot list from the script. … The work on the set is simply to record what has been chosen to be recorded. It is the plan that makes the movie." A director is very involved in the planning stages of production. Shot lists (mapping out how each scene is to be filmed) are just part of pre-production, which can take years before filming ever begins. The more planning, the more the director can concentrate on getting the pieces to fall together when filmed.

There are many aspects of filmmaking that all directors must consider:

- Story – Directors are primarily telling a story. Using natural dialogue that builds a story, with surprising reveals. Straightforward or relying upon deception, a mix of both tells a good story.

- Production Design – visual choices that build mood, and become part of the story. Set, costumes, props, lighting, sound can all be used to emphasize character elements and story themes. Look for both visual contrast to set apart, and sameness to show connections. A character is defined with words in literature, but in film we learn who a character is by what others say, and even more importantly, by the character's setting, clothing, props, and actions.

- Color – bold or subtle, color helps set the mood. Bright colors can show passion and energy, where cooler colors may do the opposite.

- Cinematography – shot choices build the tension in a scene. Don't use close ups just because, use them knowledgably, knowing that moving in close results in a sense of claustrophobia, showing the unease of a character and situation. Rack focus leads audience attention.

- Editing – When do you cut to a character's reaction? Only, of course, when that reaction is an important part of the story. Editing choices leading up to a reaction, building the scene, explaining exposition without losing the excitement of the story, are all tricky selections.

- Sound Design – sound is necessary, and some sounds (Foley effects) are used to provide a natural sense of reality. But a director can go much farther, using sound to heighten the story. Sound effects can be extreme. Sound can draw out emotion, and can draw us into a character's head.

- Music – music choices feed directly into the energy of a film, and can be subtle or obviously part of the entertainment. Sometimes, the *lack* of music is called for, to build tension, as for example the choice by the makers of tv's *M.A.S.H.* to never use a laugh-track over operating room scenes.

People think a director does everything. Wrong. Or it should be wrong (there are some directors who feel they must do everything). Other job positions exist for a reason, and the best directors (like the best leaders generally) are able to delegate. Rely upon your crew, and empower them to do their jobs. Let them, praise them, reward them, and bask in the results.

So what does a director do? First and foremost, realize there is nothing that counts in this world except people. Every story is about people. The director must break down, analyze, and understand the psychology of the characters and how they interact in the story better than anyone else. The director can then focus on getting the best performances from the principal talent, to bring out the full depth and meaning of the story. Details of shooting and running the set belong to the 1AD, DP and others. A director, as captain of a ship, is responsible for all, yes. But with a competent crew a director can focus her time to actually direct the actors' performances, which is the single most important aspect of getting good footage.

Directors must be people persons, in order to bring out the best performances from the actors. But of course film differs greatly from stage. If you directed successfully in theatre, you likely built a fun-filled environment, with your top goals including cohesiveness. When the curtain opens, everyone and everything needs to purr, right? But ultimately, in film, only the footage counts. Not to discount the value of getting along and building your cast into a family! However, unity and togetherness is much less crucial when filming. Famous examples exist of people who share frame time, while actually refusing to ever be in each other's physical presence. (One story, from *NCIS*, purports that stars Mark Harmon and Pauley Perrette refused to be on set at the same time, after some dispute over a dog; scenes with both characters were filmed separately and edited to make it look like they were in the same room.)

Have a vision, and bring it out. Be true to yourself. Don't feel like the genre you're shooting in must define you; just the opposite: genre should be defined by the artists working in the genre.

Let your 1st AD handle technical stuff. (See the section below on being an AD.) In short, while the director focuses on getting good performance out of the cast, the 1AD takes care of running the set.

Delegate. No one can be a good director without counting upon strong people to help.

WOW with personality. Good or bad. In the end, you will be remembered and loved/hated for the strength of your personality. Be a "mensch" (look it up if you have to).

Remember you're NOT the boss. No, you're not. Not unless you are also the executive producer and sole source of funding. Want to know who the boss is? Look for the money. Directors are hired help! They are hired by the executive producer. So, stay humble, all right?

You don't have to be too humble. Serve as the figurehead, and revel in it. Be a star. Quentin Tarantino is no one's milquetoast!

1st Assistant Director / 1st AD

Being 1AD (or "1st AD") has been one of the most satisfying things, for me. 1AD is the single most important position for getting the day's shooting done well, on time, and on budget. IMHO, you cannot hope to make a good production without a good 1AD.

The 1AD runs the set, taking care of all logistics on set. Think of the director as captain of the ship, but the captain delegates operation of the ship to his first officer. As discussed above, the director should spend her/his time getting the best possible performances from the actors. Whatever the 1AD can do takes that much responsibility and hassle off of the director's shoulders.

The 1AD needs to have the day scheduled out, and then needs to make sure everyone sticks to the schedule. As chaos erupts (the normal state of affairs on a film set) and tempers rise as stress gets to people, the 1AD needs to be the one keeping calm, keeping people on track.

The 1AD prepares the take, tells everyone "Quiet on set!", and then calls for "Camera! Sound! Slate!" Sometimes the 1AD will call "Action" too, but if the director is there it is generally the director who calls both "Action!" and "Cut!"

Often, a 1AD will be allowed to film B-roll footage or scenes with extras without the director. This frees up the director to work with the stars of the film.

The 1AD is responsible for keeping the production on schedule during the shoot. Preparing and shooting efficiently. The goal: get the most possible footage "in the can" for the director.

A 1AD must keep his/her ego in check; don't get power hungry. Like directing, it's all about people. Delegate and empower; don't micromanage (for example, figure out what shot you want, but then let the DP, cameraman, and sound mixer determine how to make the shot happen).

AD's need to be both stern and friendly. I've met AD's who feel they must rant and rave, to exert and keep control on set. Do you have to be an ass? No. Control with honey, and save the stick for those rare moments when you really need it.

They must be able to keep calm themselves. Keep their wits about them. Be aware of the bigger picture, even when the smaller pictures are steaming up. Be especially aware of how the director is doing! It's easy for the director to "get in the weeds" and start to panic about production problems; the 1AD needs to talk the director down from jumping off the building.

Aim at creating a smoothly running set, where everyone is working toward the success of the mission. Multitask. Pay attention to who is working, and who is not; very often, someone could be (should be) preparing for what comes next, even if they aren't busy at the moment.

Quick tip: When I go onto set as a 1AD, I carry a hard case with me (military surplus) containing essentials I'd never be without. Living in my case, I have:

- White & black 1" gaffer's tape
- Blue painter's tape (for marking an actor's place)
- Binder with the script
- Color pencils for marking the script
- pens
- (3) small LED lights, for accents – with extra batteries
- Wireless lav mic
- Clapper board
- Extra dry erase markers and eraser, for the clapper board
- 12" ruler, for making straight lines on the script
- Sun block stick
- Flappy "Gilligan style" hat
- 1/8" black paracord

What you need may vary, but I have found I need the above items on a regular basis. Yes, I hear you say that someone else should be providing most of these things. For instance, it's typically the 2AC who does the clapping, and a professional sound engineer will likely bring a digital clapboard that syncs with the time code generated by his/her sound recorder. But that will rarely (perhaps never) happen on a small, student, or indie film, where in fact there may be no 2AC or sound engineer! On indie sets where your co-workers may not be prepared like they would be on "professional" sets – it's always good to be the one who is prepared, and having these things handy can save the day.

2nd Assistant Director / 2nd AD

A 2AD is not 2nd in priority or importance. Think of it this way: the 2nd refers mostly to the idea that the 2AD is getting ready for the 2nd day – in other words, while the 1AD is handling today's set, the 2AD is preparing for tomorrow's filming.

The 2AD plans and prepares such things as:

- Permits
- Locations
- Travel schedules
- Daily call sheets

They are also similar to a backstage manager, in that they keep cast advised and shepherd them through makeup and wardrobe in time for shots.

Too bad most smaller sets that newbies are likely to be on will not have a 2AD. On those sets, the 1AD (then just called "AD") does it all.

Different Directing Styles

There is a wide spectrum in how to direct, because there are examples of successful directors as different from each other as any two actors on set. Can one compare David Fincher's brilliance with Quentin Tarantino's mastery? You, no doubt, have your favorite directors. We all do, even people who don't pay attention to who directed but love the person's films.

When you direct, feel free to do it your way. In fact, you must do it your way. Be true to your own vision and voice. (Subject, of course, to the desires and instructions of your boss – the producer.) Make bold, risky choices and live up to them.

Directing Cast

Your primary job as a director is to see that the actors create their best possible performances. The actors want you to do this, so does the crew, so does the audience, because ultimately the only thing that counts is the quality of the results. When your film is made, everything that you did to get it done is relegated to "behind the scenes" stories, or chit chat over a scotch. No one will ever care about any of it, if the end result is not worth watching, and the quality of the acting is the most important factor audiences demand. Bad acting ruins the best cinematography, while shoddy cinematography can be ignored with good acting. Hopefully, you have a strong 1AD and others in the crew to whom you can delegate most of the logistics, while you focus your energies on guiding the actors.

So how do you direct actors? Again, everyone has a different style, and you will need to chart these waters yourself. With some advice.

Beginning with auditions, and then during rehearsals, make the character clear. Give a character description, and then as you work with the actor, *ask the actor* to flesh out the character. (They should do so, anyway, as part of their acting preparations.) Have them tell you what their interpretation is, why they feel the character does and says what's written in the script, and most importantly what the subtext is in each scene. Steer them, if necessary, but don't browbeat; even if they seem way off, ask questions to get them on the right track. Questions like, "You're obviously upset at this point, but when do you think that feeling starts?" "The other actor gets pissed off by what you're saying – why doesn't that bother your character?" "You're arguing about the toilet seat, but do you think that's really what you're worried about?"

Let your actors experiment in rehearsal. Give them feedback when they do. Keep your mind open to new ideas, and be quick with praise. Don't be just as fast to shoot down suggestions, even really bad ones (if given in good faith); talk it over, and explain why a bad idea won't fit the character or the script. Often an actor makes choices based only on what they see in their character, without fully considering how those choices affect other characters and the script as a whole – help them see the big picture.

Give specific notes. Don't be vague.

Guide your actors, actively not passively. You are the director, and they want your approbation and praise – even the hard ass actors that put up a tough front. In the auditions, and rehearsals, step up to be the "king" running each meeting. A kind, benevolent king, but king nonetheless and ultimately it is your decision how each actor brings forth and expresses their character. Make sure that is understood from the beginning. You should listen and consider, but in the end make the big decisions. I've been on sets (you, too, probably) where the director wasn't directing – wasn't, in other words, exerting control to get the project done; sometimes, someone else steps up to take the empty reins, and sometimes the team of horses runs willy-nilly without a leader. Be the leader.

Directing Crew

Focus your primary efforts on getting good performances out of your actors, but don't forget that you are also the "captain of the ship" responsible for the whole crew. Every member of the crew wants to be part of a successful production – that's what moves their careers forward and puts more joy on their table. They want you to be an effective director.

Beware: some crew members will look to gain your favor, at the expense of others on the crew. They will try to toady to you. You are captain; you can't favor junior officers or midshipmen if it hurts the sailors. Put another way commonly said: parents can't have favorites. Be fair to all.

Clearly express to your crew what you want. Storyboard your shots so you can get your vision across to the people whose job it is to bring it to fruition. Make a shot list with your DP, share it on set, and follow it – while also being flexible and adapting to discoveries as you shoot.

Don't yell.

Don't micromanage. Scheduling and preparation is vital; you need strong "get it done" people to assist you. Let them do their jobs. However, make clear to them that they should not in any way adversely affect the actors ability to perform – jump quickly on any issues that disturb your actors, and get involved to find a fair solution that moves you closer to getting the production to succeed.

Hold people accountable, within their job descriptions.

An example of the above principles … I was 1AD on a film where the director was a poor communicator, and yet still insisted in a passive-aggressive manner on getting everything his way. He didn't take the time to explain what he wanted to his DP and gaffer (the person in charge of lights and sound), and instead just told them on set to "move this way" or "that way." The result, after several days of filming, was that the DP and gaffer just stood there, waiting to be told. Every time they volunteered their thoughts, they were shot down by the director … so they stopped offering ideas. On the first day that the director was not available and I took over running the set, I approached them differently. I started the day describing the scene and choosing a portion of the set where we would film, but then *asked* the DP if he thought the location worked, and how would he want to film it? I *asked* the sound guy the same. As soon as I got them talking about the set up and what they wanted, I told them to let me know when they were ready (delegation and empowerment!) and I left to rehearse the actor. This ended up being one of the best dressed and lit scenes in the movie, and the extra time working with the actor paid off nicely.

The success of the production depends upon you. Be mindful of the old Ronald Reagan line, "Trust, but verify." Delegate, and empower, to give your people the best chance at getting their jobs done, but follow up and make sure they do get done, and done well. Have back-up plans for everything, and roll with the punches that come. When "shit happens" (and it will) don't let it destroy you. Take deep breaths, and move forward, somehow – anyhow. The show must go on! Find a way to make lemonade out of your lemons. … How many clichés can I throw in here? Point is, you as the director must keep a level head and find a solution.

Production Designer

A production designer acts as the eyes of the director, designing and overseeing everything that we (the audience) will see in frame.

They help select locations, props, costumes, sets, and consider synergies between them (for example, matching costume colors with set pieces). They coordinate between departments, in order to make sure what the stunts people are doing matches, say, what the greens department is putting onto the set. They also work within budget.

Production designers are top line, involved early in the pre-production phase.

PA "Production Assistant"

Let's hear it for the lowly PA! Seriously, don't ever ignore or discount the value of having good PA's around.

In fact, listen up you ultra-low-budget types: If you have very little money and can only pay a few people, pay your PA's. Why them? Well, first, many people will gladly work for free in sexier positions, because they want the credit and experience. A director, a DP, a cinematographer, a writer … yes, they are all likely to work for free (at student film and indie levels, at least). But a PA is the person who generally does the crap work (papers and forms, organization, schlepping things around, cleaning messes) that no one else wants to do, and getting a credit for such just isn't nearly as motivating. And the real reason you should pay your PA? Because you desperately need those crap jobs done! There are PA jobs better than others, for example those that help on set during filming compared to those left behind to clean up the day's mess. If you can only pay one PA, choose the one that cleans up after the crew, because that is vital, and without a good PA you'll end up having to do it yourself, or else burn a location connection (never a good idea).

Working as a PA is the easiest and surest way of breaking into the entertainment industry. PA jobs are always available if you sniff around even a little bit. Many PA jobs require a *body* and not much else, so even without experience you can still offer your services to help a crew. And once you are on set … then keep your eyes open and learn how to be a true help. Being a PA is the quickest way to learn things, meet people, and most importantly demonstrate that you are dependable. Show up, with a good attitude, and be helpful … I guarantee you will get more work, and expand your responsibilities and capabilities with each opportunity. (Remember Woody Allen's wisdom, "Success is 80% just showing up.")

I won't use any names on this example … but let me just say I *know a guy* who spent a year or so telling everyone he wanted to make movies, with himself directing even though he had zero experience, no contacts, and worse, no funding. He advertised his "production company" in social media, went to meeting after meeting, begged just about everyone, and got nowhere. He came off as a blowhard, talking as if he were God's gift to the industry. Then I ran into him on set where he was working as a PA – in fact, he was working as the lowest of grunts, and I was pleased to see that he was keeping his mouth shut. He took a lot of flak on that set, but I think he did a good job. After that, I saw him get additional PA positions, then a spot or two as 2nd AC. He's doing well, now. I most recently ran into him at an audition Still not directing his own stuff, but he's rising up the food chain and building a better reputation for himself. Good for him, I say!

If you are a PA:

- Do what you're told.

- Shut up. Watch carefully for opportunities where your opinion is desired, and once you give it, shut up again.

- Be fast, at whatever you do. Efficient. Do not waste anyone's time.

- Be careful. Watch out for the tripod and light stand legs, especially, as well as microphone cables.

- Learn proper etiquette for talking on walkie-talkies, and follow that at all times.

- Carry extra "hot bricks" (batteries) on you for replacement walkie-talkie batteries.

- Know the names of the department heads, and where to find them. Know the set layout, the studio lot, the production company, and so on, so that you are able to run to wherever you're sent.

- Be mindful that PA's are meant to be out of sight, but ever present when needed. Pay attention to what is going on around you, so that you are always ready to jump in to assist.

Ultimately, the job of PA encompasses doing anything and everything (legally) asked of you. That changes on each set, since what needs to be done depends on the story and the people involved. Common duties include relaying calls. In other words, when the 1AD calls "Rolling!" on the walkie, every single PA needs to immediately call that out loud for everyone near the PA to hear, and then the same when "Cut" is called. This way everyone in the area knows when to keep still and quiet.

So … you've been hired as a PA (or want to be), what do you need?

Things to carry as a PA:

- walkie-talkie (usually owned by the production)
- pens
- dry-erase marker
- batteries to give to others (for their walkies)
- gaffer's tape, black and white
- small notepad
- camera (cell phone is fine)
- sides (for actors)
- call sheets

A real good addition to your personal kit is what's called a "Surveillance" (a surveillance headset). The kind of in-the-ear-thingee that you see the Secret Service wearing. Cool, right? As a PA, you will be living on a walkie talkie, and having the right kind of headset makes your life much easier. Get your own; the production will have walkies for you to use, but they expect you to get your own surveillance, and even if they had one for you to use you wouldn't want to … these things stick in your ear, would you really want to use just anybody's? Amazon has them for $15 - $30 so you can experiment until you find the one perfect for you. However, make sure you get the right kind since there are different connector types. The Motorola CP200 is a standard walkie on film sets; it uses headsets with a 2-pin "M1" connector. But not all walkies use this size connector. If you frequently travel between sets of different production companies, you may want to show your value by investing in a few different surveillances.

Script Supervisor (aka "Scripty")

> *"What if God has no Script Supervisor, and déjà vu is a continuity error?"*
>
> ~ anonymous meme

A good Script Supervisor is invaluable. Their primary task, as the name suggests, is to make sure the script is followed when filming. They are also entrusted with the heady job of continuity, i.e. making sure elements in a scene match those in other scenes.

This sounds easy, but being a good Scripty is tricky. Sometimes, a director and DP will get so excited, and so obsessed, over the art or technical challenge of a particular shot or shot combination, that they totally forget to film a key element in the script. Someone needs to remind them. Someone with a head for details, who does not get so distracted with the filming that they miss those details. Someone who pays attention to the clock, and can (politely!) remind the director that there are more shots to be covered in what time remains. Imagine the cost of redoing a day of filming (getting the location again, bringing actors back, paying for another crew day, meals, permits ….) just because a crucial shot was missed!

When an actor forgets their line and calls out, "Line!" it is the Scripty that reads enough to again get the actor going. A scripty will not interrupt filming when an actor gets a line wrong, but will point it out after the take ends if the director cares about precision (though, of course, not on sets where improv is the name of the game).

Script Supervisors take copious notes. They "line the script" during shooting, meaning they draw a line down the page through action and dialogue showing exactly where in the script a take starts and stops. That way, visually, the director (and editor!) can quickly and easily see what in the script has been covered, and what not, whether filmed by a wide shot, medium, or close up, and also which takes were considered the director's favorite(s).

Good Script Supervisors are also responsible for continuity. Whew! That is a huge undertaking in and of itself. Imagine filming a scene that comes right after a scene filmed days ago, and even the slightest incongruent detail (for example, on which side an actor's hair is parted) can ruin the final footage.

DP / Camera Operator

Easiest and best thing is to hire a qualified camera person to film your projects. Cameras are complicated. The process of getting good footage is complicated. I'm not going to even attempt to get into the nitty gritty.

But you should understand some basics. Afterall, lots a newbies end up shooting their own stuff.

Framerate

Moving pictures, both film and video, are not actually moving pictures. Just like old flip-style cartoon books, what we see is really individual pictures that are exchanged so fast in front of our eyes that our brains put them together as moving pictures.

A framerate of 1 fps (frame per second) would seem more like a PowerPoint presentation than a moving picture show. Speed up to 4 or 5 frames per second, and it starts to look like movement, though very jerky movement. Over 12 fps might seem usable, but again still jumpy. Our eyes are used to 24 fps, in part because that is the rate the original film industry used for motion pictures, and most accept it as that "cinematic look". That speed works for our eyeballs, making it look like smooth movement. You can now, in the digital world, record at much higher framerates, but some people find higher rates to seem unnatural in that the result is too sharp; faster speeds don't show blurred movement the way our eyes naturally see a moving object.

Different filmrate standards have developed around the world. North America and much of South America follow the "NTSC" standard, while half of South America, most of Europe, Africa, and Australia use "PAL/SECAM", and "SECAM" is the standard used by Russia, France, and part of Africa.

NTSC (24 fps) is the film standard in the US. But that said, it's not really so, or at least not so everywhere. Some parts of the world use 30 fps as standard. And in both cases, because the early-days television broadcast technologies had certain problems (that are no longer applicable), the actual stand in use is 23.976 fps. Odd number, but they used that number because they had to slow the rate by 0.1%. Likewise, other parts of the world using 30 fps slowed their broadcasts by the same 0.1% and ended up with a standard of 29.97 fps. Once the big companies had geared their technology to these weird framerate numbers, they've never changed. Go figure. Most camera menus just say "24 fps" but they are really shooting in the technically correct standard of 23.976 fps. There are, however, some advanced cameras that give you the choice to shoot in true 24 fps or 23.976. I recommend shooting in what your camera likely calls "24 fps" (meaning 23.976) unless and until you have reason to purposefully use a different setting.

30 fps is the standard in some parts of the world, and it might look a bit smoother to your eyes. When video cameras came out, they mostly shot at 30 fps. It's the most common option on video cameras, some of which don't give you the choice of selecting 24 fps. While not the

standard in film, a lot of sports, news, reality tv shows often shoot in 30 fps to give the footage an extra smoothness. This is why video and tv look different than film.

One reason to change settings is if you want to shoot slow motion footage. You can shoot at 24 and then play it back slower, but that results in fewer frames per second in your final product which gives you a choppy look. So people shoot in higher framerates, and then play back at 24 fps so the result is still smooth, but the time is spread out. For example, shoot at 60 fps and when you play it back you are getting almost a 3x factor. One second shooting at 60 fps gives you 60 frames, which if played back at 24 fps is 2.5 seconds. Or shoot at 120 fps, and your one second (120 frames) plays back at 5 seconds.

If you shoot at 30 fps your footage will very likely be changed to 24 in the editing process. Typically, footage is shot at 24 fps, edited at 24 fps, and then the resulting video is exported at 24 fps; it's consistent all along the process. If you import a clip shot at 30 fps, the editing software will drop 6 of those frames (or 1 frame out of every 5) to keep only 24 fps. Conversely, if you are editing in 30 fps and you import a 24 fps clip, the software will add frames (by duplicating 1 in every 5) to convert the clip to 30 fps. Unless you edit in 30 fps. And unless you change the *time* of your clip, when you edit; that's how you get the slow motion effect. For example, if you have a clip filmed at 30 fps and you're editing in 24 fps, you import your 30 fps clip at 80% speed which brings the clip to 24 fps by stretching one second out longer – giving you a slight slow motion effect. A one second 60 fps clip can be added to a 30 fps timeline at 50%, resulting in a 2 second clip.

Sound

"Sound is half the picture."

~ George Lucas

(~ also attributed to Steven Spielberg)

Movies are "audio visual" media, right? Sound then is exactly half. George Lucas (and Steven Spielberg!) knew how important sound was. We've all heard the story of George and his crew recording bizarre sounds, until they determined that the sound of a vibrating guy wire on a telephone pole was a perfect stand-in for the laser shots in *Star Wars*. I'd actually argue sound is more than half, because you can get away with bizarre, experimental, even crappy visuals, but bad sound ruins just about everything.

Sound is so much more important than people tend to initially think. I've heard this as a joke, but a truly painful one when people ask, "When do directors realize how important sound is?" Answer, "In post." Yikes. In other words, not until after filming, after it's too late to pay attention to getting good audio. And while there are many things an editor can do to fix sound (somewhat), too often bad sound must be entirely rejected and re-recorded. Since it costs money to redo things, you can see how important it is to get good sound to begin with.

Doing sound (i.e. being the sound mixer on set who records dialogue and ambient sound) is another way for newbies to break in. There is a learning curve, and some equipment to build up, but nothing too difficult even for newbies at lower levels. People usually start as a boom operator, the person who holds the boom while someone else is the sound mixer.

There are many sounds that are added in post, for multiple reasons. On set you want to concentrate on getting audio that tells the story, whether that is dialogue or a particular sound effect from an on-set item important to the script. Especially if that sound is particular to the location or a rare prop. You don't focus on incidental sounds, like someone's footsteps or the turning of a doorknob – in fact, you try to record your sound as free as possible of all incidental sounds. Editors want to have control of incidental sounds, to place them at the right point and to control their relative volume, so ideally such sounds are recorded in separate "clean" audio files. Some sounds (like gunshots or exotic animal calls) are difficult to get on set, and one might as well obtain a sound file from an on-line download. Finally, some sounds recorded on set just don't sound good.

"**FOLEY**" is the process of adding incidental sound effects in the editing process, for example the sound of footsteps as a character walks into the frame. While it may not seem important, and might never be noticed in the final film, the *lack* of such incidental sounds can bother viewers. A Sound Tech on set can record such sounds, if they think of it, but generally it's easier to add them later. Some sounds, like the sound of a punch, tend not to have the "wow" factor you want no matter how you try to record it on set; in such example, using the sound of a juicy steak landing on a kitchen counter may be just the right Foley sound you want for that big wet punch. Foley artists have all sorts of tricks like that.

On set, it's common to hold a microphone on a boom pole, close to the actors' heads, just off frame. Holding the boom carefully is crucial, because any vibration, anything clanking against the boom, even shifting hand or finger positions on the boom, can result in "noise" on the recording.

Most video cameras have a built in microphone that sucks. At best, the sound from an onboard microphone is usable when filming very close to your subject. But all film and television productions that I've ever heard of use a separate microphone and then either record sound onto a separate digital sound recorder or feed the sound back into the camera. The camera's onboard sound with the video file is helpful, primarily as a reference soundtrack to help you line up ("sync") sound files recorded by a separate recorder.

The sound recorded on set, even with a separate mic, may not be good enough. Often, the on-set sound is just used as "reference sound" – meaning it is good enough to hear what dialogue or sound occurred at what point in sync with the image. The reference sound is then used as a place holder by the editor, when replacing with good sound. This is done by some productions as a matter of course, and by others only when the on-set sound is bad (perhaps, for example, because the footage was shot next to an airport or during a rainstorm).

Do you know why a clapper board (also known as a slate) is used? Yes, it has information written on it which visually identifies the take. But more importantly, by combining the sharp sound of the clapper board's arm snapping down with the video image of the same, the editor can closely sync the separate sound file with the video file. This is why some newbie filmmakers that don't have a clapper will clap their hands in front of the camera at the start of each take; though harder to use, a clap will suffice. Hence the name "clapper board". Of course, technology has now improved to the point professionals use digital slates that sync files to within 0.001 second.

Sound Engineer

Larger productions have a "Sound Department" with a Sound Engineer (aka Sound Mixer), Boom Operator, and even a 2nd Boom Operator and 3rd. The Sound Engineer governs all, decides how to mic a scene, and makes sure the recordings are good. The Boom Operators run around like proverbial chickens with their heads cut off to get the boom mic where it needs to be in each take. On smaller productions, there is frequently just one person to do it all.

Getting good sound on set is hard, and in fact it is often impossible. That's why ADR is widely used. But even if you plan for ADR, you still want to get your sound recorded on set as good as possible.

Ever notice that the "sound person" is very often some junior know-nothing who has been handed a boom and has very little idea what to do with it? Too many filmmakers fail to give sound collection the attention it warrants.

As a result, this is an excellent way for you newbies to turn yourself into valuable assets for hire! Learn a bit, buy some minimal equipment, and you will be quickly in line for paying jobs. Oddly, not that many people are into sound, so it is the one easily attained position for which there seems to be plenty of paying gig opportunities.

Here's what you need to know: as the sound mixer, it is your job to LISTEN. It's surprising how many noises there are in any given environment that we routinely tune out. Actors and the rest of the crew come into a space, talking at full volume (of course!) while they plan the scene, block it out, even rehearse it. Then, when they start shooting, they may or may not notice the noise from the house AC or ceiling fan or aquarium or mom's tv upstairs, or the refrigerator, or creaking leather couch, or squeaky tennis shoes, or traffic outside, or airplanes overhead, or … you get the point. By the time they turn the camera on, they've become used to such noises. Like a teenager becoming "nose blind" to the stench of dirty clothes and BO in their bedroom. They just don't notice it. But you must. Before you start recording, do what you can to minimize the sources of unwanted sound. Turn things off. Unplug things. Angle mics away. Put up sound blankets. Time takes between sounds.

Test your mics and recorder before shooting begins. Always start each day with fresh batteries. (Partly-used AA batteries are handy to keep at home, for things like your tv remote or computer mouse.) Pay attention during rehearsal to check how loud the actors are likely to get; if necessary, ask the actors to run a few lines at what they consider to be their loudest point. You want to set your recording level to peak at around -6db for vocals.

Select your mic based on the mic's polar pattern (how it picks up sound). You want to get the mic close to the actor's face, to pick up the clearest dialogue. Often, lav mics are used, clipped to the front of the actor (generally upper chest area). If you are using wireless mics, check them on site before filming begins – they are notorious for picking up random interference, and you may need to experiment to find a channel that gives good results. Lavs are notorious, too, for catching the rustling of clothing; this can be minimized by taping the lav to skin and/or clothing, so that material does not rub over it. (Gaffer's tape is perfect.) If booming, make sure your mic is aimed at the actor's face, especially if you are using a shotgun mic with a narrow pickup region.

Before shooting each take, right after the lighting and blocking have been finalized, you need to figure out how you can get your boom close to the actor(s) without causing shadows that the camera will see. And you need to know how close you can get the boom, without it dipping into the frame. Every sound person ruins a number of shots, with the Director calling "Cut! That was perfect, except the boom got in there!" Once that has happened to you a few times, you will pay close attention to both lighting and camera frame. Finally, you also need to figure out where you can stand – or lay, or squat – to be hidden in the scene. You may have to move during the take.

At the start of each take, the 2AC (or 1AD, or the Director) will call out "Camera!" then the camera operator says "Cameral rolling", then comes the call for "Sound!" … and that's when you need to turn on your sound recorder, look to confirm it is indeed recording, and respond "Sound speeding." Many crews get used to working together, and the take starts simply with a grunt from the Director, then "Rolling" from camera, and "Speeding" from sound.

Depending upon the set-up, the clapper board in front of the camera may be some distance from where you are recording sound. And yet, it is important for sound syncing purposes in editing that you record the sound of the clapper. You may be able to simply swing the boom that way, or maybe just point the shotgun mic at the clapper. Or you may have to record the clapper, and then move to get into position for the shot.

During the take, everyone else is focused on the actors. You must pay attention to the actors, too, but also listen critically for any interfering sound. Wear decent headphones! If there is bad sound, you need to immediately (but after "Cut!" is called) notify the Director or 1AD. If the bad sound was only during an off-camera actor's dialogue, it may be good enough. But if there is any question, a wise Director will want another take. Just to be sure.

Sometimes, I have been asked after a take if I heard such-and-such noise, when I didn't . That's fine. What matters, of course, is only what the mic picks up, and that is what you listen to through your headphones, so some far off noise that everyone else heard during the take may not get recorded. If in doubt, take a moment to listen to the playback of that take's recording; the Director will understand and be glad you checked.

If your batteries are out, or you suspect they are almost dying and won't make it through the next take, call for a pause. Call out, "Hold for batteries!" Again, the Director will understand. Just change them and get back to your ready position as fast as you can. Try to anticipate, so that you never have to stop a take in mid action.

Boom Operator

Having done this myself many times, I may be biased when I say that the Boom Operator is one of the most important people on set.

The sound person (i.e. someone acting as Sound Engineer, Boom Op, and everything else sound-related) is actually the *only* person on set who hears, through their headphones, the quality of the recorded sound. This is a heady responsibility! Imagine how a director feels, or producer, or actor, when they review the footage in post (or worse yet, in the finished movie) only to hear that the sound is bad. This happens more than anyone wants to admit, especially on smaller budget productions where (ironically) it is even more important to get good sound on set – bigger productions are more likely to plan on using ADR anyway, or can more easily reshoot a bad scene. When you are recording sound, you must use headphones to listen carefully for every little bit of noise the mic may be picking up. You, more than most people on set, need to pay attention to the actor's every line. And you need to speak up (after the take) if you have concerns. Usually, unless something terribly bad occurs, let the take continue until the director calls "Cut"; but then, as soon as you can, tell the director or the 1AD that the sound was bad, so they can attempt another take.

During filming, listen carefully to the actor's dialogue. Make sure you catch every line, clearly. Be diligent. Be aware of distracting noises, for example the squeak of a leather couch as the actor sits down. Or an airplane far overhead, which people generally ignore in their daily lives and often don't even notice when filming. Be hypersensitive. Make the director aware of any problems with the dialogue, especially that of the actor in focus – in other words, it might be okay for a motorcycle to go by, if it happens during the line of an off-camera actor and not over your star's closeup. During a take, generally all you have to do is look at the director or 1AD when you hear a bad noise – they likely heard it, too, and will be looking at you to see if you think the sound was ruined by that noise.

Use the best equipment you can. Duh. A good boom is one which is as light as possible, while still being strong enough; as you swing a boom around for hours on a hot set, you will appreciate lightening the load by each gram or fraction thereof. A good shotgun mic will pick up sounds from where it is aimed, while diminishing ambient noise from off axis. For this reason, shotgun mics are frequently used on booms outdoors. Indoors, you may find other mics work best, though I often use a shotgun inside, too. In both situations, any time you are moving the boom around you are likely to get noise from the air moving past the mic; a swishing sound as you swing back and forth between your actors. This can be solved with a "Blimp" that encases the mic. Use good cables, preferably balanced XLR, because that reduces the risk of static caused by interference. If you use 3.5mm cables, be aware that they are quite subject to interference, the more so for cables over six feet, especially around computers, cell phones, wireless equipment, or other electrical items.

Before filming begins, set up your gear and record a couple sound tests on set. Listen to your recordings carefully. Before shooting is the time to identify noises on or near the set that you may be able to kill or significantly reduce. For example, a ticking clock in the adjacent room; it may not be noticed at all when the cast and crew are jawing, but as soon as the shot begins it looms up like a thunderous sledgehammer. Air conditioners, refrigerators, tv's, radios, pets, footsteps overhead, road noise, and the like … every set is different. Turn off or unplug what you can, and find ways to reduce the rest. Clap your hands when you enter the set; you may be the only person to notice how bad an echo is in the place. Such echoes are caused by sound bouncing off of hard surfaces. Sound blankets can be placed on the floor or hung just outside of the frame to reduce an echo.

Pay attention, as you record sound, to the camera's movement. You may very likely have to move your boom to match, or to get out of the way; you may have to dodge actors, too. You will learn to essentially dance with the cameraman. Watch the DP's movements, so that you know at all times what the camera is seeing. If it zooms in, you can get the boom closer. If the lens pans, tilts, dollies, rolls or jibs, you need to adjust your boom to both keep out of the shot and get the best sound you can. It is a dance. And you have to get into the zone.

Check the camera's framing before the scene begins, so that you can select the best (the closest) place to put your boom, and where you can stand (lay, squat, kneel, etc.) to do so. Also before the take begins, check the lighting, to see where your boom may create shadows.

Do your best to get the microphone as close to the actor's mouth as possible, pointed at the actor's upper chest (pointing directly at the mouth emphasizes the wet smacking sounds we all make while talking). All mics are different, so you need to know your equipment, but most shotguns pick up best when held just a couple feet away from the actor and pointed right at his or her chest. Of course, you can't do that in a wide shot. Get as close as you can, and check to see if the director plans a close-up shot. Directors (and editors) know the sound in a close up will be best, and they will probably use that sound anyway, so they care less about sound recorded during wide shots. If no close up is planned, then ask to record "Wild Lines", which means recording the lines of dialogue on set without the camera rolling. For example, I recently recorded sound on a basketball court, where the actors were playing basketball and speaking at the same time – bit of a challenge. Because of their movement, lav mics couldn't be trusted to get clear sound over the rustling of clothing. I boomed all of the takes, and paid attention to each line. When the director was done and happy with everything he *saw*, I told him there was still one line that one actor had not yet clearly said in any of the takes. He let me do that line "wild", meaning I approached the actor, we called "Quiet on set!" just like any take, I started recording and said, "Scene 21, wild lines, take 1" and when the director said "Action!" the actor said her line. I asked her to repeat the line a few times, and she did so before I nodded to the director, and he yelled, "Cut!" This gives the editor some good sound to plug in, if necessary.

Be sure to keep your mic at approximately the same distance during a take, and in each subsequent take. Varying the distance will greatly affect the recorded file levels. You need to get your mic in position before an actor speaks, moving quickly between actors if necessary. If one actor in frame is speaking to an off-screen actor, or in the case of the primary actor in an OTS shot (over the shoulder) where all you see is a bit of a second actor, then keep the boom on the actor in focus; the shot is about them, and the other actor will likely get their own turn. Same with close up shots; don't worry about swinging the boom to record an off-camera actor because all the director and editor care about is the sound of the close up actor.

Knowing where to be, how to cover the actors, and stay out of the camera's frame while not creating shadows is hard. It requires concentration. You should watch the rehearsal blocking, check with the DP, and look at the camera's frame if possible. While you're doing all this, the gaffer is checking lighting and may very well change something last minute. Likewise, the DP may change a camera movement, or the director may change an actor's blocking -- point is, you have to pay attention to all this, and be ready to get that boom in there for the shot. I recommend booming for the shot even during rehearsals, that way it's clear to all where you intend to be, and you can see ahead of the shot whether your placement is good.

Almost everyone booms from above. Keep in mind, though, that many times the best approach might be to boom from a low angle. Pointing a shotgun mic up toward the sky can potentially introduce the sound of distant airplanes, or make birdcalls louder, but sometimes it's the best or only way to get close to an actor's mouth.

Stay flexible. That boom pole is adjustable, so keep it as short as possible. Or nix it altogether. Be prepared to take the mic off of the boom pole and just hold it (in a shock mount) in your hands, in order to get close to the actor in confined spaces. Think about placing the mic in the set ("Planting" it), perhaps in a table's centerpiece or sitting on a couch next to the actor; there may not be room for you in there, but the mic fits. Lav mics are often planted on set, since they are easy to hide and (usually) omni-directional. Sometimes you need to ask the actor to hold a mic.

Rehearsal is a good time to set your sound levels. The actors may run lines, and if not you should ask them to run a couple of their loudest lines. Let them know you'd like to know how loud they expect to be in the scene. You should set your levels on the recorder to record between -24Db and -12Db, peaking no hotter than -6Db, which gives you a solid signal with good noise ratio and about 10Db of "head room" before an outburst reaches 0Db and gets distorted or "clipped" in the sound file.

Be hyper-aware of your own noise. You must be silent. This means learning to move silently. Move the boom pole around efficiently and carefully, with total concentration so you get where you need to be without hitting anything, brushing up against anything, or even rubbing your hands on the pole (as happens when you shift grips or rotate the pole in your hand) since that noise frequently transmits to the mic. Dress your cable(s) so that nothing bangs against the boom during a take; I use 4 – 6" lengths of Velcro tape, which works nicely. If you have to make noise getting into position, make sure the director understands to "hold for sound" so that he/she waits to call, "Action!"

A special note about clapping. The clapper will hold the slate in front of the camera, call off the scene information, and then snap the clapboard arm down. You need to swing the boom over to cover such action, to be sure the slate info and snap are recorded for the editor to hear.

If, *before* Action is called, you hear a noise – perhaps an airplane, a loud car, or people talking elsewhere on set – speak up. Call out, "Hold for sound" and then say "airplane" or whatever, or call "Quiet on set!" then nod to the director when you're happy the problem has been fixed. But once Action is called, stay quiet. Let the scene play out, and only after the director says Cut should you speak up about any sound concerns.

During the scene, check your levels. Make sure they aren't exceeding -12Db, and adjust if necessary. This is called "riding the levels" and in some takes one must continuously do so.

A director or AD may ask to hear the sound. Be prepared to hand them a headset (your own, if need be) and replay the file for them. Good directors / ADs should do this, though few do. Don't take it personally if they do ask; getting good sound is vital, and they should know it. If they ask to listen to a file, it means you are working with someone intelligent and professional enough to care about sound.

Let's get technical
Learning to get good sound is an art, far beyond the newbie scopes of this book. YouTube is your friend, so is Google. Do your research and learn. Here's just a peek at some technical aspects of sound.

Sampling & bit depth – Soundwaves are sine waves. When a digital recorder processes a soundwave into an audio file, the recorder must sample the wave by breaking it up into slices. The more slices, the better sound quality, since each slice carries information about the wave. Such slices are expressed in kHz. For example, low quality Internet audio is 11 kHz, which means that the soundwave is "cut up" for analysis 11,000 times per second. CD quality sound is at 44.1 kHz, or 44,100 times per second, so you can see how CD sound is much better. For digital video audio, the standard sampling rate is 48kHz (you can look up the precise reasons for this). Many people (myself included) record in 96kHz, which is twice the sampling rate of 48kHz, and gives a better quality to the recording (although honestly, you'll rarely hear the difference). My Zoom F4 records up to 192kHz (four times the 48kHz standard!), but I can't hear the difference at all.

Bit depth refers to the number of different possible values each sample can have. "16 bit" sound means each sample can have one of 65,536 values (2^{16}). This is what most good cameras record. But a good recorder can record 24 bit sound, meaning each sample is at one of 16,777,216 values (2^{24}). Think of it as extra resolution for sound.

WAV files – some cameras record compressed sound, which is what MP3 files are. Recorders usually have such option. Don't. For film, you want the quality of uncompressed WAV files.

To summarize, for highest quality set your recorder for 96kHz 24 bit WAV file recording. You may want to check with your editor, because some programs (like Premiere Pro) may only accept sound at 48kHz.

Preamps are the electronics in your camera and sound recorder that boost the mic signal. Camera preamps are notoriously weak and unreliable, which is one of many reasons to use a double system (i.e. record sound separately) because dedicated audio recorders have much better preamps.

Line Level – many recorders and other preamps have a switch for "line level" or "mic level." Line level signals are much stronger than mic level, so much so that you may cause harm to equipment by plugging the wrong thing in. Professional line level signals are at +4dBu 1.228V$_{RMS}$ and consumer line level signals are at -10dBv 0.316V$_{RMS}$. No further amplification is needed. Mic levels, however, are much weaker and they do need amplification. Mic levels typically range from 2 – 50 mV. If you plug a cable carrying a mic level signal into a line level input, you'll probably hear nothing at all because the line level input needs a more powerful signal. But if you accidently plug a cable carrying a line level signal into a mic level input, you will get seriously distorted audio and potentially cause harm to the mic level recording equipment.

Phantom Power is an option in many recorders. Usually 48V. This is electricity that goes back down the line to power a condenser mic. Some mics don't need power, and some do but they have their own battery. Sending phantom power to a mic that doesn't need it can cause harm.

Sound Levels need to be set before you begin recording, and monitored during recording. As we talked about bit rates above, we were imagining each slice of a sound wave being registered at one of many values. But what if the amplitude of the sound wave exceeds those values? Imagine a sine wave with its head cut off. Looks ugly, and sounds ugly. This is called "Clipping" and it happens when the gain on your recorder is set too high. Unfortunately, there is nothing to be done that fixes a clipped recording. Your recorder probably has red lights to warn you of a too-hot signal, because it is very important to avoid recording clipped sound. To avoid clipping, we give ourselves "Head Room", which is another way of saying you need to set your recording sound levels low enough that an actor's occasional outbursts don't overload the signal. Keep your recording levels set between -24dB and -12dB. Watch where an actor's dialogue peaks, and make sure it never goes above -6dB tops. (0 is the clipping point on most digital recorders.)

Room Tone should be recorded for every location. This is a baseline recording of the ambient sounds in any given environment, without any dialogue or action taking place. There are two reasons one does this. First is to give the editor a sufficient amount of clean background noise, which allows them to identify and remove such from your sound files. So important, and yet hard to remember, and hard to get people on set to cooperate fully. I found I was having problems in particular when I would plan on doing the room tone last, after filming the scene. When "Woof" is called, everyone is immediately hustling to move onto the next setup, and no one wants to give you a minute or two of silence for doing a room tone recording. Finally I got smart. Do the room tone *first*, before the scene is filmed, when everyone on set is prepped for that call of "Quiet on set!" and will actually comply. I recommend you get into this habit.

The second reason for recording room tone is that there are times when you and your editor will want to build a scene by inserting footage from some other source. Perhaps you're adding B-Roll that you shot separately, or perhaps even stock footage from a third party. You want the soundtrack of that inserted footage to match, to sound like it was shot in the same location at the same time as your other footage. You can get that effect by adding the room tone.

How to put a lav mic on actors
Lav mics need to be close to the actor's mouth, but not too close. On the chest, around "nipple height" or so. If you mic under the shadow of the actor's chin, the sound will be restricted.

Ideally, you'd clip a lav mic on top of clothing, and for some types of filming it's okay to see the mic. For instance, an interview in a news show or documentary – no one would object to seeing a microphone. But in narrative stories, seeing a mic would take the viewer out of the experience. Sound engineers are forever wrestling with ways to hide a mic on or under clothing.

Hiding a lav is problematic because the mic will likely pick up a rustling sound as it rubs against clothing. One trick is to fold two pieces of gaffer's tape into triangles, sticky side out, and place those "tape cushions" on either side of the mic so that (hopefully) nothing rubs against the mic. Sometimes a mic can be clipped or taped inside of clothing where it won't rub against anything, such as inside a jacket or under a shirt lapel. Taped on the inside of a shirt collar near the actor's mouth can work well, although sometimes that creates an obvious bulge.

In any event, it is difficult to wire someone. Many actors are squeamish, and you need to be sensitive to the humanity of the situation. Especially when wiring someone of the opposite gender. Always ask before approaching! Even if they expect you to wire them, even if you've wired them multiple previous times, always announce your intentions. Make sure they know what you're doing. Give them the opportunity to run a wire themselves (perhaps down a shirt, or down a pant leg); actors can do it, and will greatly appreciate you not presuming that you should do it.

Things to have on hand:

- Hand sanitizer, for both before you touch someone and after. Let them see you clean your hands before you work on them, as they will be comforted by your professionalism.
- Breath mints (always a good idea when working close to people) (I credit Rudy Garcia for this tip, which he claims leads to more work when you get known as "the sound guy with mints"!)
- Alcohol prep pads. Clean the lav right in front of the actor. Actors know how sweaty and gross the job of acting can be, and God knows where that lav has been.
- Windshields for your lavs. These can be just foam, or the furry type that do better at stopping wind noise.
- Tape to attach lavs to clothing, and to skin. Gaffer's tape works well for clothing, and it will also work on skin, to a degree. Fortunately, gaffer's tape comes off without much screaming. But gaffer's tape sweats off, too. If you are taping to skin, I prefer to use KT tape that is sold for athletes who sweat a lot. When you tape the cable to clothing or skin, add a loop so there will be some slack in the line should any sudden tug pull at it.

Prep the night before recording
Not too much preparation is needed for sound, but you need to stay on top of a few things.

Make sure you have enough batteries. Always start the day with fresh batteries, and plenty of spares. Take more than you expect to need. If you use any form of rechargeable battery, make sure the day before that you have a full charge. Running out of power on set sucks.

If possible, ask ahead of time about the location, script, and wardrobe. Location because you may have to think of creative ways to deal with noise. Script because you should prepare for any particular sound needs, and it's also helpful to think about recording action sounds for Foley use. And wardrobe because you may have challenges to work around, for instance where an actor needs a lav but has insufficient clothing in which to hide a lav.

Decide which mic(s) you plan to use, and test those mics with your recorder. Testing them on set is too late. Make sure the day before that you have what you need. Also, carry a backup mic or two.

Make sure your prior sound files have all been transferred to where you need them to be, and are not still on the SD cards. Reformat the SD cards, and test them with a test recording. Also, carry extra SD cards.

Voice Over

There are times when an actor's dialogue is "OS" (off stage) or "VO" (voiceover), which is pretty much the same thing, soundwise. In such cases, an actor is called upon to record into a mic, without being filmed at the same time. Actual voice over artists (actors who do only voice over work) are rarely on set; they are elsewhere, typically hundreds or thousands of miles away in a sound studio which is carefully insulated from exterior noise sources so that a very clean recording can be made. Ideally, all voice over recordings should be done in a sound stage. But sometimes you need to record lines on set, because that's when and where the actor is. The last time I recorded a voice over, we had the actor phone it in, literally. (The sound worked well enough since the script called for a voicemail message.)

"ADR" (Automatic Dialogue Replacement – though some say it stands also for Alternate Dialogue Recording) is the process of recording an actor's dialogue separately, and matching it to the footage. This is done whenever the sound recorded on set is, for any reason, not good enough. This happens frequently, very likely more often than you expect. Some projects (in fact, most Hollywood blockbusters) are entirely ADR!

What this means is that the actors come into a sound studio and re-record their dialogue. As you can guess, it is an expensive and time consuming process. First, the project is edited to the point where the appropriate takes have been selected and pieced together (a phase called "picture lock") -- it would make no sense to clean up footage that doesn't get used! Then the actor comes in and views their performance, to refresh their memory on precisely how they did their dialogue, including inflection, breathing, and any other idiosyncrasies. They then go into the sound booth and try to repeat the same lines, with the same tempo and feel of the original, so it sounds natural and exactly matches the recorded images. Unless, of course, the director instructs them to change something in the line or the way they did it. In both instances, the new vocal recording must match up closely with the visual movement of the actor's lips in the footage. This can be a slow, line-by-line process.

In case it sounds easy to you … think how hard it may be for an actor alone in a sound booth to recapture the emotion found during the performance. I've heard of sessions where it took an actor over 100 attempts to get just a single line recorded convincingly. It's vital to have the director on-hand, coaching the actor during ADR; don't presume the sound tech can or will help the actor.

For good results, try to record your ADR in a like environment. If the scene is outdoors, ideally it is best to record the ADR outdoors – provided you have an outdoor area free from interference with bad sounds. ADR recordings in a sound booth would need additional work (EQ and sound effects) to make it sound like it's outdoors.

ADR can be used to swap one actor's voice for another's. Famously, Darth Vader's voice in 1977's *Star Wars* was added in post-production by dubbing James Earl Jones for the part, although visually played by British character actor David Prowse.

ADR is not always done to correct sound recording problems. It is also done routinely for release of the film internationally. Replacing the original with another language is also called "Dubbing". When a film is intended for international distribution, it's important to have the dialogue on its own track, separate from all other sounds. For example, when a character shouts "Leave me alone!" and slams the door shut behind them, both the dialogue and sound of the door slamming would be recorded on set on the same mic, and therefore the sounds get mixed together forever. If that film gets dubbed into another language, the English track gets removed, and in this example, the sound of the door slamming would be lost. So, it's better practice to record all incidental sounds separately (Foley), and put them on a non-dialogue track (called "M&E" for Music & Effects), so that in the ADR / dubbing process those sounds are retained, even when multiple language tracks are used.

Other uses for ADR include inserting a new line, or corrected line, of dialogue; inserting or changing a name – either for product placement, or because of a trademark issue; cleaning up swear words for a broadcast-safe version; and to improve comedic/dramatic timing.

"Looping" is another term for ADR because an actor's line will be selected to loop (repeat) over and over, allowing the actor to hear it in her headphones and then speak the line several times. The editor then uses the best recording. Looping is also used to describe when VO actors record voices for background actors, bringing the background to life. This adds depth to the film. It's recorded separately (rather than trying to mic the BG actors during principle filming) so that the volume of the tracks can be manipulated.

Logic Pro X is recommended software, which includes a "Music for Picture" template to begin ADR.

Clapper / How to Slate

Another job for newbies hoping to break in. This job is often given to just about anybody standing around, which is a mistake because there are some important things to know to get it right. The

2AC is typically the clapper, on sets large enough to have a 2AC – luckily for newbies, most indie and student sets where you're most likely to find yourself early on won't have a 2AC.

The job of slating a take is easy to understand if you know exactly why it is done at all. If you've ever edited video files together, you likely already know. An editor's job is not an easy one. It begins with first collecting all of the relative footage and sound files together, which often includes many poorly done takes that won't get used in the final project. The editor has to pull all of this stuff together, make sense of it, and decide which are the best takes to use - and yes, you directors get a say in that, too! The process is already daunting; anything that can be done to help, should be done. Slating each take is incredibly helpful to (1) identify which section of the script is being filmed, and (2) sync the video and sound files together. Writing scene number, shot, take, and other identifying information on the slate accomplishes the first goal. Syncing sound is done by the editor matching the visual descent of the clapboard arm in the video file, and the CLAP sound on the reference sound recorded in camera, with the sharp CLAP sound on the sound file. Even though there is now software that helps with syncing, it's still vital to get a clearly focused shot of the clapboard arm while also recording the sound of the clapboard both in camera and in the sound recorder. It's good practice to slate the beginning of every take.

The slate or clapper board is typically used by the 2AC, if you have such a person. Slating can be learned quickly, and is frequently done by just about anybody handy. It's an easy job, but easy to do wrongly, also. Most boards are dry-erase, some are still old fashion chalk, some use pieces of tape for labels, and the really nice ones now are digital (and expensive). Remember, the purpose of the slate is two-fold: to identify the take, and help the editor sync the sound files.

Write the take information legibly. Boards vary, but I prefer to write the scene number, shot letter, and then take number. So, for example, let's say we want to shoot scene 5 from three different angles, first a wide shot, then a medium, and then a close up. The first (the wide shot) is simply "Scene 5, Take 1" on the clapper – and successively "Scene 5, Take 2" "Scene 5, Take 3" and so on until the director is happy with the shot. For the second shot, the clapper will say "Scene 5, Shot Alpha, Take 1". Of course, the boards are pre-printed, so all you're writing in the appropriate boxes is "5 A 1" and for the next take "5 A 2", and so on. The third shot of course begins with "5 B 1", which would typically be read off as "Scene 5, Shot Beta, Take 1".

The clapper needs to hold the slate up where the camera is in focus. The cameraperson will tell you where. Ideally, you put the board where the camera is already focused for the scene (in other words, pretty much where the actors are), instead of having the camera refocus – but sometimes it needs be the other way – especially on long shots or panning shots, where you'll need to slate close to the lens for the slate information to be read. You also need to slate where the sound mic picks you up, which again is typically where the actors are, but can be different in special set ups. For example, a wide shot of actors sitting in a car where the actors wear wireless lav microphones and no boom is used. You would need to hold the slate in front of the camera, to identify the scene visually, and then move closer to the microphones before calling it out and snapping the arm down.

A director saying "Mark the scene" or just "Mark it" means to slate. The 1AD (or director) calls "Camera" and the cameraperson answers, "Camera rolling." Then the 1AD says, "Sound" and the sound engineer answers, "Sound speeding." Then the 1AD says, "Mark it" and you read out the scene, shot and take, snap the clapper board down, and after it hits, say "Mark." Then you clear the frame (move out of the way) and take a quiet position. The director will say "Action" and the scene begins. Do not say anything over the sound of snapping the arm down, and make sure that action is clearly facing the lens; finish the snap before you begin to remove the slate. By the way, the reason you say "Mark" immediately after slating is to help the editor find the snap sound – in the example above where actors are sitting at some distance in a car, there may be a considerable time gap between the identification part of slating done in front of the camera and the snap of the arm done where the mics can pick it up. Also, the snap may be difficult to hear on some mics. Getting in the practice of saying "Mark" after the snap will make a difference on those difficult takes. But say it AFTER your motion is totally complete. I see too many people snap the board almost as an afterthought, already removing the board from view and saying "Mark" on top of the sound. No no no. You must keep the sound and movement clean.

Some productions want you to also note the sound file number on each take. Ask the sound engineer for the number.

Not all shots have sound. For example, B-Roll shots of skylines or clouds or a close up of a pencil in someone's hand – whatever. Those shots will get added in with music or some other sound score, and there's nothing in the shot to sync. For those shots when there is no separate sound recording being done, there is a special convention by which the clapper signals this to the editor, so that the poor editor doesn't waste time going crazy looking for a sound file that isn't there. When you fill out the slate, write "MOS" (or circle such, if pre-printed), which means no sound. What it actually stands for is a bit of a mystery. Some say it is bad German for "mit ohne sound" but there are other explanations, the subject now of film lore. When you slate MOS, grip the board at the top, with your fingers under the clapper board so the clapper cannot come down; this visually shows the editor that the take is MOS.

A clear, sharp SNAPPING sound is all that is necessary, and so long as the sound reaches the mics it is sufficient. Clapping louder serves no further function. Actually, there are times when clapping loudly hurts the take and you may want to purposefully clap quietly, for example when children or animals would be easily startled. Also, don't clap loudly in front of an actor's face – besides being rude, that might take the actor out of the scene mentally, resulting in a less than ideal performance. If clapping quietly, call "Soft Sticks" when slating, so that the editor knows to listen carefully for the snap.

Finally, sometimes it's impossible to slate at the beginning of a take, or not desirable, anyway. For instance, a take starting with a very emotional moment may require the director and actor to work up to such performance and slating would just interrupt it. "Tail Slate" means slating at the end of the take. When "Cut" is called on the action, but BEFORE the camera and sound recording is stopped, slate the take by first holding the clapboard upside down while saying "Tail Slate", then hold the board right side up and slate normally. I find half the time a tail slate is intended, the camera and sound operators forget and reflexively end recording when they hear "Cut", which makes it important for the clapper to yell out "Tail Slate!" to hopefully remind them before they stop recording.

Acting

> *"Some directors expect you to do everything; write, be producer, psychiatrist. Some just want you to die in a tragic accident during the shooting so they can get the insurance."*

> ~ John Malkovich

Talent

"Talent" is a word long used in the Entertainment World, and it doesn't mean what you think it means. (Apologies to *Princess Bride* fans because I know what's running in your heads now.) The word "talent" is not good; it is a word sometimes (often) used derogatively.

"Talent" refers, of course, to the actors on a film set. Actors are seen as meat – bodies chosen to look good and sound good – and they are *not* seen as being actively involved in the technical process of making the movie. Many crew members would gladly make movies without actors, if they could, and that day will come. (Many big-time actors have already been fully scanned – there will come a day when computers will be able to use those digitized actors and make movie after movie, without that actor having to ever again learn a line, travel to a set, eat from the catering truck, or age another day ....) Many filmmakers (especially at the lowest levels) are easily annoyed at the apparent weakness of actors. The crew almost always work much longer hours than the cast, carry heavier loads, rest less frequently, if at all, and usually receive far less attention, gratitude, and compensation. How do suppose they feel when an actor bitches about the wrong crackers on a craft table? Remember before you bitch too loudly that talent is lowest on the set's totem pole, and easy to replace, too.

It's more fun, many actors say, to be a stage actor. Stage acting is communal, where you must play off of your brethren's performances. Actors get together for a longer period of time, including rehearsals and multiple performances. Sometimes performances run months or years! Film acting is lonely. You learn your lines, typically on your own, then show up for a limited number of filming hours or days, during which you may perform by yourself just pretending that the other actors are there. It's no surprise to me that many film actors take a break now and then from film and spend it doing legit theatre.

You can't lie to the camera, and it sees even the smallest things. On stage, your mole or limp can be easily disguised with makeup or blocking tricks. But in front of a camera, the tiniest defect shows up larger than life, literally. On the flip side, film tricks allow manipulation of reality more easily than is possible on any stage. If you have a director and film crew willing to take the time. For example, making Tom Cruise look tall in films. My point? Embrace who you are and use it to your advantage; don't worry about hiding things. Unless you are at Tom's level of clout – in which case, order the smoked salmon and garlic-roasted brie.

For continued success, you still need to be nice. Support your crew, give them props, recognize that while you were called to set at 9:00 am, they started at 5:00 and will likely be there all night, long after you've gone home. Be sympathetic. No, there's no need for little violins, because they chose their jobs and love doing it. But don't be a dick, okay?

Here's one quick example – something you actors can easily do, which helps other actors and even makes life better for the crew: when another actor is being filmed, offer to help by running your lines off camera. This helps the other actor get into and keep character. And it helps the crew, because otherwise one of them would get stuck reading lines. It also helps the filming go faster, more efficiently, because the actor on camera is dealing with you – the real McCoy – instead of getting thrown off by the Scripty or someone else reading the lines differently than the actor rehearsed. Don't be that actor that leaves the set and relies upon a crew member to feed lines. Even better, work with the camera crew to position yourself in the eyeline that the actor on film needs. Everyone will appreciate this! (On some sets, this is common sense; but it's not always required by a director, so sometimes lazy actors will head off for their trailers. Some actors mistakenly see this as one of their perks of stardom.)

Acting on film requires a leap of faith. Faith and trust in what the camera and microphones are getting, in the crew, in the director, and in the vague idea that the divers bits of footage will be edited into something that works. Ever wonder why really good actors sometimes make flops? Better to ask, why doesn't that happen more often? Films can go wrong in hundreds of ways, some of which can be "fixed in post" -- but some can't. Many problems aren't apparent to the actor on set, and they are shocked to see how bad the final show is. An actor can only do the best job at acting, and cross fingers on all of the rest!

Act locally. Hire local actors. I've seen problem after problem on film sets, arising from the fact that the actors did not live nearby. Filming days were dependent upon travel days. Costs increased (whether hotel, travel, or incidentals as simple as "oops, I forgot my charger"). The first feature film where I was employed as 1AD was also that director's first attempt at making a feature; when we were done, I asked him what he thought the biggest lesson learned might be. Without hesitation, he said he'd never again hire non-local actors. We had lost two principal actors early on (before filming, thankfully), due to travel difficulties, and had several days limited to when people could be in town. This was an indie film, low budget ($200,000). I know major Hollywood films deal all the time with distant stars, balancing travel schedules and other filming conflicts. But there are many differences between indie film and the majors, and one of the key diffs is simply that they have people to take care of scheduling headaches! So, my advice to filmmakers at all levels *below* the Hollywood level, hire actors that live in your area.

Hiring local actors has another huge benefit -- built in support groups and potential audiences. When you screen your film, that young actress who lives locally will convince everyone she knows to come to the premiere: her friends, family, co-workers, other acting students, other actors she's worked with, casting agents she hopes to impress, agents she wants to sign with, newspaper critics … and on, and on. These people buy your tickets! (Well, I suppose you will comp a number of them, especially the press, but still – take my point. Think like a business MBA. Hire local.

What does an actor need on set? Not much more than a good attitude and memorized lines. Here are things I try to have with me, and see others tote around, too, in a backpack:

- Full script (it's important to understand how your character fits in with the whole, and even on set you may want to refer to other scenes, plus you may find yourself helping another actor with their lines)
- Your sides – i.e. your scenes, which by filming day you have broken down and made oodles of notes upon. (Please, don't just look at your phone. You need a paper copy, on which to make notes.)
- A couple granola bars – the production should have a craft service table (catering), with snacks and/or real food, but you should never count on that being available
- Keys / wallet / purse – these are things you typically have in your pockets or otherwise with you, but when you get into costume will have to be put somewhere; I recommend a backpack to hold all (*"…and one ring to rule them all"*)
- Your cell phone on silent (not vibrate)
- Portable battery charger, to recharge your cell phone. Such a life saver! I love my HUAF 24,000mAh power bank (Amazon $30.99), which lets me recharge 4 or 5 times.
- Water bottle – again, the production should provide, but ….
- If you film outdoors, get solid-stick sun protection, and maybe the same for bug protection – don't carry around sprays or lotions, because sooner or later that will spill in your bag
- Floppy "Gilligan style" hat – great sun and rain protection, and won't hurt it to be wadded up until you need it

Extras / Background

One of the quickest ways to break into the Entertainment World, many people begin as an extra. An "Extra" is simply any person visible in the frame who is not one of the credited actors.

In other words, a character with no dialogue or any key function to serve. Sometimes an extra will have a specific job, which can make them a "Featured Extra" – for example, a ticket taker at the carnival, who may even get a short line or two, "Here's your change." "Background" is the term for everyone … wait for it … in the background. They are extras, too.

Being an extra is an exercise in patience. You will need to be on set for hours, most of which is time spent doing literally nothing. You may be in costume and placed where your movement is cramped, if you can move at all. You may be able to read a book if you're lucky. You may be able to talk with others around you if you're lucky. You may be in the shade if you're lucky. Or you may be unlucky – if so, tough it out.

But being on set as an extra is a great way to learn how sets are run. Because your duties are minimal, you have time to watch and learn. Notice how the command system works. Watch how shots are set up. Pay attention to how the actors work (how they perform, and more importantly how they prepare). Look at the lighting, and at what is done to alter natural light to fit the scene.

Don't expect to be "discovered" as an extra. Your job is to blend in. If you stand out, you've probably done something wrong, which could backfire on you. For example, an extra looking into the camera in the middle of a scene can ruin that take. You may be kicked off the set. And if whatever you've done is only caught later in editing, you may have a problem getting future work.

There are people who do BG as a career. Yes, they get paid, and enough to make a living if they stay active enough (which pretty much means only in LA or New York). Why would anyone do this as a career? 'Cuz it's easy, it pays, and it's fun. Why not? There are talent agencies that specialize in extras and BG talent. Sign up, give it a try. Earn, learn, and yarn (i.e. network with other BG actors).

But you may be thinking a bigger question, Why do productions hire BG actors? I mean, it seems there are always random people eager to be in a movie, even if not paid at all -- people who can walk the street in your background, or whatever other simple task is needed. And those people are likely out of focus, anyway. Just throw any random *bodies* back there, for no money or dirt cheap, and forget out about it.

Oh, no. Let's look at this from the filmmaker's perspective. We all know filming is not easy, and it takes time – so much time – to set up each shot, film repetitive takes, and then repeat the scene from a different angle or with a different lens. In each of these takes, the BG needs to be consistent. Extras need to do precisely the same thing, at precisely the same point in script time, over and over. Same clothes, same props, same movements, same mimed dialogue, same gestures, same looks, and of course the same extras! Imagine what it does to a scene if even one extra is suddenly gone. A whole days shooting can be lost just because one BG actor disappears. Almost anyone will agree to be in a movie, but few people have the patience and fortitude to stick it out for hours, presenting the same look and attitude throughout. Production companies know how crucial it is to maintain continuity, and how expensive it is if shots have to be redone because of BG problems, so they are willing to pay.

A film I just finished (as 1AD) was an independent feature, with no budget for paying extras. We had to beg for people to come for free. This is very common in the indie and student film environments. But it meant real problems for us. When we filmed, we had to work with what we had, even though in one case the "crowd" called for in our script was a meager 20 or so people. We had to film quickly, knowing that the nice people who volunteered their time cannot be counted on to stay all day, and that their interest would fade if we delayed for any reason. When we filmed a court scene which required two days of filming, we had to plan to film all of the shots which showed extras on one day, because we couldn't rely upon any of them to return the next day. These are all examples to show why bigger, established productions gladly pay their extras.

Extras are actors. Every person in the frame is a "character" in the film, even an extra. You will be told where to be, and what movement may be needed from you, and probably not much more than that. It's up to you. Decide who your character is, and make whatever choices will help you stick to that character. Have fun with it. For example, I was a "patron diner" in an indie feature film recently, and told where to sit in a small restaurant. In the scene being filmed, two main characters were conversing in a booth, when the town sheriff comes to arrest one and a fight results. I was told where to sit … and nothing else. Because I knew I'd be bored silly just sitting there all day, I pulled out a notebook and pen so that instead of just "patron diner" I decided I could play a "writer working on his manuscript." I could sip on my coffee and write. Then react when the fight starts. No one told me what to do, but then again no one objected – so I did it.

How to behave if you are an extra:

- Do what you're told.

- Shut up.

- Cellphones are ubiquitous in the modern world, so much so that it would be strange for extras not to have one – depending of course on the time the film is set in. Ask. You can read or play games on your phone, but be sure doing so is OK on your set.

- Do NOT take pictures of the set or anyone there. This is a major no-no and can get you kicked off the set in a hurry. No selfies! Not unless you are really sure that it is allowed. Many sets require you to sign an NDA (Non-Disclosure Agreement), and they are very serious about keeping details of the filming secret. In fact, there are often signs posted around the set, stressing secrecy and no pictures.

But taking pictures may be okay on some sets. Ask.

- Do NOT post anything about the production on social media, unless you are certain they want you to.

- Do NOT interrupt, even if you feel you have the best idea in the world.

- Do NOT speak to the cast, unless and until they speak with you. Especially recognizable name actors. You would love a picture with that actor – but don't do it. Don't bother them, don't even approach them. Don't even look them in the eye! Eye contact during a scene can be very disruptive to the actors. Even off set, when they look like they're doing nothing, be mindful that they may be preparing, rehearsing their lines, or otherwise getting into character; don't interfere!

  It may be alright to photograph an actor, even get a selfie with the actor – but it is always safest to follow that actor's lead. Don't ask for a picture, don't put them in an uncomfortable situation. If they're cool with it, they will let you know.

- It's OK to bring snacks or a book in a small backpack or other bag, small enough to keep out of sight during filming. You may be required to put it off set, so make sure there is nothing in it that you really care about.

- Do NOT help yourself to the craft services table, without being told to do so. There may be a separate table for extras, or nothing for you. (Sorry.)

- Do NOT leave the set without letting someone know, even to go to the bathroom. At any moment, you may be needed, and people need to know where you are.

Billing

Actual billing varies, depending upon the medium, as follows:

In commercials all actors are Principals, unless they are extras. Difference being if you have a line.

In <u>television</u> actors are Series Regulars, Recurring Co-Stars / Recurring Guest-Stars, Co-Stars, and Guest-Stars. (Plus Extras / Background.)

<u>Film</u> roles are *not* "Starring" or "Co-Starring" – those are terms used frequently by the general public and the media, but they are too vague for use within the film industry. Actors in film are either Leads or Supporting Actors. (Plus Extras / Background.) "Principal" generally refers to both lead and supporting roles.

On your resumé, use character names only for theatrical roles. Record film roles only as lead or supporting.

"Uncredited" is used to refer only to a principal actor whose performance ended up on the cutting room floor. But with the growing use of IMDb, the term is now used by many for extra positions.

You ain't much, you know

I grew up thinking movie stars were the topmost shining examples of all humanity, the ultimate status that anyone could hope and dream of obtaining. Cary Grant, David Niven, Brad Pitt, Harrison Ford, Jack Nicholson, Tom Cruise, Kenneth Branagh, Jimmy Stewart, Spencer Tracy, Michael Caine – I'm naming guys because I am a guy, and dreamed of being these guys – but there are certainly as many wonderful female stars, especially Kathryn Hepburn, Myrna Loy, Shirley MacLaine, Emma Thompson, Bernadette Peters, Jennifer Lawrence … I could go on forever. These are stars of today and yesteryear. But even back then, in the film industry actors are referred to generally as "talent" and they are treated mostly like garbage unless and until they hit "star" level.

Talent is considered to be among the lowest possible creatures on set. It takes incredible skill and knowledge to know how to put films together, and to be honest no real skill at all to "just be an actor" which means on any given set the crew is probably more important to the success of the project than the actors. At least, this is the attitude you will find commonly on many sets. And it doesn't take any skill to "be an actor" … anyone can stand there, look pretty, maybe say a few lines repeatedly until they get lucky and something sounds good. There are sooooooo many "actors" like this, people who call themselves actors but don't bother learning the trade or exercising their talents. Might be the director's boyfriend, her cousin, or her dry cleaner's nephew. Might be someone with millions of Instagram followers, which producers sometimes confuse with an indication of real talent.

Not all actors are crap, of course. There are still great actors that rise far above the derogatory label of "talent" and deserve the fame and special treatment the industry eventually gives them. But they had to prove themselves. Unless and until you are an A-Lister star, it's best to swallow your ego and realize you can be replaced with a phone call. Actually, your replacement is probably standing next to you, working as a PA. With the horrendous amounts of money on the line, you should expect the money people to throw you out if you can't prove your abilities. Never rest on past laurels. You are only as good today as what you can bring to the table today.

I'm stressing this point, really, to emphasize two things: (1) check your ego; and (2) prepare yourself to succeed.

Preparation

Arrive on set prepared to do the scene, as written.

This is one of my biggest pet peeves. Too many actors arrive on set thinking they can "wing it", that they'll learn or make up the lines as they go. They're wrong. No one can do that, not even the absolutely best actors. Try this, and you will look like a fool. Worse yet, you will be doing a tremendous disservice to your co-actors, and to the production as a whole, because everyone else will be forced to wait for you to figure out what the hell you're doing. An actor prepares – perhaps many even over prepare, but that is far less a problem.

Know your lines. Memorize and rehearse until you know the dialogue and can pick it up from any point. Michael Caine has said that you need to be able to run your lines despite distractions, otherwise you get to the set and when the crew calls "Quiet!" "Camera!" "Rolling!" "Sound!" "Speeding!" "Action!" you forget absolutely everything.

Michael Caine also recommends that you rehearse your action, with props. You may not know exactly how a director will block your scene, or precisely what props you will be given, but get what the script calls for and practice. Get comfortable with the scene, before showing up to do it.

Be yourself, said one of my heroes, director / actor John Huston. I met Mr. Huston on the very first set I worked on, where I was a lowly teenage extra (the 1981 film Victory, starring Michael Caine and Sylvester Stallone, although I did not meet either luminary). Ignorant 16 year-old me didn't have any idea who Mr. Huston was, other than some old nice guy breathing with the help of an oxygen tank. But we chatted for an hour or so, sitting on a picnic table, and I've remembered his advice ever since. Be true to who you are. Don't try to be anyone else.

Actors prepare. This often means acting classes, and studying different acting methods. A thorough study of acting methods is way beyond the scope of this book; I'll just mention a few tidbits.

Acting Styles

Acting instructor Stella Adler focused on setting. People may say things like "Find your soul" but the young don't have souls, they haven't found them yet in life's experiences. Stella Adler said that theatre is 99% imagination. You don't have to recall your past emotional experiences. You don't act words. You act the character, what the character wears, how they move, everything the writer wanted, everything. "No background is lost," said Ms. Adler, "Use all of your background."

Uta Hagen, famous for acting and teaching, said to bite off what you can chew. Like Adler, she advised that actors spend time to know your space. Ask yourself, What do I do in this room? Always connect your first beat with a physical activity. Consider 3 steps as you analyze each scene, or each beat: What did I just do? What am I doing now? And what do I want?

"When I go to the theatre, if I can see the acting, I already don't like it. If I can see the actor's choices, it's bad acting. When I believe that there's a human being in action up there, in that moment, alive, right there and then, I get spellbound." (Uta Hagen)

When you first get your script, Uta Hagen advised that you cross out all of the action, all of the adjectives, all of the parentheticals that writers use to tell actors what to do. Figure out your own motivation from the dialogue.

Stanislavsky said look at the character, and act as real as possible instead of presenting / pretending. This led notables (Elia Kazan, Lee Strasburg) to create "method acting", which is the actor trying to stimulate genuine feelings from real experience. Sanford Meisner was part of the method acting movement, but split off and said the focus should be on what your effect is on the other characters.

Mark Travis' approach says an actor's biggest obstacle to finding the character is the actor's intent to find the character. Stop directing the actor, and start directing the character. Interrogate the character. This is now known as "interrogation process."

Wendy Alane Wright, who teaches currently in LA, says acting is not pretending. Acting is being. Your job as an actor is to hear the words as written, then decide who this person is, what they want and need, where they came from, where they're going. You have to make the character human.

I wouldn't advise studying any of these teachers. I would advise studying them all. Find what resonates in you, what best helps you to bring a character to life in your acting.

Training

Train every chance you get. Every day, every situation, every place you go, you have opportunities to absorb what's around you and practice your art.

Like going to a gym to work on your muscles, you should act regularly to exercise your acting abilities. Discover, improve, fine-tune ... practice, practice, practice! Practice makes perfect – OK, perfection isn't possible, but you'll get closer and closer the more you practice. You can't expect to get better without practice.

Learn monologues. Find fun stuff that you enjoy, because you will need to do the piece over and over, so don't saddle yourself with one you hate. Many auditions will give you a page or more from their script (called "sides"), and ask that you tape yourself doing a video audition. Very common. However, you will still find yourself in auditions where you are asked to give a monologue – sometimes without advance notice, because some CDs just expect actors to be able to riff out a monologue. It shows an actor is prepared, and that is a sign that the actor is professional ….

Learn and practice a funny monologue, and a serious one. Lots of times a CD will only want a one minute monologue, but be prepared with one that's longer (3 – 5 minutes, tops); they can always stop you if they need to move on to another actor. It's good to have a Shakespeare monologue ready, although more so if you are auditioning for theatre than for film. There are many ways to find monologues. You can pick something from a tv show or movie, even if you have to write it out yourself, but if you pick something done by a famous actor be sure not to copy that actor. Your expression of the piece should be your own interpretation of what the character is feeling and saying, and the worst thing you can do is attempt to parrot the performance of some other actor doing the part.

Do cold readings. This is where you get together with other actors and read a script out loud, usually just sitting at a table or around the living room – don't try to act it out. Great practice for hearing and delivering vocal inflections.

Go to auditions. Go! Force yourself to go, no matter that you're scared of the probable rejection and hate the waste of time. Every time you go physically to struggle with the nerves and fears of performing in front of strangers, you will get better.

Find other actors to work with, even if just fooling around with a scene. They need to practice, too!

Self-tape. Create scenes, even if just for your own amusement and viewing.

Break apart your favorite tv shows and films: write out scenes, find the beats, and study why it is that you like the show. Do the same for shows you hate.

Take acting classes. Even free classes that aren't very good will still help you. There's really no such thing as wasting your time because you can always learn from each experience.

Concentration

Acting is work. Concentrate. Focus. Pay attention. Remember your action from take to take, so the master, medium and close up shots match.

~ Michael Caine

Michael Caine also said:

- Don't fidget. Don't move props, unless and except as required.

- Don't blink in close ups, unless doing so for effect. A steady gaze makes people listen to you; blinking makes you look uncertain and confused.

- Forget the camera is there. Forget the crew and any audience. The only people that exist are the other actors you are working with.

- Look the other actors directly in their eyes. Acting is all about the eyeballs meeting.

- Go slow, take it easy. Let your reactions develop. Let the viewer catch up.

Find the subtext when you analyze your scene, and then drill in on that as you perform. Stella Adler said, "Listen with your blood."

Comfort

Most important? Underwear. Victorian posture derived from stiff corsets. Humans have always been humans, but fashions change. Pour carefully if it's important not to ruin your cuff, or get fingerprints on the silver. Find the reality of the time, and use it.

~ Uta Hagen

Jack Lemon said, "Sometimes you can't get a character until it comes alive with the costume." Combine preparation and concentration, and wardobe, so you can be comfortable.

Don't put on a costume; put on your clothes. (Uta Hagen)

Movement

If you're going to stand, take the cameraman up with you.

~ Michael Caine

In film, the slightest movement can be hugely meaningful. Cameras get the smallest details. Here are more nuggets from Michael Caine:

- To hit a mark on a certain line, start at the mark and say the line as you walk backwards. Then that is your starting point.

- In a closeup, ask the director how much freedom you have. Don't move out of frame, but feel free to move within the frame; don't freeze or present a blank face, just because you know the camera is close.

- Theatre is about big movements, to be seen by the audience; film is about small, seen only by the camera. In film, just shifting your eyes is a big movement that can indicate someone's coming or create tension.

Michael Cain said, "Movie acting is relaxation. It's easy. If you are knocking yourself out, you're doing it wrong."

Jack Lemmon coming to film out of Broadway was told repeatedly by George Cukor to "do less", until finally Jack says "pretty soon I won't be acting at all" and George replied, "Now you're getting the idea."

But always be doing something. Nobody does nothing, ever. If you are waiting, you are doing something, always. (Uta Hagen)

If you don't know where you came from, what you're doing, and where you're going, then your body will tense up, as you focus on where you think you need to be to act. But when you know these things, then your body is at ease. (Uta Hagen)

Any physical confrontation has to be worked out like ballet, so that it can appear spontaneous. (Uta Hagen)

Eyeline

As the Crab says in Moana, "Pick an eye." Don't shift your gaze back and forth between an actor's eyes, because the camera will pick that up as if you are talking to two people.

Never look at the camera (except the rare instances when breaking the 4th wall is desired), but instead look as close to the camera as possible. The other actor should be next to the lens. That will look the most natural in the camera.

Reaction

The art of conversation has fallen on hard times (compared to examples of how people conversed in literary works written prior to electronic entertainment), but one thing remains true: conversation is as much listening as it is talking. I'd argue one should listen much more than talk.

Just as true in film. We've all worked with actors who parrot their memorized lines in sequence and are not responding at all to the other actors. They listen only for the last word cue in the other actor's dialogue, and without that word they are lost because they aren't engaged in the conversation. Their physical reactions are preplanned, delivered with their own lines. While the other actor speaks, they just wait. But such actors are missing half the conversation! Such actors are not acting half the time. Such actors are boring on stage, and never shown on film.

Michael Caine said nothing exists except the other actors; listen to them. The only story is the story being presented. Keep the rest of your world out of your head while you perform. Your character is not thinking about the audience, cues, blocking, or lighting; none of these things exist in your character's world – these are only distractions existing in the actor's world. You must push everything aside, other than what the other actors are saying and doing.

If you are on stage or in front of a camera, you must act. Even if you have no lines. You existing there at that moment says something, and you must determine what it is that your existence is meant to say in the story. An extra sitting in the background of a courtroom drama would not be dozing. In real life, people sitting in court may be totally bored by the current case in front of the judge, and they may look bored. But that most likely does not fit in the courtroom drama story that you have been hired to be part of (unless that *is* part of the story). Don't invent rationalization based on your knowledge of real life that goes against the script. The writer put you in there for a reason.

Michael Caine advises that when you have no lines, you should think about all the things you would say. Not saying things still shows in your physical reactions. Not saying anything can scream something.

React to the other actors. Don't make it clear that you already know what they will say. Listen and discover their words and meaning, as they deliver it. React as you have determined (in your scene preparation) your character would react. No need to overthink that, just get into character and let it happen.

Per Uta Hagen: If you do it for the other actor, it's correct; if you do it for the audience, it's bad acting.

Auditions

"Auditioning sucks hippo dick."

~ William H. Macy

Did you ever have to stand up in front of your class as a young child? Maybe for a spelling bee? This is nightmare stuff! I remember knowing how to spell every single word that other students got, but as my turn approached … I'd lose focus, as if my world were closing in on me … a buzz would fill my head, almost like a voice shouting "You're going to fail! Everyone is going to laugh at you! You're a loser!" … short breaths, clammy palms, a sudden bad taste in my mouth, and an overpowering desire to sit down …. Until, as you'd expect from this story, I failed at my word and had to (or is it *got to*?) sit back down, the horrible ordeal over at last.

Some people can easily stand up and perform naturally in front of an audience. If that's you, I hope you realize how lucky and fortunate you are. Most people have a hard time with it. They freeze, or just as bad suddenly get diarrhea of the mouth. My first theatre audition was in high school, and I was poorly prepared – although, at the time, I thought I was good to go. I stuttered my way through a dead monologue, just proud of myself for getting over my fear of standing up. (No, I did not get that role.) Fans of Shakespeare in Love will recall the audition scene with a number of truly stinky attempts – I was just as bad.

The fear of auditions is what keeps many people from acting.

I can audition now. In fact, I just did so the night before writing this, and it was a very fun and rewarding experience. So let's talk about how you can get to that point.

Have you ever driven to an audition, sat in the car yelling at yourself, and then left without going in? Or signed up, but chickened-out before your name was called? I have come to believe, the worst part of auditioning by far is the waiting, the anticipation, the worrying. The best way to stop fretting is to stop thinking about the process from your own perspective, and look at it from the show's perspective.

"You're there to solve their problem, remember that."

~ Jeff Daniels

Think about Jeff Daniels' quote, that the casting director and everyone else involved in the production has a problem, and it's a big one; it's not easy to find actors that they can be comfortable choosing. They need actors that can (1) do the role, speak the lines, move around, etc.; (2) look the part, which means satisfying the preconceptions of the director, producers and other money sources; (3) get along with other actors and the crew; (4) take direction; (5) commit to studying and preparing for the role; (6) show up on time, dependably, every time; (7) not be a disruptive force, whether talking politics or just standing in the way; and (8) not whine about all the little bumps in the road that are sure to arise. When actors think of auditioning, they think typically only about the first two factors, hitting the character's performance and looking the part. But believe me, when I'm on the casting director's side of the table, we are thinking about finding someone who can meet all of these criteria – especially the "commit to show up" part! We don't want a fantastic actor who will make the set miserable. To make us want to hire you, you need to present yourself in a way that demonstrates all of these points. Sure, we want to see you do the part ... but much more than that, you have to show us that you're a good person we can rely upon.

So, when you go to an audition:

- Whatever the instructions for the audition, be sure to follow them precisely, and cheerfully. If they tell you to sign in and wait, then do so with a smile. You're proving you can be a team member.

- Take with you whatever they may have asked for, perhaps a headshot and résumé. Don't show up with excuses, because they will then suspect that you will arrive on set unprepared, too.

- If they asked you to prepare a monologue, have it ready. Practice, practice, practice, until you are able to give that monologue with barely any thought. When you are asked to start your monologue, there is a good chance that – for a split second – everything you practiced will suddenly disappear, leaving you that frightened little child standing in front of judgmental monsters. The more you practice your monologue, the less likely you will blank.

- Even if the audition instructions do not require a monologue, it sure is a good idea to have one or more ready!

- Choose a monologue that roughly fits the genre of the role for which you are auditioning. Comedy for comedy, drama for drama, in other words. Remember, you're helping them see how well you fit the part, and unfortunately casting directors seem to have little imagination.

- When you enter the room, realize that from that moment on you are performing. Say, "Hello" in a friendly manner, greet the room and everyone in there with at least a quick smile.

- There will likely be an asshole or two in the room (this *is* the Entertainment World), so don't be nettled by scowls or any other reaction from people in there. They may be tired, overworked, bored, hungry, or whatever else humans frequently feel. Ignore them. Don't ignore them, though. Address everyone with the same "can do" attitude.

- You may be asked to stand in front of the production table, where typically sit the casting director, maybe the director, maybe the producer, and probably a PA, or two. Make eye contact as you introduce yourself. But when you do your monologue, don't go for eye contact; don't make them part of your performance, because that might disturb them. Pick a point at a slight angle from them, or below, or above, and address your performance to that point. Make sure, however, that the CD can see your eyes. The exception to this is comedy; everyone enjoys being looped in for funny moments, so with a comedic monologue you may choose to address is straight to them.

- Instead of (or sometimes in addition to) a monologue, you may be given pages of the script, called "sides." You are, of course, at a huge disadvantage in doing so, because you don't know the character, don't know how the character fits into the script, and haven't had a chance to determine the purpose and subtext of the scene. You may or may not get some time to work with the sides, but even then you will have to make certain fast assumptions about what the director wants from the character. You'll have to guess. Relax. The CD and everyone else knows what situation they pushed you into. They know they can't expect you to find the perfect performance by magic, and they will take that into consideration as they watch you. But what they want to see is that you try to do the part. This shows them more about *your attitude* than about the character, and that's what they want to know.

- If you're given sides, look for the meat. You're not expected to have the script memorized, and therefore it is okay that you are looking at the script, reading it. But as you do so, identify that meaningful passage and nail it (advice from Jeff Daniels), and look up as you do so. Make that point sing, even if you have to repeat the lines.

- More on that point: feel free to repeat yourself. If a line sounds like it came out poorly and you feel you can do better, go right ahead and redo. That's perfectly acceptable in auditions.

- You may be asked to read lines you've never seen before. Yikes! This is called a "cold reading" and it happens, so expect it; don't let it throw you off. Take your time; don't feel pressured by the tense atmosphere. Take pauses before your lines, and within your dialogue. Follow the punctuation for clues on inflection. Practice, practice, practice this at home, by reading books out loud. You will find that, like everything else with practice, you get much better at it.

- With both sides and cold readings, the dialogue may include other parts. These lines will probably be read by a PA, who may or may ham it up. The PA *should* just read the lines neutrally, to simply give you the necessary cue, but sometimes the PA is also a wanna-be actor, goofing off, or playing with it because it's the 22nd time that day they've auditioned with the same sides … whatever. Focus only on your part; react only as you see the character reacting, and not in reaction to what the PA is doing, unless what the PA is doing seems right to you.

- When you've finished, some actors say, "Scene" to make it clear that they are done. I don't do so. I'll finish by freezing, dropping my head, then lifting it back up with a cheerful smile, as if I've just performed on stage.

- When you are done, they need to get you out of there as quickly as possible. They are always short on time, always running late. Be considerate of this. Smile, say, "Thank you" and answer any questions they may have with short, friendly but direct answers. Then say "thank you!" again, and leave.

- Don't look for reactions to your performance. They may smile, they may applaud, they may stand up and cheer – all wonderful, and if they do so, don't gush about it; simply nod and say "thank you", with a smile. They may glare, they may look at you with disgust, they may play with their cell phones or doodle on papers, they may even tell you that you sucked – that's right, it's a cold world. But if they do so, your reaction should be the same! Nod and say "thank you" with a smile. Their reactions at the time (good, bad, or indifferent) mean nothing. They may praise everyone, or may be rude to everyone, but they will determine *later* who to cast, after further reviewing and thinking about their choices.

- The only reaction to your audition that really matters to you is your own. If you recognize that you didn't do your best, then you have learned where you need to work on your preparation.

Stage fright

Fear affects more than just auditions. "Glossophobia" (the fear of public speaking) is said to affect as many as 75% of all people.

Al Pacino says you may be inhibited, personally, which causes you to think about yourself as an actor. But when you have a character to inhabit, you can just let go. Do your research, prepare, find out who the character is, know the character fully. Then, step into that character. Become the character, and in doing so step away from the insecurities inside you – because those fears are not in the character. This is, I think, the trick to getting over stage fright. Stop thinking about yourself.

Do you know why the room where actors wait to go on stage is called the "Green Room"? You'll see different explanations (because no one knows, for sure, how the phrase came about historically) but I think it's because nerves and fear turn you green. Actors get "green about the gills" or they are "greenhorn" beginners. I feel like puking every time, every single time I'm due to go on stage or in front of a camera … but then, stage or camera, that feeling goes away as soon as I focus all of my energies into bringing out the routine of the character for the audience. Think only about the character, from the perspective of what the audience needs to see and understand in order for the audience to understand and enjoy the story.

The more prepared you are, the less fear you should feel. Preparation into the character, and preparation generally as to what kind of actor you are, even what kind of person you are. Preparation leads to self-confidence, which allows you to get up and perform despite fear and nerves.

If stage fright controls you, spend more time preparing. Break down the script and each scene to determine who your character is. Create backstory, the character's history, which isn't in the script and will never be part of the production, but is nevertheless consistent with everything in the script. That depth of understanding is just for you. The deeper you get into your character's world, the more meat you have to work with during your performance – which means, ultimately, far less time for you to think about your performance.

There are other solutions people recommend to get over stage fright. Whatever you do, please don't be one of those who think they can benefit from a "mother's little helper" of any sort, whether drugs or alcohol; substances can help you deaden feelings, like fear, but at the same time they affect your ability to give a good performance – I don't care how good you think you are, when drunk or high your capacity to accurately bring out the intricacies of a character is reduced. Have you tried:

- Picturing the audience wearing nothing but underwear
- Think only good thoughts
- Imagine success, applause, awards
- Practice meditation, yoga, deep-breathing, anything else to calm your nerves
- Prick your finger before you go out, and focus on not getting the blood on anything
- Visit with a psychiatrist
- Have a hypnotist tell you that you are not afraid
- Tell yourself that no cares about your small part
- Pick a focal point

- Perform to one single person in the audience

You may have success with some or all of these methods. Still, I recommend you follow Pacino's advice: focus on your character, instead of on yourself.

Intimacy

This is a fear of almost all actors, even those who don't feel stage fright! Physically intimate scenes, where you are required to act in close proximity with other actors. (Hey! I'm not talking about porn. Read some other book for that. I'm not even talking about actual sex scenes, but really *any* scene where you are close to others.) We all have varying degrees of comfort, in how close we can stand to another; cross a certain line and suddenly it's just "wrong".

Michael Caine's advice: carry a mouthwash spray (Binaca, etc.) and take a blast before any close talking or intimacy. When your co-actor asks, "What's that?" offer them a blast. You may want to pull the spray out and use it yourself, for the sole reason that you hope the other actor takes the hint!

Be professional. This is a business for stars, day players, and extras alike. Don't offend anyone by telling them, publicly, that their breath or body odor stinks. If you must speak up, do so in private so as not to embarrass the person.

Michael Caine also warns against the risk of becoming too intimate. Do not rehearse the intimacy on your own, prior to shooting. That leads to disaster. You are likely to go farther, and the next thing you know you're in a relationship, and then halfway through the shoot break up. Don't subject yourself or the production to all that negativity on set. This is a recipe for disaster for you personally, and also something the production worries about.

Self-Tapes

With the rising popularity and lower prices of good video cameras, including those within most smartphones, it's becoming more common to see casting directors ask for video auditions. Actors can typically do these themselves, without any great fuss. Actors have also come to realize how important it is to have an "acting reel" – a collection of short videos showing their best acting – which can be scenes from productions they've acting in, or scenes they videotape themselves, too.

When self-taping, put yourself in front of a background that will not distract the viewer. There should be nothing moving in the background, no other people, no odd things to draw the eye. People sometimes put up a sheet or blanket on the wall behind them; if you do so, make sure it is stretched tight to reduce or eliminate wrinkles that catch the eye. A dark background may make the whole shot look dark, while a white background may bleach out the whole shot. If you're shooting digitally (as I presume you are) then experiment; video yourself and then look at the results, and alter what you want.

For every gods' sake, don't shoot a bathroom selfie! Avoid using a greenscreen or bluescreen background, because those will make casting directors think you either don't know what you're doing with chromakey, or else they'll wonder what kind of background you meant to add – in either case, distracting from your performance.

Set the camera on a tripod. Don't rely upon a friend to hold it still – even small movements are distracting.

Light yourself from the front, at a flattering angle, and add a back light – just enough light that your background is not completely lost and it will help highlight your hair from behind. Make sure your eyes are lit! This is most important. There should be a "catchlight" visible in your eyes, which is the reflection of your light source(s). Eyes without catchlights seem dull, dead, not at all likely to catch and hold the attention of the casting director.

Position the camera to show you in a close up, from mid torso up, unless the script absolutely calls for some other shot. Speak your lines, looking just to the side of the camera lens, as if the person you're talking to is standing very close to the camera. Most instructors advise against looking into the camera lens, as this can seem jarring to the viewer; but for every rule, there are exceptions, and you may want to address the camera directly at times.

Obviously, the whole point of self-taping is to do what makes you look like a solid, competent actor. Rehearse as if you are going to perform the audition in front of real people, not a camera. Memorize your lines, unless the CD has specifically instructed you to read from the script – even then, I'd recommend memorizing and only holding the script to show your compliance with instructions, or for a quick reference peek. Dress for the part – not in costume, but choose clothes that fit the character type. And dress ALL of you, not just your top half, because filming yourself barefoot or with no pants will affect your performance, no matter what you think. Make up? Not recommended. Only as you might if going out anyway; don't put on film/stage makeup, or prosthetics that the character may need.

If the sides you've been given call for a prop, get a prop – doesn't have to be anything special, but something to hold and use as directed.

Since video is free, shoot your scene several times. You will get better each time. Don't be lazy and send out one of the first takes, when you could send better. Tape until you have a complete run through that you like. Even if you are incredibly skilled at video editing, do not edit your self-tape together. The CD wants to see a complete run through, to show you can do it.

I do recommend that you learn how to edit your own videos. Software is not that expensive. (Actually, one of the best – Davinci Resolve – is available for a free download, although it requires a good computer.) Before you send out your self-tape, edit it to remove anything and everything that you don't want seen. For example, if the beginning of the take shows you are walking from the camera and turning around to get ready, edit that out. Many CD's ask that you begin or end your tape with a "slating", which is where you identify yourself. Film that separately, and then edit your takes so that you can present the best slating with the best take. If you want, you can find plenty of people who will shoot these tapes for you, and edit them, but that takes time and money; you will be much better off in your career if you teach yourself how to do self-tape and edit on your own.

Comedy

Comedy is hard. Is it any wonder most independent films stick to horror, drama, crime stories or romance? Comedy is great when it hits, and terribly bad when it falls flat. And it's a fine line between.

Jack Lemmon used to say, "The minute an audience thinks you're trying to be funny, you're dead." He recommended that an actor should play even comedic roles straight; let the audience find the humor. Noel Coward said the same thing: "You can't get a laugh if you're asking for a laugh."

And timing. Did I mention timing? Like the old Rowan Atkinson joke, "Ask me what's the secret of great comedy?" "What's the --" "Timing!"

We spend ¾ of our lives trying to make people laugh. If you have a funny line, try to get the other actor to laugh. This advice is from Uta Hagen.

If you get involved in a sitcom, whether you are writing, acting, or directing, remember that the golden rule – and the great expectation – is that the show have as a minimum one laugh a minute. Minimum. Which is why many sitcoms have teams of writers cranking out the jokes. This is also why, as an actor, you have to consistently hit it. It's why standup comedians can fit so well into a sitcom acting spot; they already know what it means to live and breathe comedy on stage, hitting it regularly, delivering the right timing.

My personal theory is simple: comedy is pain. Whether physical pain, as in a slapstick routine or any of the *Jackass* movies, or emotional pain brought out by awkward situations. We humans laugh at the misfortunes of others. Just try to find an example of something funny, without some pain to someone! I can't claim to be a comedy writer, but when I do – I focus on that pain.

I started a comedy sketch group recently, but it has not risen to any great success yet. Years ago, I had Fox Television interested in developing a new tv concept for which I put together a team of ten writers and we had a great ol' time creating the show. That concept died on the vine, due largely to the fact I was going through a divorce. I would love to revive the idea – in the years since, still nothing has been done like it, and the idea is just as ripe as ever. But the concept includes comedy sketches, which need to be fresh and timely, especially those that refer in any way to current events. The sketches we wrote long ago are no longer interesting or funny. So, in 2019, I started a new group of writers and performers, with the intent to revive that tv concept. Here's the problem. Twenty years ago, I found writers and performers dedicated to the hard work required to make something new. Now, I've found many people who say they are excited to be included, but they all want to ride piggy-back on my success and none are showing any willingness to actually work! Is this a sign of the times? Or perhaps a sign that I'm trying to do this in the wrong geographical market (Tampa), where the last time I was in Chicago?

Many comedy shows are ensembles, probably because comedy is so fast-paced and really benefits from mixing up the character interactions arising from different viewpoints. But it's not always easy to get along in a group.

Working Together

The success of any project hinges largely on the ability of its people to get along. True for marriages, where there are only two people, and exponentially true for productions with more people. When I first got into filming, I joined a couple groups and … the groups were so horribly dysfunctional that nothing ever got done; one group filmed three whole days (in my house!), and had less than five minutes of footage to show for it – crappy footage, at that. My first short film which got accepted into film festivals was done by me – me alone, as writer, actor, director, cinematographer, editor, special effects artist … you get the point. I made it on my schedule, the way I wanted to make it, and without any problems. Maybe this is the way we should all make films? Although, it seems rather anti-social. I seriously wondered whether I was the kind of asshat that couldn't work with people.

Thankfully, I've since discovered that I can, indeed, work very well with people. I've learned some lessons, along the way:

- No actor is irreplaceable. Not me, not you. Put your giant ego aside.

- Don't criticize other actors. Learn. When you watch others perform, ask yourself, what is it that works? Or that doesn't work? And learn from it. (This is more advice from Uta Hagen.)

- Don't criticize other crew members, creatives, productions. Don't criticize even major movies – you never know when your comment might turn people off, especially as you rise in your career and you begin to run into the people involved in making the movies. Focus you comments and energy on what you think is good in everything.

- Work out all physical confrontation so that it is believable and doesn't hurt anyone. Play nice, play carefully. When I studied Tae Kwon Do, we upper-belt students were most comfortable sparring with other advanced belts, even black belts; the most dangerous to spar with were, by far, the beginning students, simply because they had not yet learned control. In film, and on stage, working with newbies is dangerous, because they likewise have not yet learned how to balance their zeal with the ever-present need for safety.

- Safety is even more important since the risk of COVID19.

- Be there for your cast and crew. Help people be successful. Be a "mensch" in all you do, and you will find good people who, together, can make wonderful things happen.

Mistakes

Mistakes are literally "miss takes" that you can learn from. Go with it, use the mistake. Never break character or stop the action, until the Director has called "Cut"

Even bad takes can have usable portions, and who knows? Maybe the mistake is really a happy accident that results in a new discovery.

But never skimp on safety. Don't hesitate to stop the action if there is a safety concern. A mistake that puts people at risk is not the kind of mistake made worthwhile by being able to learn a lesson.

If you haven't failed, you haven't tried!

Language

Uta Hagen taught that even Shakespeare can be natural, normal, if you just get used to it. Have you seen the Starz show *Spartacus*? (If not, I highly recommend binging it on Netflix!) The show *Spartacus* takes place in Roman times, with much of the story lines revolving around slave gladiators and the fancy elite slave owners. The show is in English, mostly, and it is a modern form of English that is easily understood by today's viewers … and yet, there is a certain style to the dialogue that helps sets the show in historical context. Choice of words, patterns of speech, sentence construction – I recommend watching with subtitles turned on, so that you can truly admire the beautiful writing of each episode. The dialogue is unique, but after a moment it seems perfectly normal and right within the context of the show. None of the actors appear to have any difficulty (even if they may have had when first rehearsing).

Learn to enunciate! And learn to mumble, too; mumbling in a way that is still understandable is an art form, in itself. Ultimately, no one cares if you are "spot on" with your character if what you are saying cannot be understood.

Practice with diction exercises (for example, how Greek orator Demosthenes cured his speech impediment by learning to talk with pebbles in his mouth). Listen to accents; speak with people and try to copy them (without making fun of them). Read your fiction books, not just scripts, out loud. Understand and play with sentence structure and stressed inflection points.

When you get to a higher point in your career, there will be opportunities for you to take on certain roles that require particular accents. Fortunately, there are dialogue coaches to help you learn and practice. Until such time (and budget), tape record yourself and listen critically, or have friends listen to you.

Improv

Improv is the general term for making it up on set, or on stage. It is potentially fun and creative, provided the actors are clever enough and follow a few simple rules. Acting like this is probably how we all began. It's the child inside of us getting out to play. None of us (I suppose) were reading from scripts when we play acted with our childhood friends and siblings.

I got involved with a form of improv called Commedia Dell'arte, which has been around since long before tv and film. Traveling minstrels would present these shows in towns across Europe. Per Wikipedia, Commedia Dell'arte began in Italy in the 1500's, and was popular all the way through the 1800's. What makes the art form fun for actors and audiences, and easy to follow, is that there are well-known set characters (for example, the love-blind lover, the devious servant, the foolish old man) that always stay true to character. The devious servant never relents, the clueless lover never sees his mate's faults. Storylines are improved (with, of course, a lot of repetition from show to show), provided that each actor stay truly within the bounds of their character.

If you're a fan of John Cusack and live in the Chicago area, you may be aware that he has for years been active with a group of his friends doing Commedia Dell'arte improv. I believe he does it purely for fun, but it is also excellent training.

In fact, there are a number of fine actors who use Commedia Dell'arte acting to rehearse, or to adapt other plays. Tim Robbins formed "The Actors' Gang" in 1981, which has since involved such stars as Cusack, Robbins, Sabra Williams, Jack Black, and Jon Favreau. The success of improv depends largely upon the cohesion of the actors involved; they must totally trust each other, listening closely, playing off the slightest clues. Training this way creates an incredibly strong ensemble. Sabra Williams is quoted in 2014 as saying her theatre company was still rehearsing, even after a year of performing *A Midsomer Night's Dream*, because they were constantly discovering, constantly trying new things, constantly changing the action of the show each night.

Improv must, I think, always follow a couple rules, no matter what style. Even without the set character types of the classic Commedia Dell'arte. Whatever you do, wherever you are, and whomever you're with, these rules should be followed. First, all actors must be in a safe environment at all times; there is no way you can build the necessary trust within an ensemble if anyone is afraid for either their physical safety or for their mental and emotional well-being. You must treat each other well, be aware of the needs of each other, and work toward allowing each other to succeed. This is why acting groups, and in particular improv acting groups, tend to be tightly knit and hard to break into. Trust is earned slowly.

The second important rule in improv is that one is not allowed to refute. When an actor brings something into the scene, you must run with it. An actor can't say to another "No, you can't act it that way", although of course you can (and often should) turn it into something else. If I am playing a mailman who delivers only candy hearts and another character says I instead gave them a poisonous snake, about the only thing I then *cannot* do is say, "No, I didn't." My character is now a mailman who delivers candy hearts and poisonous snakes, because that has been established.

Improv on film sets

Improv can be fun, and a great tool to help you learn to be comfortable acting, but I'm going to get up on my personal soapbox and argue that it is one of the worst things ever to happen to film production.

If you are a fan of improvising, make sure you're not doing so just as a crutch for failing (or refusing) to learn your lines. I'm sorry to say, but I find this to be the case time and time again. Short films, feature films, SAG and non-union, paid and non-paid. So many actors arrive on set unprepared – meaning they have not studied and memorized their lines, let alone fully analyzed their scenes. They trust that the director will film short enough takes for them to "wing it."

I am primarily a writer at heart. I can tell you from first-hand experience how writers struggle, often (very often!) rewriting and rewriting a script through several drafts. Many writers, myself included, read their dialogue out loud as they write, and then put the draft scripts through table reads with actors, to fine-tune and perfect the dialogue. Writers agonize over each word choice, comma, stopping point, inflection, stress. Then along comes an actor who doesn't take the time to study the character, or break apart the dialogue to discover how that character lives in the script, or even read the whole script, but suddenly announces, "This doesn't feel right. I wouldn't say it this way." You think you know better than the writer? You must realize the writer chose that dialogue because it fits in with plot and/or character points of the script, for the character – not for you, as an actor.

The dialogue belongs to the character, not you. If you improv, have you done the homework to understand and bring to life that character, or are you merely saying "This is what sounds right to me?" The character is not you, and would not speak exactly like you; sorry, but you are not in the film; the character is. It's your job as the actor to bring that character to life. It is not your job to turn that character into the person you are.

I think improv is the bane of all directors. In the long run, it is an actor's bane, too: improv that brings out the actor is the same (or at least very similar) from role to role, leading to stagnation as an actor, and likely cast typing. If you approach your characters with the intent to bring yourself into the role, then your characters will all be essentially the same person (you).

On the other hand, an actor who strives to bring out the character as written will always be different from role to role. That actor uses his/herself as a physical and vocal instrument, but strives to be a different person: the person the writer wrote about!

Consider, too, how rude you are being to other actors. They learned their lines, which they expected to be able to play off of your lines and cues. They need you to deliver your character, as written. Even if you are able to mystically channel Robin William's intellect and improv wonderful lines, in doing so you are throwing off your co-actors, most likely trying to make yourself look good at their expense. That is not the way to build trust. Not the way to build an ensemble. Not the way to get hired back on the next production.

(Obviously, improv has its place and time. If you are part of a cast that improvs, and everyone knows that you are all improving, well then … have at it. As I say above, it can be great fun and an excellent way to train and perform.)

Photographer

Headshots

In addition to acting, filmmaking, and entertainment law, I have also been a headshot photographer for many years. In the 1980's I shot with black-and-white film, and had to make multiple trips to the darkroom facilities to develop, print contact sheets, adjust the print within limited abilities, and finally print dozens or hundreds of 8x10's for my actor clients. Now, the standards have changed drastically. Now, color is the norm, and almost everything is shot digitally, which allows for immediate review and editing of the results. I no longer bother with darkrooms at all! Now, I give my clients a number of digital shots, and leave it to them to get prints made (if they ever need hard prints).

So, what is a "headshot"? Where there use to be only a few photographers doing headshots of actors, there now seems to be someone every 10 feet who thinks they can do it. Actors frequently set up a camera and take their own headshot, or ask a friend to shoot it. But let me point out that a headshot is a tool that can (and should) get you work. It is not an "identity picture" like you find on a driver's license or passport. It is not a pretty modeling picture. It is not your school yearbook photo, nor any other sort of candid shot. I'm going to plug my own photography site here – not really because I want you to hire me, but because my site contains a more detailed explanation of what a headshot is, and there are many examples you can see for yourself. My portfolio is at www.nauticproductions.com.

Your headshot must be an accurate and complete image of the current you. Update annually, or following any major change in your image. Kids should update every 6 months, because they change so fast. Make sure your headshot looks like the "you" you are, deep down in your essence, when you walk into the room for an audition. Don't ever provide a headshot that no longer looks like you, because casting directors hate to be surprised. If they call you in for an audition, they are expecting to see the person shown in the headshot.

A word on scars, tattoos, birthmarks, moles, and anything else that is part of your image: it must be shown in the headshot. Again, don't ever surprise a casting director! Yes, a mark can be covered with makeup, but it is up to the casting director to determine whether or not that is a viable approach in any given production. I advise my photography clients to go the other way: showcase whatever makes you unique. For example, a young male actor with a large birthmark on his cheek showed me his prior headshot, which was shot from the "good" side and barely showed any of the birthmark; I shot to show both sides, and very clearly the birthmark, because that is a prominent part of his image. It also helped, in his case, that he wanted to go for villain roles, and he felt the birthmark would help him with that. (BTW, his name is Donovan Davis and you can see on my site what a good looking guy he is, birthmark and all!)

Like many things in life, you get what you pay for. Get the best headshots you can – from a professional photographer that specializes in headshots, even though that likely costs a bit. Don't believe just any photographer can take your headshot. Any of them can shoot a picture of your head. But … they need to understand what a headshot really is, and how it is used in the industry, or your headshot will not be all it can be. A headshot is really a tool, the key to open doors with Casting Directors, Producers and Directors. It must be what such people want and need to see. And different industry people need to see different things. There is a different style accepted in Los Angeles versus New York City, and such styles change with the years. Commercial (film and television) is different than Theatrical. Don't waste your time by going to a photographer who doesn't know these things.

One of the best headshot photographers is New York City-based Peter Hurley. Look him up. Hire him if you can afford him and are incredibly lucky to find him available; he charges thousands of dollars and is typically booked for months. Read the book he wrote, titled simply "The Headshot", check out his many YouTube video appearances, and examine his work on his site www.peterhurley.com.

One of Peter Hurley's tips, never look like a deer in the headlights. You want your headshot to make you seem confident and approachable. It helps if you "squinch" your eyes a bit, not enough to make you look sleepy, but just enough to make it look like you have an important secret to tell.

Casting Agents have little to no imagination – and you can't blame them, really, since time is money, they are afraid of risk, and so many actors are flakes. It helps them select you if you look like the role they are casting. For this reason, many actors get different headshots, to show different character types they can perform. A strong villainous look is probably not the best to submit for the leading man in a romance, and vice versa. Know your acting "types" and try to capture fitting looks in your headshots – another reason it is important to go to a photographer that knows the importance of acting types. Hopefully, you should be able to present a headshot that fits each type of role you want.

Behind the Scenes (BTS)

Productions of all sizes should have a stills photographer on set before, during and after shooting. More and more, productions also hire videographers to shoot behind the scenes, for added DVD "making of" videos. BTS is fun, especially if the production allows posting on social media (many do not!). But BTS is not just for fun; it is also invaluable for marketing. The images you use later for posters and other marketing are best shot the day of filming, and yet you and your crew are far too busy to think of such. Get a good photographer, and tell them you want both fun candids and artsy photos that show characters, sets and/or props.

An example of this comes from the first short I did. The storyline included large jars of blood. Only once I saw the jars of blood under the set lighting did I realize how perfect that image was for the movie's poster, and yet I would have hated trying to make up all that blood again on another day jut for the picture!

Doing BTS is an easy way to get onto a set and meet people. It's not much of a job, and rarely pays much, at least at the newbie levels. You'll have to be very careful what and when you shoot, to be sure no noise or flash interferes with filming. But you'll generally find that actors are more than willing to help you get good photos, and they often have plenty of down time between wardrobe / makeup and the start of shooting.

Be sure to understand your role. I too often see BTS photographers setting up to get the same shots that the primary camera crew is recording, perhaps because they hope the director will choose to use some of their own footage in the final film. Don't do this! Your job is the "making of" not the actual scripted story. The crew will love seeing you get shots of them at work, but they will absolutely hate you for trying to share the space to film the story they are filming.

If you have time and opportunity, suggest to the actors that they practice getting into character by shooting a short video with you off where you don't interfere with the primary filming. I've never had them refuse, and I've had Directors praise me for helping actors get into character. By the way, don't shoot the actual dialogue the actors will be saying – that could come across as if you're trying to prove something, and you could face copyright issues. Also, keep in mind that the characters are not yours, and any video you create is to be used only in connection with your BTS duties, absent specific authorization otherwise.

Cinematographer

The DP is usually the cinematographer, i.e. the person actually running the camera. On smaller productions, there's probably just one or two people on the camera crew. If it's you, you got some work to do.

Much of the work is preparatory. Figure out ahead of time what shots you want, and what equipment you will need (camera and lighting) to get the shots. Check the location the day before, or earlier, because you may need to buy or borrow equipment. For example, you need to examine the windows to know what kind of natural light you may wish to use, or block as the case may be. If you are shooting "day for night" (making it look like night) you may need large blankets or heavy-gauge trash bags to tape over windows, doorframes, and other light sources.

Every Director has a different approach to filming. Generally, however, you let the Director figure out the blocking in rehearsal with the actors, and once they have the action down then it is your turn to figure out how to shoot it. Don't be shy about speaking up, if they've come up with blocking that you simply can't shoot; but otherwise, figure out how to get the Director's vision. Most Directors are open to including cool shots. Discuss ahead of time. Don't be that person who constantly derails the filming schedule by monkeying forever with equipment and camera angles.

Costumes

So many of my theatre friends in high school and college wanted to "break in" and "make it big" in the entertainment world. So many that for years I diligently studied the credits at the end of every movie I saw, anxious to see my friends succeed. But I never recognized any names. Mark Wahlberg was around my campus, but I barely knew him – so he doesn't count. Likewise visiting actors (Kevin Kline, Kenneth Branagh, Bill Irwin, and Chip Zien, for example) don't count, either. Of my friends … Dino and Brian had strong starts, then faded away. Doug likewise – a couple movies, then POOF! Only one of my old friends that I know of has actually gone on to a true measure of Hollywood success. She did it as a Costume Designer.

In their own words – Costume Designer Jennifer L. Soulages
Jennifer L. Soulages has done costume design for many Hollywood films, including *Atlas Shrugged, Veronica Mars* and *Saw*. She's worked with Rhea Perlman, Dane Cook, Pink, Danny Glover, Michael Madsen, Lou Gossett, Jr., Lucy Lawless, John Larroquette, Cary Elwes, Kathy Griffin, and Robert Englund, just to drop some names! Well done, Jennifer!

I asked Jennifer for some help with this section, and she was kind enough to send the following:

"Are you sure you don't want to make a living doing something else?"

asked my mother as I complained about the challenges of the current costume project I was working on. She was used to my rants, usually about working the long hours, receiving small paychecks, and worrying about my next job.

My mom had a right to worry. "What kind of a person loves finding clothes to fit an odd-size actor at the last minute, driving in Los Angeles traffic and standing in a frozen bog covered in fake blood at 2:00am?" she'd ask me. "And with no job security? We sent you to college for that?"

She wasn't wrong. I often wondered myself…. I guess I am someone who is wired differently, enjoying the work involved, lost in the creating and collaborating with other artists to tell a story, often forgetting about myself and my real life in the process. But to be honest, even with all my valid complaints, doing "something else" was never an option. (Sorry Mom!)

What the average person doesn't know is that there is a lot of work involved.

As a Costume Designer my job is to let the character shine through the clothes. By the time I meet the actor at his or her fitting, I have carefully considered the clues from the script: the character's socio-economic status, his/her job, the season and location of the story, and what happens to that character in the story.

It all starts with the script, which I read once through, getting into the story and seeing it as a movie in my head. I also write down my first impressions as I read. I then take my notes and put together visual mood boards that reflect my thoughts in a visual way. Making the boards is one of my favorite parts of the design process. I usually cut out tear sheets and other visual references to glue down in separate collages for each character. These boards help drive the discussions with the director and the other creatives about the overall look of the project and the characters within it.

I then read the script again and break it down. This process takes time, entering the script day and night intervals into my breakdown program denoting where the characters change clothes. Actions and events, such as taking a shower, a formal dinner, a Halloween party, a love scene, or getting shot are details that are also added. The same breakdown applies to stunts and background players.

The breakdown then becomes the roadmap for the budget, and I have to get creative in how I spend the money. For example, stunts usually denote multiple outfits, shower scenes call for nude wear (yes, there is such a thing!) and the department is always running out of hangers. Most of the money is usually spent for those items that get placed in front of the camera.

Once the paperwork is in place (although it will continually change through script revisions, budget requests and production meetings), my team and I can go shopping, pull from the costume house, or build costumes. I always ask myself, "how am I going to achieve the look I want for these costumes within the confines of the script and budget, and make everyone happy in the end? Especially myself?"

Luckily, I don't have to go it alone. I usually collaborate with talented costume assistants, costume supervisors, cutter-fitters, ager/dyers and set costumers to create the individual looks for the actors, getting them all to camera through hard work and resourcefulness.

And suddenly, ready or not, we arrive at the day of the actor's fitting! Since I'm usually the first person to meet the actor after they get cast, many actors are grateful for my input, because the clothes help them to get a direction about the script and character they're playing.

It's the ultimate game of "dress-up", in which the actor tries the selected outfits on and the character emerges: a different posture, a swagger in the walk, or a badass attitude that comes from within. And very subtly, that actor transforms before the mirror and can use those clothes (now his/her costume) as a clue to the character's inner life.

Of course, the fun part includes lots of discussion about fit, color, and whether we both like the outfit, or maybe those shoes look better, or yes, this jacket is more appropriate or "more the character". There are a lot of pins, tags, clothes, and accessories strewn all over by the time we're done, but the effort is always worth it.

Once the character's outfits are approved by the director and producers, they are dismantled and processed. Some pieces go to the seamstress to be altered, a bigger belt needs to be bought, a smaller dress needs to be ordered, or all the clothes need to be washed down and aged to look lived in. More fun still, the custom made pieces need to be altered and tweaked to fit perfectly. Sometimes, all this has to happen before shooting the next day at 6:00 am. Or I'm called to fit the actor on set at 6:00 am and alter the clothes before he's due on set that morning by noon!

Once finished, the pieces get put back together as outfits (they'd better be, or my set costumers will be calling me with tons of questions!) and loaded onto the costume truck, ready for the set.

Being on set, watching all of the actors wearing their costumes together with hair and make-up, is the final head rush for me. It's unfortunately short lived, since there is usually more work to be done, as new actors are cast, and more fittings are needed to get ready for future shooting days in the crammed production schedule.

And so the process goes for the Costume Department of film and television. Script. Run-around-gathering-clothes-and-accessories-with-hair-on-fire. Fittings. Shoot. Repeat.

After all these successful years in the Industry, I've come to realize that the complaints to my Mom barely scratched the surface of all the work that is involved in my job as a Costume Designer. Some days, usually after a challenging problem in production comes up, I still sometimes ask myself, "Are you sure you don't want to make a living doing something else?"

My answer has always been the same: Yes, I'm absolutely sure!

~ Jennifer L. Soulages

Respect the costume

Once you are in costume, have some respect for the time and cost that went into making it and getting it ready for you.

Don't eat or drink anything after you get into costume, except water. If you must, then take great care not to spill anything on it. Great care! One little slip by you can set the filming back by hours or days.

Prop Food

Those of us with community theatre stage experience learned early: don't ever eat or drink the prop food! It's "whiskey" in your play, and you've done a good job pretending that the iced tea really is whiskey, right? Until that one performance where your castmates play a joke on you. Then you take a big gulp of real fire water and choke and sputter your way through your show. So funny! And so common.

But there are other reasons not to eat or drink. It might not be safe, for one. It might not even be real food. The yummy-looking grapes could be plastic. Or real food could have been sprayed with polyurethane or something else to make it look good longer.

In film, continuity in another concern. People notice when an actor picks up a half-full glass, and then his next sip is from a full glass. Or the quantity on a plate changes. Fake your eating. (Actors can act, right?) Eating the food can create real problems, especially if it turns out there is no more food to film and you still need another take.

Only in an extreme close up might you need to truly eat, drink, chew or swallow. And then continuity is not important, because the plate is not seen. Such a close up is usually shot last.

PART V: HOW TO MAKE A FILM

Films get made in pre-production. This bears repeating: films get made in pre-production. Planning is vital. The shortest short film should still be thought out and planned meticulously. You can just fire up your camera and film something, but whatever it is you hope to accomplish will benefit from thinking it out. Even simple B-Roll shots need to consider location, lighting, framing, frame speed, and sound; plus additional factors if you add actors. These details are what makes the final footage usable or not.

Even more so for larger budget productions, where so much in terms of expenses depends on everything fitting well together. In fact, the bigger the production the more important planning is, and the more likely the production has budgeted pre-production time.

"Prebiz" is the slang term I've heard. Prebiz increases the likelihood that the production shoot day goes smoothly, which is greatly appreciated by cast and crew alike, as well as by the production's financial backers.

Process

Films are made in 3 phases: pre-production / production / post-production.

Pre-production – Come up with an idea. Write a script. Plan a million details. Meet actors and crew people, and get them excited to join you, with or without pay. This is usually the longest phase, and can quite often span over years, even decades. Just writing a script can take years. Reaching out to get people interested, and to find funding, can again take years. Once the ball gets rolling, however, it may suddenly take off fast. And getting the right big names attached can make an instant difference. For example, I was writing a script with Shirley MacLaine in mind; if I shopped it around with someone (just "anyone") in that role, it might eventually get attention, but if I first got Ms. MacLaine interested … Touchdown!

Production -- Get your people together to film (easier said than done). Shoot your footage. Feed and thank your people. Repeat many, many times. This is the fun, exciting, terrifying phase. One director I worked for told me, "Movies are made when written, and when edited. What we do here on set doesn't matter." Well, I don't think I'd go that far, but his point was I should relax and have fun with the filming.

Post-production – Select the best takes that tell the story and put them together (edit) in a way that makes sense, looks good (color grading), sounds good (ADR), and is fun to watch. Don't make the mistake of spending all you have just to film because the editing process is expensive. Good editors are hard to find.

Three phases … and you have a movie! Now, what?

Actually, there are really four phases to making a movie, the fourth being <u>distribution</u>. Having a movie is pointless if no one gets to see it. You can start by distributing the movie yourself, which is done in a few ways. Show your film in film festivals; it's easy to submit them on www.filmfreeways.com and if your film gets selected and wins awards, it will start to get buzz. You can also put your film online on YouTube, Vimeo, Hulu, Amazon Prime, and the like, again with the idea that you hope it will get buzz. And you can rent theater space yourself, to hold local screenings – again, to get buzz.

You want buzz. People talking about your work. That is what will, eventually, get the attention of distributors, and you can then dream about selling your film – and maybe even actually do it. Success at some of the larger film festivals can actually lead distributors straight to you.

Sample schedule for a short film
Let's say you want to make a film. Here, briefly, is how that might go. (We'll talk details in the following sections.)

Pre-production:

- Concept. Someone (you, or the writer most likely) has an idea. And you want to film it
- Script – writing, rewriting, and more rewriting to tell a compelling story
- Line the script (break it down into elements)
- Start the union process with SAG-AFTRA, if you want to be able to hire union actors
- Develop the production: get people working at top levels (designers, producers, director, DP) to flesh out how to tell the story
- Enter into deal memos with key people
- Scout locations; get location releases
- Work with director, DP and designers on storyboards & shot lists
- Cast actors; sign deal memos
- Hire payroll company
- Rehearse actors
- Practice blocking & choreography
- Prepare location / sets / props / wardrobe
- Obtain all needed filming equipment
- Obtain permits (which might include street closures, off-duty police and/or fire marshal, and porta-potties)
- Arrange for craft services (food)

Then Production:

- Shoot the film!
- Transfer audio & visual files at the end of every day, and review for quality
- Some people start editing even before principal shooting is completed

Then Post-production:

- Collect all audio and visual files, and deliver to editor
- Get all BTS from photographer
- Prepare rough cut
- Review rough cut; revise
- "Picture Lock" when done selecting and editing takes
- Clean up sound – get actors back for any necessary ADR
- Color grade the film
- Add soundtrack / score
- Create credits
- Premiere for friends, cast, crew
- Show to test audiences; revise edit as desired after feedback
- Present to distributors (if you have contacts)
- Submit to film festivals
- Use social media and press contacts to build buzz
- Take to film markets
- Sell

In a nutshell, that is the process of getting a film done and out for viewing.

As you can already see, it's not a simple process. I recommend using some sort of "Project Management Software" to keep everything organized. Things like Celtx.com (which is for filmmakers) or generic project programs like Monday.com.

Now, let's look at the process in more detail.

Pre-Production

Prebiz is vitally important. It's such a broad category. A film may be in "pre-production" for years, even decades.

Pre-production means everything before filming begins. Typically, beginning with a script. Sometimes, though, a producer begins with an idea and hires the writer. Then that script will get re-written over and over.

Besides polishing and/or re-writing the script, during pre-production the producer puts together the "above the line" creative team: those people who influence the creative decisions prior to the start of principal photography. This usually means the producer(s), writer, director, designers, and lead actors.

Script vs Shooting Script

The purpose of a script is to tell the story; it should not include camera directions and other filming notes. It is helpful, then, before filming to convert the script to a "Shooting Script" which does include such details. Think of the shooting script more as a tool than a story-telling device.

A shooting script will have numbered scenes, and the numbers are locked down so that they are not changed in future revisions of the script. This allows everyone to keep focused on the same scene.

The amount of detail in a shooting script depends greatly upon who is doing the shooting script. For example, the director and/or DP will add specific shot ideas. Where a script might simply say "Montage", a shooting script may break each shot of a montage down. Specific equipment may be noted. Scene transitions may be added. Anything that can help get the film done.

Shot list

Many newbie directors get on set and then think of the shots they need. It's good to be open to inspiration on set! But starting your day without a shot list can be horribly frustrating to the people you work with, and the process of shooting will be the slowest possible.

Very commonly, a scene is filmed wide first, then from a mid-range, and then close up. But there is so much more one can do to add interest to the scene. The thought given in planning the shots will show in the creativity of the end results.

For each scene, consider how to best shoot it. List the shots you need. The biggest advantage of doing this is the saving of time and energy, because you will be able to film all of the shots you need with a particular lens and lighting set up. Those who don't use shot lists are constantly needing to set everything back up the way it was earlier!

Story-boarding

Story-boarding is the process of drawing out (using freehand sketches, computer graphics, and or photographs) how you imagine a scene should look. It is most helpful in communicating one's vision to others. It also helps you fine-tune your vision.

You don't have to be a wonderful artist. There are people who will do the art for you, and there are computer programs to help you, and actually you don't need to be worried at all about the quality. Stick figures and scribbles work. All you need is the ability to convey what's in your head.

Some storyboards are art worthy, and can be sold or published themselves. That's up to you. I tend to see storyboards only as a tool that helps get the production done, but that's probably because I can't do much more than doodle.

Story Telling
If you want to be a filmmaker, you must be a good storyteller. Telling a story is the essence of filmmaking, and no one at all wants to see you put images and dialogue together without a story. Be a good storyteller!

Script Consultant Jill Chamberlain says that 99% of screenwriters fail to tell a story. She says they just write situations.

As a "Script Doctor" I've been hired to fix scripts, to rewrite scenes and hopefully improve them. Other writers frequently ask me to review their work, and when they do, I always warn them that I will give brutal feedback; constructive criticism of course, but it really doesn't help to tell someone what you *like* nearly as much as it helps to tell them what you *don't like*. Because I use a red pencil, I tell them I "bleed" on the page, and sometimes the whole page looks like I literally slaughtered it! I'll markup formatting and other technical errors. However, when I review a script, the primary thing I look for are the story elements. It is surprisingly sad how many times one sees a script that fails to tell a good story, or falls off the track midway, or spends valuable time on tangents and little nuggets the writer is so proud of but which really don't help the story.

If you have teenagers handy, try telling them your story. Even if your project isn't aimed at that age group, you can judge how exciting your story is, and how clearly you are expressing it, by how long you hold the teenagers' attention.

Preparation: Breaking Down a Scene
Before you begin filming, it is crucial to make sure you're happy with the script. Can you make a bad movie from a good script? Yes, unfortunately, that is easy to do. But can you make a good movie from a bad script? Uh … probably not. Address plot holes, wordy dialogue, empty (motive-less) characters, needless filler, on-the-nose dialogue, and un-filmable action *before* you start to film. I know most of you will ignore this paragraph, especially if you wrote your own script and think it's all that. But believe me, even the best scripts can be fine-tuned, and the more you do ahead of filming, the happier you and your cast/crew will be, and the better the results.

Your script is final? Cool. Oops, no it's not. No script is ever final, at least not until after the film is released and someone goes back later to match the script to the final edited film. For fun, use Google to look up script-to-scene comparisons. Actors may change lines on the fly, directors may change lines and/or action, and editors rearrange bits as they see fit, sometimes resulting in a film that is vastly different (one hopes improved) from the original script. It's rare to find a finished film scene that precisely follows the script.

When you are happy that your script is ready to film, the next step is to "break down the script" or "do a breakdown." There are several YouTube videos that explain the process. Basically, you want to go through each scene and mark certain items in different colors (I use colored pencils, some people prefer highlighter markers, and others use software). Once you get used to the color code, you can very quickly scan a scene to see what is needed. Different people and groups use different colors, and you are free to use any system you want, but what follows is pretty typical:

- RED – underline the named characters when they first appear in each scene, whether that's in the action block or dialogue column.

- YELLOW – underline extras

- GREEN – underline background extras – What's the difference, you ask? Extras are un-named characters, for example when a script says "They are brought to their table by the hostess, and a busboy approaches to fill their water glasses, before the waiter brings them menus." These people are extras (color them YELLOW), as they have a specific function to fulfill. The script can also call for "diners at other tables", or maybe the script is silent on the point but you feel it would be good to show people at other tables. Such other people are background extras (color them GREEN).

- ORANGE – underline stunts. Basically, everything other than standing, sitting or walking is a stunt. A double-take, a spit-take, arching one's eyebrows – when these are called for in a script, they are stunts. Underline the big obvious stunts, too, like running, tripping the bad guy, crashing the car, throwing a hand grenade, etc.

- BLUE – underline FX

- PINK – underline vehicles and animals (Don't ask me why both are pink, they just are. If your script has a lot of both, then you may want to change one or both colors to differentiate.)

- BROWN – underline sounds

- PURPLE – underline props

- BLACK – make a circle around wardrobe items

- BLACK – make a rectangular box around special equipment (for example, a crane)

- BLACK – underline production notes (for example, if the script calls for "intercutting" between two scenes)

You may have guessed already that breaking down a script serves multiple functions. First, it helps you as the filmmaker get organized, and perhaps identify problems that need to be fixed. Second, it helps you prepare for filming each scene, as it simplifies the task of identifying which actors are in a scene, what props are needed, and so on, and minimizes the risk that you realize on set that you've forgotten something crucial.

Subtext

Perhaps the single most important thing to consider when looking at your script is the *subtext*. Not what the characters are doing (action) or saying (dialogue), but instead what is really happening. In other words, what's going on "between the lines." In our everyday lives, people rarely ever talk about what is really on their minds. A character may, for example, scream at another for leaving dirty dishes in the sink, but the problem isn't really the dishes, it's that seeing the dishes there means the person doesn't love and respect them. If your scene does not have subtext, then re-write it! It's boring to yell about dirty dishes, but high drama to yell about not being loved. Find the subtext, discuss the subtext with your actors, and film for the subtext. (By the way, actors are trained to look for the subtext, to find their motivation in a scene, but not all of them are good at it.)

Storytelling in film, tv and theatre is visual and audial. We see and hear not only the dialogue and obvious sound effects, but also the *subtext* in a scene. Body language, if you want to think of it that way. But so much more: the lighting, movement of actors (blocking), movement of the camera, camera angles, sound, and the editing (sequencing) of shots – everything works together to tell your story.

Or not. Newbie filmmakers tend to place a camera and tell the actors to start. That director says "Cut" when they finish the scripted lines, the editor links the takes together, they throw some music on top, and call it a film. They might consider it fancy enough if they start with a wide shot to establish the set, then a couple medium shots, then a couple close-ups. Ooooo, wow. If this is all done scene by scene, because "that's how you make a movie" … the end result is boring, lacking energy, because the filmmaker caught the written lines and failed to film for the *subtext*.

Finding the subtext is what actors are trained to look for, and all filmmakers must do the same. Writers, too (honestly, if a script is written without the writer focusing on subtext … well, that's a script probably not worth filming). Ask yourself, "That's what the character says, but what do they mean?" In our everyday conversations, people rarely speak directly about what they mean internally. A character doing so is said to be too much "on the nose" – i.e. too obvious. We speak, often without even meaning to do so, in veiled references and nuances, using stresses, inflections, metaphors and allegories which only hint at our deepest desires.

Tear every scene apart until you fully understand the subtext. Then film to express that subtext. You do this through all of your choices: casting, lighting, costumes, locations … and in every scene, you bring out the subtext by your blocking, shot selection, and editing cuts.

Types of shots

Your shots should work to tell your story. Each and every shot, ideally. Not the full plot, of course, but the story of what the character is doing, facing, thinking, and feeling at that point. A character may say, "I'm lonely" and you could film that and move on. Point made, right? Yeah, but … you need to show it. Film it in a way that also, visually, tells us she's lonely. A wide shot showing physical separation; a zoom from a crowd to isolate the actor in a claustrophobic close-up; other characters turning away from her; place her in shadow, while happy people are in sunshine.

Understand the types of shots, and what emotion you can get from their use:

- Close Up (CU) – a shot where the actor's face fills the frame. It's meant to show facial expressions, emotions. Use this when that character's emotion is the most important thing.

- Extreme Close Up (ECU) – a tighter shot, showing just part of the actor's face. For example, a shot showing the eyes from just above the mouth to the ridge of the eyebrows. This can be used to show emotion, or to direct the audience's attention to an element of your scene.

- Wide Shot (WS) or Long Shot (LS) – shows the actor's entire body and some of the set. Useful for showing bodies in motion, and characters interacting.

- Extreme Wide Shot (EWS) or Extreme Long Shot (ELS) – where the subject is a small part of the frame, and the setting is important. You may want the subject to look small, in comparison. Often used for exposition at the beginning of a scene.

- Master Shot (Master) – usually Wide or Extremely Wide, the Master shows all of your characters from a perspective that shows them doing the whole scene.

- Medium Shot or Mid Shot (MS) – roughly, half of a person. Useful where body language is important, or the actor is carrying something.

- Medium Close Up (MCU) – mid chest and up.

- Single or Solo Shot (Single) – one actor

- Double Shot (Double) – two actors

- Triple Shot (Triple) -- three actors

- Point of View Shot (POV) – shooting from the eye position of one character, toward whatever that character is looking at

- Eye Level Camera Angle – "normal", where you're not evoking any particular emotion with the camera angle

- Low Angle (Low) – shooting up at the actor, making the actor look larger. This empowers the character, shows strength and dominance.

- High Angle (High) – shooting from above eye level, which makes the actor look smaller, reduced in power and importance.

- Top Angle or Bird's Eye View (Top) – from an aerial perspective, useful in showing where the actor is in the setting, as well as weakness.

- Dutch Angle (Dutch) – where the camera is tilted. Useful in showing that the character or the film's entire world is literally off balance.

- Over the Shoulder (OTS) – shooting one character as primary, with another character barely in the frame, facing away, for reference. Typically, this shows conflict between the two. It's usually a confrontation, but can also be used to show emotional bonding or separation.

- Panning Shot (Pan) – camera position remains the same, but the frame moves right or left

- Tilting Shot (Tilt) – camera position remains the same, but the frame moves up or down

- Tracking Shot (Track) – camera position moves, left or right

- Dolly Shot (Dolly) – camera position moves, front or back

- Crane Shot (Crane) – camera position moves, up or down

- Zoom Shot (Zoom) – camera position remains the same, but the shot moves in (closer) or out (farther)

- Random Motion Shot (RM) – where the camera moves around in a given area, turning up, down, right, left, whatever. Used to provide energy, chaos.

- 360 Degree Shot (360) – where the camera moves around the character, which really showcases the character in a given setting

- Single Take Shot (Single Take) – a combination of shots, where camera and actors move, without stopping and starting the camera.

Types of Cuts

Transitions between scenes should be considered. There are many ways for an editor to go from one to another, some smooth, some jarring, depending of course upon the desired effect. Yes, you can let the editor worry about this … but you'll be happier with the results if you plan for the transitions. For example, you may want to do what's called a "match cut", which is something like ending one scene by zooming into a close up of someone's hand, and then beginning the next scene by zooming out from a closeup on the same hand, but in a different location. An editor can't do that unless you have shot the right footage.

Know the cuts and transitions:

- Match Cut: as described. A neat example is when Dustin Hoffman, in the *Graduate*, emerges from a swimming pool and flops down on top of a woman in bed. But they don't have to be visual match cuts: you can also tie scenes together with audio and/or lighting similarities.

- Cutting on Action: common, and effective. Zooming in on a punch, for example, or just when a character turns. Or when a character throws something. Or goes through a door. The action begins the movement, which makes the change in camera perspective seem more natural.

- Cut Away: insert something into your footage. For example, a character hears something and you cut to show a close up of a mouse squeaking, then back to the character. In *It's a Wonderful Life*, Jimmy Stewart points up, referring to the moon – then next cut is an insert of the moon, before going back to Jimmy. This is used, also, for showing what a character is thinking. Stock footage is great for the inserts (so long as the footage can be matched in color and lighting).

- Cross Cutting: cutting back and forth between two locations, such as between two people in a phone conversation. This is very powerful when showing two characters in action, approaching some doom. Or when a character is struggling with a memory.

- Jump Cut: often used to show the passage of time, this is when an editor jumps from one point in the shot to another in the same shot. Good for montages, too. They can add a sense of urgency because it is a jarring effect.

- Dissolve: where one scene slowly fades out, while the next fades in. Useful in montages, and also for showing the passage of time. You've probably seen the hands of a clock dissolving from one time to another. Dissolves are also used for effect, for example a ghost disappearing – you simply dissolve the ghost scene to show the same scene, without the ghost.

- Smash Cuts: abrupt transitions, like someone walking into a sucker punch, or waking up from a nightmare. An intense scene into a quiet one, or vice versa, with the intent to startle (or wake up) the audience.

- Iris: like closing down a camera's aperture, circling a portion of the frame. This is a stylistic choice. It's useful to highlight exactly what you want people to dwell on.

- Wipe: a line, vertical or otherwise, on the screen literally dividing the shots and moving to close one and open the other. Sometimes matched with the action in the scene, as when the cut follows the line of a door opening. Useful to show two different scenes occurring simultaneously. (Wipes don't have to be straight lines, and can pretty much be anything.)

- Invisible Cuts: used to hide a cut, as if it were not a cut at all but instead part of the first take. Generally, this type of cut is hidden by zooming in on darkness, or out of focused movement (as in a whip pan), so that when we come out of it, the whole shot seems to be a continuation. Sneaky stuff. Fans of *1917* have fun trying to discern the hidden cuts.

- Audio Cuts: keep in mind your next scene's audio can come in before the scene changes (a "J Cut") or continue after (an "L Cut"). Used frequently when characters are talking to each other. These cuts help smooth the transition.

When planning transitions, keep in mind you can combine effects. In fact, you can combine multiple scenes, such as panning right, wiping right into the next scene, then panning right in that scene, and wiping right again. Why not?! There are no limits! Dream.

The quickest way to learn transitions is simply to watch tv and films now that you know what to look for. Jot down notes on transitions, as you watch.

"Line" your script. By this, I mean draw a line down the page of your script to show the coverage you want. For example, you may draw a line down the whole scene and mark it "wide" to show that you want to film the entire set from a wide angle perspective. But then draw shorter lines through the spots you want to film as close ups. This is different than what a script supervisor does (called "lining" the script, which sounds confusingly similar), the difference being when you line you are planning how to film, whereas the scripty is noting what was filmed. Of course, the two results may look very similar.

Location Scouting
Finding a location that fits the script's look and feel, that provides space and everything else you need to film, and that is available for your use, is hard!

Larger productions rely on "Location Scouts", people who are expert at finding and maintaining relationships with the owners of locations for just about any need. In smaller productions, the filmmaker is the one driving around, talking people into allowing the use … and it does not take long for the filmmaker to appreciate and want to hire a location scout.

The night before you film …

Holy shit, the nerves will get you. Good luck sleeping!

But if you have prepared, you should be able to get some good rest, comforted by the idea that your creativity, hard work, knowledge, people skills and connections will get you through.

Your confidence comes from being prepared. Always do a "Gear Prep" session the day before. Major productions budget a full day on site to make sure everything needed is there and working. You may not be at that level, but you must still be sure that you will have what you need on set, and that you know how to use it. If you are relying upon someone else to, say, direct … then prep with that person! Don't rely *blindly* upon anyone. Work ahead of the scheduled shoot day with everyone. Then you can sleep the night before.

Equipment Prep

Set up and test everything the day before. Do this where you can spread everything out, and collect everything together, until it is all ready to be packed to go. Ideally, do this where you have power, so that you can charge batteries right there next to the equipment. Keep it all in one place, to reduce the chance of forgetting something.

Everything you take should be labeled. Small stuff, especially, like SD cards and batteries. These things get swapped around and are easily misplaced. A paint pen (Amazon) is great for marking most surfaces, and a plain old Sharpie will usually do, too.

Food / Craft Services

General rule, you must feed your people every 6 hours. This comes from SAG-AFTRA union rules, so you may not have to comply, but even if you are non-union it's still true that your people will do better if they're fed and watered. Often on small projects, food and drink is the only payment the crew is getting.

Even small, indie and student films should prepare a menu and give particular thought to when and where to stop for food. Be considerate of allergies and food preferences.

"Craft Services" is the name given to the food department, initially because food was laid out on a table in the crafts (i.e. props) section. "Crafty" is slang for the people working in craft services. This can be catered, of course, and many larger productions do so. Smaller productions will generally send someone to get a platter of subway sandwiches, or boxes of cheap pizza.

In any event, plan ahead.

Parking / Directions

Even small productions involve numerous vehicles – more than you'd expect, typically. Consider parking needs. And put out clear instructions to your cast and crew about parking. This is the quickest way to blow your filming day, if neighbors or nearby businesses complain about your vehicles.

Make maps, too. Give clear directions. Assume that your people are blind and idiotic, and make your directions so clear that even the densest of them will find your location and know where to park.

This is a huge need that you must think out ahead of time. Don't get caught wasting time on parking issues the day of. You may need to rent a lot near your shoot. Or find a public garage that doesn't fill up. Or park remotely and shuttle people in. Or cut your cast and crew down to bare minimums.

Restrooms

Consider the number and availability. You may have to rent porta-potties. If you have pulled a permit, this is a factor high on the bureaucrat's list.

Safety

Be prepared!

Have a good first aid kit on set. Know where the nearest hospital is. Have a list of emergency telephone numbers.

Larger productions even hire medics to be on hand, especially if stunts or anything else dangerous is planned.

Safety is also high on bureaucrat's lists. You may be required to hire off-duty police.

Permits

Unless you are indoors on privately-owned property, you probably need a permit. Even inside, if you have a large number of vehicles you may need a permit. Permitting varies by jurisdiction.

Do yourself a favor and get to know the people in your local film commission office. It is always better to be on their good side before any problems erupt. Find out how to get permits and then comply with a smile.

Production Meetings

Not only do you, as filmmaker, need to prepare, so do your department heads. Weekly production meetings are common.

Set ground rules early. You are the leader, and you will not allow unprofessional or harmful behavior on set, so you should not allow such in pre-production meetings. Establish your hierarchy, and begin enabling your lieutenants; give them power and authority to run their squads, but observe them closely in these meetings so that you can steer them and correct any missteps early on.

Rehearsals

Contrary to what many newbie actors think, "winging it" on set on the day of shooting is not the way to get your best results.

Approaches and styles vary, of course. Some directors throw people together with a minimum of rehearsal, or none, on the theory that they will get more natural reactions that way. I personally think that is a load of horse shit (sorry, Ridley Scott!), but perhaps my bias comes from a theatre background where of course you must rehearse, since there's no second take possible.

A "Table Read" is helpful. This is where you get your actors to sit around a table and read the script, out loud. They should perform, vocally, although no one expects them to have lines memorized at this point. Assign someone to read the action sluglines and scene headings. Encourage your key crew members to be present, as it is helpful that they know and understand the story.

Following one or more table reads, you should work with actors on scenes. Help them understand the script, and understand specifically how you see the script. Your actors need to know what themes you are bringing out in the story.

Transportation

Everything you need on set needs to get there, somehow. It's too easy to forget something, and sometimes the smallest item can derail your shooting plans. Be Santa: make a list, and check it twice.

Production – Shooting Day

Good preparation and planning is the key to a smooth day of filming. There are hundreds of logistical things you must keep in mind, constantly.

Producer's Checklist

Here are some common things producers / filmmakers should consider taking to the set:

- Walkie-talkies with extra batteries
- Cell phone with power bank recharger
- Script: full script + multiple copies of the sides to be filmed
- Lined script breakdown
- Director's chairs
- Folding tables
- Shade tents
- Wardrobe racks
- Printer
- Laptop with card reader
- Paper
- Phone numbers for cast, crew, and all location contacts

Call Sheet

Send out a call sheet the day before (or earlier). The call sheet should clearly state who is needed, when, where they should go, and what they need to bring. All of the essentials: location, call time, which scenes are being filmed, which actors, what props. Call sheets also frequently contain other helpful information: nearest hospital, where to park, and the weather forecast.

Refer to your script breakdown. You should know exactly what each scene needs. Make sure no necessary element is forgotten.

Staging Areas

On location, the first question each person will have is simply, Where can I put my stuff?

Define your set location boundaries, so that no one drops their stuff in a place that interferes with the set.

Actors need space to dress, prepare, and relax as they wait. Makeup needs a place to set up and work on actors. The camera crew needs a place for setting up camera equipment, and likewise G&E (gaffers and electricians) need a place, and the sound person(s) need a place. Craft services needs space to set up and serve.

Think this out prior to shooting, and communicate clearly to everyone.

Running the Set

On set, you (filmmaker) should be able to trust your crew. Let them get the day done!

Let your DP figure how to film each scene. Camera, lens, lighting, angles, camera movement, all of these are factors to discuss ahead of time, but on the day of shooting let the DP take your shot list and get it done.

Let your Gaffer figure out how to light the scenes, to get the effect you want.

Let your Sound Mixer determine how to get the best sound.

Let your director work with the actors, to get them ready to give their best performance. (This might be you, as so many indie filmmakers are also the director! If it's you, concentrate your energies here, on your actors.)

Let your 1AD run the set. Let them take the nightmare of logistics, better them than you.

Let your Script Supervisor track your filming, with what's called "lining the script" to show what each take covers.

Let your Makeup / Hair / Wardrobe artists turn the actors into characters. Let them monitor the filming, and jump in when needed with a refresher here and there.

Let Crafty worry about feeding people. The "craft services", as it's called, is so important. People need to be fed and watered; they need it, they expect, they demand it. If you're doing a SAG-AFTRA project, it's required. But make someone else responsible for this major headache, and understand what a headache it is for them – be appreciative! Break for lunch when you can, without stressing people.

At the end of shooting, you call "It's a wrap!" (or "That's a wrap for today!") and then the rush to pack up and depart begins. Nobody can clear a room like a director yelling "Wrap!" – whoosh, like magic people disappear.

Before people leave, there is one absolute crucial thing you must do. Get the memory cards! Before you party, turn your attention to securing the cards, both video and sound. Tell your camera and sound crews that you want to copy the cards, while they pack; don't wait until they pack up. Sometimes cards are collected and returned to the crew member at a later time. Or sometimes the cards are immediately copied onto the DIT's laptop, and the cards are then returned right away.

Personally, when I work for someone else and record video or sound onto one of my cards, I expect to leave with that card in my possession; I don't at all like anyone presuming that they can take my property, and some cards (like the Cfast cards in my URSA) are expensive. One of the reasons I want my cards (besides pure selfishness?) is that it is my practice to copy files back at home, before deleting from the card. As I write this (and frankly, the reason I'm writing this), I've just gotten a frantic text message regarding the sound files I recorded this morning – it seems somehow someone deleted the copy they made while I was on set, or failed to copy the files over correctly. Lucky for them, I will be on set again tomorrow and will take a copy of today's files. But not every cameraman or sound mixer keeps copies of files, and all of today's work (the sound files) would have been lost!

White balance

The digital sensor in every camera is slightly different, which leads to slightly different footage. Color values vary by brand, due I suppose to the engineering inside each camera. Matching the shots from one camera with those taken from a camera of a different model and/or maker can be difficult, or even impossible.

Each sensor reads the colors of light and translates those readings into numbers through that camera maker's proprietary algorithms. What you should do when you first get your camera running on location is do a "White Balance" which means simply pointing the camera at a plain white surface and telling the camera that it is looking at what we all call "white." (Every camera has a button or menu by which to do this.) It is smart to carry a white card with you, designed for just this purpose. The camera then calibrates itself to that white. This is very important because a white object will look considerably different in different locations under different ambient lighting conditions. Resetting your white balance at each location will help your footage match from location to location.

Makeup

Another subject where you are best advised to hire an expert.

On your own, it's best to ask your actors to "just look normal", typically meaning women would use whatever they usually do, given the situation, and men probably do nothing. The thing you should watch for, before you film and as you go, is any sheen on an actor's face.

Get oil-reducing blotting papers, pretty cheap on Amazon. That's *blotting* papers, that you blot with; don't wipe with any strength, or you'll make the skin red. Natural skin oils are the most common reason for a shiny face. Sweat is the other. If it's hot, pause frequently to *blot* off faces. If you don't have specific blotting papers, use paper towels.

Newbies often gravitate away from "simple" stories about human nature, and instead choose to write and film projects about alien creatures and horror plots. I truly believe we'd all do better if and when we learn to tell the small, human nature stories that don't require end-of-the-world dramatics. In fact the surest sign of a newbie filmmaker, to me, is making films about zombies.

But when you're doing horror, you'll want makeup effects. That's fun stuff! YouTube is your best friend on how-to make wounds and other gore. And again, consider hiring an expert.

Blocking

Blocking is simply the word we give for character placement and movement. The script will call for certain actions, but to bring the scene to life you need to get the actors moving naturally.

First, think about what the characters were doing right before the scene begins, where they're coming from, what they might look like. Consider how movement is needed or helpful, to keep the scene interesting. Use blocking to introduce visual depth, or even set up scene transition.

Blocking is ideally done in rehearsals, before the day of filming. You fine-tune, then, when you get on set. By blocking ahead of time, you are able to clue your DP and crew in on what they need to do to set up their equipment. Storyboards help. If you wait to get on set, then your crew will need to sit and watch the blocking, before they can select lenses, lights, microphones, etc., which not only slows the day down but demoralizes your crew.

Lighting

Hire a good gaffer! And a good director of photography. Trust these people. Getting the "look" of the film is their responsibility, once they know the look you want.

Good lighting is the most important factor making your work look cinematic. All that is truly required of a scene, is that the audience be able to ascertain what in your script is happening. It need not look good. However, regardless of the genre, your audience will appreciate well-crafted looks, even if they do so subconsciously. So, how do you get good results?

Approach each scene as follows:

Start with framing your shot, and choosing the lens to best fit the action. This is highly dependent upon the blocking, what set elements the director decides should be emphasized, and of course what lenses you have to choose from.

Once you have your lens mounted, open the aperture to its widest point (lowest number), which will allow the maximum amount of light into the camera. In most cases, you will want to shoot at the widest aperture, which is most likely to give you the out-of-focus-background (called "bokeh") that is so desired. Then set your camera's shutter speed to 1/50th of a second (the standard for film, presuming you are filming at 25 frames per second – or 24, or 24.98 – close enough. If you film at a higher framerate, select a shutter speed roughly double.) Now, the lower your ISO, the less noise in the image; select the ISO you want. With ISO, shutter speed and aperture selected, you'll see whether you need to add light to the scene, or not.

If you need lights, add them selectively. Don't just flood the scene because your camera is thirsty. Consider the effect you want to form. This is art; play with the light. Start with any source of natural light, say by opening the blinds on a window. Natural light is almost always the best. You may be able to reposition your actors further from a dark background, and closer to a natural light source, which will help them "Pop" (i.e. stand out distinctly from the background). Before you add lighting instruments, consider first the actual lights visible in the room ("practicals"), such as table lamps or overhead fixtures, which may provide the light you need and in a manner that is logically convincing. All light in the scene must have an implied source, to feel right to the audience.

The standard approach to lighting any scene is called "3 Point Lighting," and is commonly used for portraits. It will make your subjects look their best. Start with a "key light" (main light source) first. If there is a window, that is likely your key light source. Other lights are used to bolster the key (make the key light source seem brighter) and fill in from other angles, so we call them "fill lights." Third, a "back light" is helpful, just to give a slight edge to your subject and further help them stand out from the background. Also called a "hair light" for obvious reasons.

A "reflector" is anything that bounces light, to brighten the shadow side of your subject; tinfoil on a tripod or light stand works well, as does any large white foamboard or similar item. Make yourself some "Brooklyn Reflectors" (see DIY Section VIII), or buy the real things (Amazon). If you can't reflect enough light, add a lighting instrument to the shadow side – but don't brighten the shadows too much, or the subject will appear flat and boring.

Your scene should have depth. Look for dark spots where a dim accent light would help define the background. This could be a hidden LED, to brighten a dark hallway, or even just a lit candle flickering on a shelf.

"Cinematic lighting" can truly be anything at all. As a filmmaker, your choices are unlimited.

Tips to get good lighting
If it looks good, it is good. You don't have to be able to see everything clearly, only what is important to your story. In each scene, to get a cinematic feel you should ideally be able to see a wide range of values, from dark blacks to bright whites. Check your frame. Make sure it looks good to you. There's no real law, so develop your own style.

Your DP is important to the look of a film. It's your vision, and the DP is tasked with bringing your vision out in the way everything is filmed, but a film is also the artwork of the DP. You and the DP must share the vision and work together to make the film look good. If you haven't worked before with your DP before, check out their prior work. You need to have confidence that they know their stuff and that they can get the "look" you want.

Some lighting tips:

- Match your lighting to your story. A documentary should not have dark, moody lighting; a horror film would definitely benefit from darkness. Use lighting to reinforce your themes, perhaps soft "romantic" lighting for a romance, or harsh jarring flashing lights at the moment your character is shocked and surprised.

- Maximize the natural lighting and existing practicals in each location, to minimize the number of instruments you bring in, and also to end up with the most natural looking result.

- Go small. Lights are big, heavy, clunky, and expensive. Plugging in too many lights causes electrical problems.

- Put depth into your scenes. You don't want distractions, but neither do you usually want black dead areas. A small light source or item catching reflected light adds interest, especially if significantly behind or in front of your area of focus.

- Have plenty of flags and reflectors, even if you have to make your own Brooklyn Reflectors. Plus c-stands to hold such. This way you can bounce light into where you want it, or conversely block light from where you don't.

- You almost always want a catchlight in the actor's eyes. Not getting a catchlight, or in the extreme not lighting a person's eyes, can dehumanize them – which looks bad, unless that is the effect you want.

- The bigger your light source, the smoother a face will look. Sharp, narrow lighting will enhance every wrinkle and flaw. Bouncing the beam off of a light-colored wall is a way of effectively making a light source seem bigger.

- Haze your scene. Add smoke. Not enough to make it look smoky, but some haze in the air gives your light something to hit and softens the whole set.

- Use dimmers to adjust practical lights. You may also want to swap out the bulbs to match the color temp of other lights.

Chromakey (or Greenscreen)

Many film and tv productions today use the process referred to loosely as "Greenscreen", which has become so widely used that all actors should understand the principles and be ready to encounter it. Correctly called "Chromakey", it is a filming technique that allows the editor during post-production to remove the set background and replace it with a different background. To do this, the set background is made to be one color, usually green, but it could technically be any color. In the editing process, that color is removed, and once removed then the remaining imagery can be laid over other film, to create the appearance as if the actor were in front of the replaced background all along.

It's fairly easy to do, although like most things in the entertainment world it is difficult to do it well. I believe most, if not all, editing software (like Final Cut, Avid, Davinci Resolve, Adobe Premiere, etc.) include this ability.

Chromakey was originally done with a blue screen background, because the selected blue tint was not in skin tones. Getting actors to look right is the most important thing. If using bluescreen chromakey, then everything blue in the shot is removed, which means you can't wear blue clothing. Unfortunately, it was discovered that the blue tint was in the skin of some black skinned actors – plus, some people say blue was a problem given the popularity of blue clothing. Now, greenscreen is mostly used. Unless your name is Shrek, your skin shouldn't have a green tint, so you should look fine once the editor removes green from the frame. However, blue is still used here and there, for blonde hair with a green tint, for example.

Whatever color, it is important to evenly light the background. Uneven lighting results in different color hues, which can make the editing process more difficult and the result choppy. It is especially important to place the actors well in front of the chromakey screen, so that there is no back spill of light bouncing the color onto the actors. A green back spill adds a greenish tint to the actor, which then results in an ugly pallor and bad chromakey result when that green is removed.

Of course, the hardest part about acting in front of chromakey screens is simply the lack of setting to play off of. Imagine Emilia Clarke in *Game of Thrones* having to climb onto a big green box, acting as if the box was her dragon. Or even more difficult, Zoe Saldana in *Avatar* acting essentially in an entirely green set, with literally no setting or props to help focus her performance. You can imagine Drogon the dragon or the world of Pandora, because you've seen these shows. But think about the poor actors who had to imagine it all before seeing what the special effects department ultimately put on the screen!

Sound

Hire a good sound engineer! A good boom operator! Rely on such persons and talk over what you need in each scene before shooting. You may plan to shoot MOS, presuming good sound can't be had, but the expert may surprise you with some good ideas. Conversely, they may be worried about sound when you can tell them that it's not that important in the particular shot. Film is a collaborative art, so collaborate!

Tips to get good sound

Getting good sound is all about the details. Here are 21 detailed tips:

1. Don't try to shoot in noisy locations. If you must, then plan on redoing the sound. Plan on ADR and Foley. If it turns out, by some miracle, that the sound you get on set is usable, hooray! But don't count on it.

2. Check out your sound engineer / boom operator, if you haven't worked with them before. Listen to sound done in their prior projects. Ask around for recommendations. Chat with them, to make sure they "fit" with your personality and that of your production. Make sure they have equipment that meets your standards.

3. Decide if you are using a single or double system. Recording sound using the camera's mic (single system) is the worst quality, but might be sufficient depending upon what you are doing. Or run the sound from an external mic into your camera (still single system), which is better because the mic is better, but still utilizes the (probably bad) preamps built into the camera. Or run the sound into a separate mixer with better preamps, and then into the camera (still single system) which works, but you've got all this equipment and cables tied to your camera. OR … record external mic(s) into a separate sound recorder, and sync the sound files later in post (double system).

4. Choose the right mic. Pay attention to the polar pattern. Shotgun mics are best outdoors, but indoors they may pick up interference caused by sound bouncing off walls. This is because the same slots in the body of the mic that reduce off-axis noise outdoors will allow bouncing waves in, so you end up with too much off-axis noise. Indoors, a super-cardiod or hyper-cardiod polar pattern condenser mic will do better, as it does not have the slots in the mic like a shotgun. Lav mics have their own challenges. If you hide a mic on set, you may need an omni-directional polar pattern.

5. Clap your hands and listen for any echo. Bare rooms with hard surfaces, for instance. You can use sound blankets on walls and floor to try to dampen the reverb. Put the blankets as

close to the actor as possible. Pay attention to angles. Soundwaves hit a surface and bounce back; the more off axis you are, the less echo. Studios have special sound absorbing tiles on their walls. You could buy some and carry them around with you, but they are very expensive, bulky, and heavy, so I don't know anyone doing this.

6. Listen. Identify noise, and unplug anything you can unplug. Turn off AC systems, and refrigerators. Pay attention. In our daily lives we have trained ourselves to ignore airplanes overhead, or the distant sounds of traffic, kids playing, or even sirens. When filming, you must be aware of everything.

7. Be aware that noise you hear may not be a problem, because mics only pick up certain things. If, during a take, you hear something like a distant plane, don't cut unless the sound person is signaling you. After the take, ask if the sound person heard what you heard – many times they will not have heard it, and on review of the recording the mic did not either.

8. Block your shots to avoid noise. For example, if you must have your actor plop down onto a squeaky leather couch, make sure that action is done *between* dialogue lines so that you can cut the bad noise out without losing what you need.

9. If there is noise in your location that you absolutely cannot get rid of, you can always record without sound and plan on adding sound later (ADR and foley). But there is another option: you can establish the sound. "If you can't beat 'em, join 'em." For example, noise of loud business equipment in an office can be really annoying to an audience as they wonder, What the hell is that sound? But it's fine if you've established that there is a loud machine running.

10. Position the mic about 6" from your actor. Maybe 6 – 18 inches. Using a shotgun on a boom, this is easy to do in a close up shot. But impossible in a longer or wider shot, right? Don't worry, you'll use the longer/wider shot to establish, and then cut mostly to your close ups, so as long as you get good sound there, you're golden. Even if you have to use the sound from your close up over a bit of the longer/wider shot, no one will be able to closely see the actors' mouths so it should be easy to sync.

11. Don't aim a shotgun mic between two actors, unless you are some distance away and can treat the two speakers as essentially one sound source. Shotguns are designed to pick up from in front (on axis), and reduce any sound from off axis. If you point it between two people thinking the one mic will cover the conversation, you have put both actors on the fringe of the mics polar pattern. Instead, your boom op needs to aim the mic at each, as they speak; you'll probably need a blimp to reduce airflow noise caused by moving the mic.

12. Consider hiding a mic on set. Get creative. Sometimes a mic can be visible, but in a place no one would ever recognize it as a mic. Don't forget an obvious option that almost everyone neglects: actors have hands. Have an actor not facing the camera hold the mic.

13. Make sure sound levels are in the sweet spot, between -24dB and -12dB (peaking). Rehearse your actors at full volume, so the sound engineer can anticipate and adjust accordingly.

14. Do make sure to slate every take, and make sure that the mic is picking it up. It's hard to match a sound file just based on what you think is happening. This often means the boom op must swing over to cover the slating, and then before "Action!" is called, get back into position. Sometimes you'll have a long shot, where the only mic is a lav. In that case, call for a second slate near the actor. (In post, try software called Pluraleyes which syncs multiple files for you. This is a timesaver, and a real asset especially if you have sound files that were not slated.)

15. Record redundant files, so if one is bad you hopefully still have a good take. Two ways of doing this. First, use two mics. Many people routinely lav and boom. On some sets, you'll see two mics on the boom. You'll see two lavs on politicians giving live speeches. Using multiple mics gives you multiple sound files; your editor can use the best. Second way is an option available on some recorders, and some mics: they automatically record a second file at a lower sound level, so that if an actor suddenly screams loud enough to cause clipping, the lower level file is probably not clipped. This extra work insures against having to refilm a scene or bring in actors for ADR.

16. Monitor the sound. Your engineer / boom op should monitor each take during filming – it's their job. But you as the filmmaker should check in with them. Ask if sound is ready before shooting, and ask if they got good sound after the take. No, don't do this every take, just enough to establish that you care and expect them to let you know if the sound is in any way questionable. Borrow a headset and listen to a take or two if they are less than confident (or if you've never worked with the sound person before).

17. Be aware that you can use sound to get certain effects. For instance, you can adjust the EQ to reduce higher frequencies and the result is the voice sounds like it came from another room. Or raise just the midlevel frequencies and it sounds like the person was talking on the telephone.

18. Look for unique sound opportunities on set. Get the sound of that teapot lid closing, for example, rather than expecting your editor to find a suitable sound later in some online collection of effects. This helps your editor, but more importantly it means your finished

film will better reflect your creativity and skills as a filmmaker. (Great stuff to point out when you're presenting your work at a film festival!)

19. Always get a room tone recording, from each and every location. You may need multiple room tones, if shooting for a long time at a single location and anything significant changes during the day. Your sound engineer knows how important it is to get room tones, and how helpful they are for editing, but it's hard to remember to get them. Make it your habit to get the room tone at the beginning of your shoot, instead of the end when everyone is anxious to go home.

20. Work with your actors on voice control and projection. Classically trained actors prepared for stage work are used to this, but many film actors have weak voices that don't register well. An example, in my humble opinion, is Orlando Bloom whose voice is soft and doesn't carry well. In ideal situations, the mic will pick soft voices up just fine, but in any adverse situation those actors will not give you good audio. If you know you will be filming is less than ideal circumstances, you best keep this in mind as you're casting.

21. Get your sound files transferred right after the shoot. Most recorders record onto SD cards. Make sure you have someone with a computer that can read the SD cards and copy the files over to you. Don't "cut" the files off of the SD card, just "copy" them; that way they aren't lost if the process goes awry, plus many sound engineers keep files just in case.

Sets

Use what you have!
Indie filmmakers most likely do not have the budget to build sets, so it is very important when writing or planning your film that you place your actors in settings to which you already have access. Hopefully, free access. My first scripts were written with the use of my own house and yard in mind, because I knew those spaces were available. Make a list of places your family and friends could let you use.

Check with the film commission offices found in many larger cities. They often keep a database of "film friendly" locations, which may be available at no cost even.

Be careful with public spaces. First, you never know who might be there to disrupt your filming and you can't chase people off of public land. Second, permits may or may not be required. (Permits can be a sticky topic.) Third, when you find a buyer of your film, should you ever be so lucky, they will ask to see written location releases from the owners of all locations – and good luck navigating the red tape involved in getting written approval to use a public space! If you get a permit, you should generally be safe, at least in terms of proper authorization.

If you do need to build sets, don't worry too much. You can do it. You might need, however, to dial down your expectations. In other words, think about the sets used for the original *Star Trek* tv show – pretty hokey, right? Laughable. A starship bridge made of plywood and blinking lights. And did you notice that very alien world they visited looked exactly like the California desert! And yet, those sets sufficed for the purpose of the storytelling, so well so that *Star Trek* has survived to become a cult classic. Today, I think there is too much concern about authenticity, and too little about storytelling.

Construction

I took set design and construction classes in college, even worked as a Teaching Assistant in a set design class, but don't let that intimidate you. Honestly, it ain't rocket science. Every trick used on stage for centuries can be used in film – actually, it's even easier in film to get away with cheap and minimal sets, because you have control over lighting, camera angles. and sound.

One big give away that immediately tells audiences that you have a fake set is the *sound*. Cheap sets sound cheap. That window or door that shuts with a weak hiss instead of the realistic thump, for example. But cheap sets don't have to sound cheap. You can build solidly. Anchor walls and doors. Use woods and metals, not foam or plastic. Or not. You don't have to build solidly, if you pay close attention to the sounds, and add appropriate sound where needed to cover a deficient set piece.

Don't be afraid to build your own sets. It's simple carpentry. For walls, build 4x8 flats either New York theatre style (wooden frame with stretched canvas), or Hollywood film style (wooden frame with plywood facing). This is easy. Use simple 2x4 or 2x3 boards to build a frame, over which you either staple canvas or nail a thin sheet of plywood (usually ¼ inch plywood or lauan). Flats are usually 4x8 feet, but you may need to make them shorter if you are shooting somewhere with a low ceiling. On set, tie the flats together. This sounds much harder than it is. All you need to do is pound large nails into the side frame boards – on the *inside* edge parallel with the front side. Tie the end of any heavy cord or thin rope at the top, and weave it diagonally down, hooking it over the nails on each flat alternatively, until you pull it tight and tie it off at the bottom.

Flats, once painted, make a very convincing background.

Set Dressing

Make it look real. I know I just said you shouldn't worry about using hokey sets, because you're telling a story not creating a perfect documentary. But make your set as "real" as you can within reasonable and budgetary terms. Make a set looked like it has been lived in, and used. I am so tired of seeing perfect papers in the hands of cops, or laying upon their desks. Really? Handle a piece of paper for 2 minutes and it gets wrinkled or torn, yet some productions want us to believe papers can look pristine even in cold cases from years ago.

If a cabinet is opened, or a drawer, please give some thought to the mess that one would typically find inside.

Give your set age. Paint on some grime. Throw clutter around. Ding up the edges.

Virtual Sets

Building the world of your script may be more cheaply and easily built in a computer. Greenscreen is fairly easy to film, and a good visual effects person can create digital worlds that look amazing. Not easy. Not cheap. But perhaps easier and cheaper than building the world you need in physical form.

For example, I've got a film in production that is set primarily on the bridge of a starship. I've been building a physical set, with large greenscreens for the starship's windows. I want my actors to be able to live in the space, so most of the bridge equipment consoles and chairs are real, but in the finished result we will see outer space out of the windows. The same result could be accomplished without using greenscreen, by building projection screens on the other side of the windows … but that would require a significantly larger set space and cost more.

Another example from the same project: I plan on a couple of the key bridge control consoles to be enhanced with a holographic effect. That can be done virtually, and I *think* it could also be done in real life … but at what cost?!

Continuity

It pays to have someone watching for continuity. Audiences today are super quick to point out mistakes. Especially things like water bottles or Starbucks cups left in *Game of Thrones* shots!

We know films are made up of individual shots pieced together to look like they naturally belong together. Two people, for example, having an argument. In reality those actors may have been filmed in separate locations thousands of miles apart. Even in the same location, no doubt they filmed many takes of each shot, and many shots to cover each scene. It is very easy to make a mistake somewhere that results in an incongruity (like a left behind Starbucks cup) that can shake the viewer out of the story. Continuity is rarely given the attention it deserves, but problems like this can ruin footage and force a re-shoot.

Often the Scripty is in charge of continuity. They take detailed notes and pictures, so that the next time or place you are shooting you can match the details. Wardrobe takes pictures, for the same reason. Actors should take it upon themselves as their responsibility to remember what they did and how, so that successive takes match. Eat with the same hand, part your hair on the same side, move at a certain cue in the same way, and so forth.

Post-Production

You guessed it! If there is "pre" then there is also "post" – meaning everything that happens after principal photography is finished.

Editing is the largest post-production task. It's often said that a film is made three times. First, when the screenwriter writes it. Second, when the actors perform it. And third and final, when the editor puts it together. (I suppose an editor said this.)

I worked with a director on a feature film who says a film is made twice: when written and when edited. (Sorry actors!) That director let all sorts of things happen during filming, as if he didn't care, and as I watched him struggle in post it was hard not to repeatedly tell him, "I told you so." It's dangerous to blithely float through filming days with the expectation that all problems can be fixed in post!

Post-production is largely the process of cleaning up the visual and sound files, and melding them into a final film.

Improving Sound

Three tools in sound software will get you pretty much all you need. Suppression to even out volumes, EQ to alter good and bad frequencies, and a De-Essing filter to minimize hissing and clicking sounds.

ADR

Alternate Dialogue Replacement (ADR) is the process of re-recording dialogue and syncing that new dialogue recording to the video images.

Like many people, I initially thought ADR was only to fix mistakes. Something to be ashamed of, because it means you failed to get good sound during principal photography. OK, I still feel that way, to a point. But only to a point.

ADR is widely done, and not just because someone put the microphone in the wrong place or forgot to turn off the air conditioner on set. ADR is, like Foley, a means of controlling the quality of the sound the goes into your production. It's similar to the recording of music in a studio. In times past, a band would gather around a microphone and play. But now every instrument, every voice, every sound effect is recorded on its own track, so that in the final song the relative volumes, tone, and quality of each track can be adjusted separately. You can't do that if the group just sang into one microphone. Similarly, large productions want to be able to tweak every aspect of the sound, which can't be done if a scene was recorded on a single mic, but can be done if each of the separate sounds is recorded separately.

On film sets, we generally see one microphone. Typically, it's that big bulbous thing on the end of a long pole that someone is holding just out of frame over the actors' heads. Bulbous because the microphone is usually a shotgun microphone (meaning it can be aimed at the subject and is designed to minimize sounds from other directions) and to further block noise from the sides and rear it is usually in a protective cover called a "blimp". But this single microphone is, as with old music recordings, just able to record all of the dialogue and set sounds on a single track. Lav mics worn by actors likewise pick up everything around them.

As with music, the development of surround sound in movie theaters has led to higher expectations for dialogue and other sound recording.

Nowadays, the sound recorded on set is often considered just a "reference sound" which enables the editor to match other sound recordings with the visual action. Lots of the final sound you hear when watching a show has been recorded separately, on separate tracks that can be adjusted appropriately, and recorded in controlled environments that are rarely possible when filming on set.

But, of course, there is a cost to all of this. ADR means getting your actors back, because they need to repeat their dialogue while watching their own performance. Otherwise, the little pauses, breaths, interruptions, and movements that affect sound would never exactly match the visual recording. This is done well after principal filming concludes, because you want your actors to match the precise footage to be used in the film, and that is only determined during the editing process after filmlock.

Your contract with actors should include access to them for ADR.

Insurance

In our litigation-happy world, you better have insurance. Location owners will insist (they should). Actors and crew should insist. Equipment rental companies will insist. Permitting agencies will insist. SAG-AFTRA will insist. Any distributor you might hope to find will insist. You yourself should insist. It's smart to be covered.

And there are many different types of insurance, so this is a tough subject. Get some help from a reputable agent! There are online companies specializing in film production, with agents who can explain what you need and the cost. Some of these companies are Film Emporium (www.filmemporium.com), Filmins (www.filmins.com) and Supple-Merrill & Driscoll (www.productioninsurance.com). These are entertainment insurance brokers. Could you get coverage from your household agent? Yes … but. Seriously, the agents in the industry know what you need and how to package the coverage correctly.

For example, you will find yourself needing to get a Certificate of Insurance at the worst possible times – it always happens. That location you planned is suddenly unavailable, but luckily the place next door is willing to let you in … if you can show insurance. Or your replacement gaffer will only set foot on set when s/he sees proof of insurance. How do you get that fast or after hours? Here is another reason to use a good entertainment insurance broker. They understand and make it possible for you to generate COI's (certificates of insurance) at any time.

Good filmmaking policies protect your people (producers, filmmakers, cast, crew), your equipment (cameras, lenses, sound gear, lighting) and also your locations. Let's look at what you need.

Film Production Insurance

It's nice to know your own gear is covered, but what you truly need to worry about is liability coverage. One stumble that results in injuries, or one ladder falling onto someone's head, and without insurance you could be looking at thousands of dollars and even bankruptcy. Most run-and-gun indie productions don't have insurance, or are underinsured; they take the risk of complete ruin. And let's face it, film sets are often a place for fun and hijinks. Shit happens. You should think twice before joining any production without insurance.

A film production policy protects the purchasing company from liability, up to a certain amount. How much depends on your level of comfort, just as with any insurance. You may be required to get a certain minimum by your permitting agencies.

Each policy will be different, because each policy takes into effect the history and operations of the company (if you're getting an annual policy), and the size of a film project (if coverage is just for a specific film). You can get a policy for as short a term as one day, for as little as $30. Small productions are often insured on a daily rate basis, for a specific number of days only; if they continue past the cut-off date, they do so without insurance coverage. If you do one or two short films per year, this is the way to go – just make sure you don't operate on extended days without also extending your coverage. But if you do a number of films, then annual coverage is probably more cost effective and safer for you.

Insurance will cost you. Some suggest that 2.5% of your budget is a good ballpark for insurance. Even newbies doing just a handful of films can expect the cost to run to $2,000 - $3,000 per year.

General Liability. Your policy must include coverage for general liability. This is for bodily injury and property damage that occurs to third parties. GL is required by SAG-AFTRA, because having it protects the actors on set from exposure. It's also required by most permitting offices. The standard coverage level is $1 Million, for starters.

Liability for vehicle accidents is covered under the GL policy. However, the coverage may only apply to your company employees; if so make sure the vehicle isn't driven by a volunteer, friend, or intern.

Equipment Coverage. Optional, unless you are renting gear from a rental house; they will have their own requirements, which can easily amount to $500,000 in coverage, even if the value of what you rent is much less.

Geography. Most policies are limited, so you will need to buy a policy that covers where you will be rehearsing, pre-producing, filming, and post-producing. You may need international coverage. Your US policy may cover the US, or just a part of it.

Worker's Comp. This protects your company in case any company employee is hurt on the job. Note that you yourself, if you work as an independent contractor, may need to get your own separate WC policy.

Deductibles. Just like any insurance, there is usually a deductible. Standard is $2,500 but of course you can lower that number by paying a higher premium.

Quick heads up: some equipment rental houses require you to deposit the amount of your deductible with them, up front.

Errors and Omissions

An E&O policy covers mistakes you may make in the actual project, its marketing, and its circulation. Things like claims for unauthorized use of characters, or claims of libel and slander. This coverage is required if you want to sell your project for distribution, because no distributor will touch your project without it.

Other Types of Insurance

Your production may have unique needs, which you should discuss fully with your insurance broker. There are all sorts of specialty insurance policies, for example coverage for:

- Stunts
- Pyrometric effects
- Weapons
- Animals
- Drones
- Recreational vehicles
- Aircraft and aerial photography
- Underwater or on the water

Contracts

This book is not a law school textbook and I am certainly not giving legal advice by writing this. Get an attorney, preferably an entertainment attorney.

That said, I will touch on some of the contracts commonly used by filmmakers. When money is on the line, you are well advised to have certain people commit to performing under the terms of well-defined contracts. Not to be too "lawyerly" about it, but they say good fences make good neighbors. Having clarity on the terms, by writing things down, is crucial.

If you are fortunate enough to create a show that someone wants to buy, that someone will most likely ask to see your location releases, performer releases, and contracts with talent and key crew. They want to be sure you did the legwork, so that they can be assured there is little risk of problems pertaining to ownership of the film's intellectual property rights.

If you sign with SAG-AFTRA you will need to use many of their form contracts. That's a whole other subject.

If (when?) I write a sequel to this book for more advanced filmmakers, I plan to go deeper into the legal aspects and even provide sample contracts.

Financing

Each episode of *Game of Thrones* reportedly cost $15 Million to make. Blockbuster movies routinely cost $100 - $200 Million. Money makes things happen.

But there are other examples, though rare, where quality shows were made on the cheap. Robert Rodriguez' directorial debut *El Mariachi* famously cost him only $7,225 to make, and it grossed a very nice return over $1 Million. Kevin Smith made *Clerks* for $27,575 -- it also grossed millions. When you get an ROI (return on investment) like that you become a hero, even a household name.

Rodriguez and Smith made their films without any major financial backers. They dug into their own pockets, begged from friends and family, maxed out credit cards and, in Smith's case, sold a comic book collection. In the independent film world, the question I see most often is, "How do I get funding for my [film?] [pitch?] [series?] [tv pilot?] [idea?] [dream?]" There are good and bad answers to that question. Unfortunately, when you ask people online or in groups, most of the answers are negative; people seem to relish telling others that it's hopeless to follow dreams. I'm very thankful that Kevin Smith didn't hold that attitude!

I'm an executive producer in a film and tv production company called FILMAM. That name is an anacronym, and the name comes, honestly, from a chance remark Kevin Smith made to one of our founders, Chris Neumann. (Shameless plug: www.filmamproductions.com) At an indie film convention years ago, Chris met Kevin and asked him essentially "How can I make a movie without money?" Kevin told Chris to stop focusing on the negative details, and instead push forward to get the film done. Stop making excuses, in other words. I don't recall if swearing was part of the answer, but … well, it was Kevin Smith. In any event, Chris translated Kevin's advice into "Fuck it, let's make a movie." We take this motto to mean that a project worth doing is worth doing – despite excuses like lack of funds (or other excuses like poor equipment, bad actors, no vehicles, inhospitable locations, etc. etc.)

Don't use your lack of financing as your excuse. Reduce the scope of your project so that you can make what you can, without putting yourself and your family in the poorhouse. That way, instead of "one and done," you can make *multiple* movies! Build up to the level you want to be at, instead of killing yourself in the jump.

"You got $10?! Go shoot a film, fool!"

~ Darious Britt

But, not all of you will accept that advice. So, here are some suggested ways for you to possibly find money:

Crowd source funding on sites such as www.gofundme.com, www.kickstarter.com and www.indiegogo.com has become intriguing. And no wonder! There are examples that make one giddy, where it looks easy for people to get investors to back their ideas, no matter how far out or crazy.

For example, someone started a Kickstarter saying he wanted money to make potato salad. He only asked for $10 … but investors pledged to give him over $55,000! Look it up – it's a great story. Of course, besides potato salad he was also promising to give investors hats, t-shirts, photographs, and other perks.

If you try this route, take a long hard look at the successful funding campaigns. Like the potato salad guy, the successful campaigns almost always return tangible results. Another key selling tool is posting a heartfelt video on the site, showing people who you are and making your pitch as personal and fun as you can.

Like Robin William's Genie says in *Aladdin*, "There are a few provisos. A couple quid pro quos." First, such sites aren't free; they keep 8-10% of the money raised. And second, I'm afraid the newness has worn off, Mr. Potato Salad got lucky, and none of the film-funding requests I have seen managed to gather any significant amount of money.

Kickstarter is the crowdfunding site which seems most focused on film and other creative ventures. But there are also other, lesser known, funding sites that you can try (and probably others to come): search the names Crowdwise, Razoo, Fundify, I Patreon, Pledgemusic, and Give.

Beg from family and friends, though this is a good way to lose said family and friends.

Borrow if you must, though banks need to see collateral that is comfortably valued at more than the loan amount.

Adjust and adapt. Write and plan your projects based on what you have available in locations, sets, props, and people. Be smart. Cheat. Make that $5 ring look like a gem worthy of a queen, rather than spending money to rent a Queen's jewels for a day of filming.

Spend wisely what little money you do have. Feed your cast and crew as a first priority, especially if they are donating their time. Pay for lower level (but important) jobs, like PA's who do the vital stuff that no one else wants to do; the higher, sexier jobs, like directing, can be filled with people who want the experience and exposure. Don't give into the temptation to buy more gear; you can almost always do the job with what you already have, and if not then maybe change the job.

Make your pitch count. Everyone knows that most films don't return the investment, so only someone who believes in your project will fund it. The question you should be asking is, How do I make potential investors believe my project will succeed? That answer hinges entirely upon you. What have you done already that you can show to them? Who are you, and what makes you the person to do this? Why do you believe that the idea is a good idea?

Prove your concept. An idea can be too ethereal, too vague, too creative for any words to do it justice. Create a "proof of concept" video that you can use to visually demonstrate what you have in mind. This is frequently done for new tv shows, where the creator of the show first films a "pilot" that can be shown to investors. If the pilot generates enough buzz, the money people will back production of the show. (The pilot, by the way, often does not reflect the resulting show. Actors, characters, settings, and plotlines are all subject to change. When you make your pilot, don't worry about getting everything perfect – it just has to be good enough to prove to the investors that the idea is worth funding.)

If you can't afford to do a full pilot episode, make instead a short film that includes your characters or otherwise presents the gist of your concept, even just a single scene. All you need is something visual, to impress and convince all of those people who don't have sufficient imagination or trust to see the potential in your script.

Siphon from some other business. You want to make movies, but maybe in the meantime you can succeed in a different line of business, and use the profits from that to fund your dreams. One of my best friends, Dejan, had to go to work for his father's plastic manufacturing plant in order to fund his dream of starting a theatre company in Chicago; the deal paid off, and Dejan's theatre was a huge success, even reviewed by New York City critics!

Win the lottery.

Or marry well. Or rob a bank. Or find a Genie in a bottle. Or kill your rich uncle. Or print some cash yourself.

Before you rob, kill, or cheat anyone, I hope you go back to the initial advice: make the film that you can afford to make without ruining your chances to make your next film.

Provide Food

An observant visitor from an alien planet could be excused if they concluded that the job of a filmmaker (Producer, Director, AD, what have you) is to feed the cast and crew. Food is a hugely important part of many productions. I swear it seems that many people are involved (actors and crew) just to get free food.

SAG-AFTRA requires that you provide regular meals for cast and crew, with no more than 6 hours after the last meal. Even non-union productions are expected to feed everyone. And I suppose they should, especially if people are working without pay!

Working on sets, I constantly get cheap pizza. Hey, as a director and producer, I've fed cheap pizza to my own people. It's kind of an Entertainment World staple. Everyone likes pizza, right? Even when I hung lights in legit stage theatres, pizza and beer was the currency for payment.

The better the food, the more praise you will get. But of course, just about anything more than cheap pizza is more expensive. When you figure out your budget, don't skimp on the food. You can impress people even with cheaper options:

- Grocery stores and subway shops will put together sandwich platters.

- Some catering companies can provide basic staples at reasonable prices. Things like large trays of fried rice and small chicken breasts.

- Fast food restaurants will sometimes cut a deal on a large order. On a recent set, my crew was thrilled with chicken nuggets from Chick-fil-A.

- Family members can help you whip up large orders. I did sound for a guy whose parents wrapped up dozens of Cuban sandwiches in tinfoil.

Safety
Safety on set is your duty. It is everyone's duty!

The safety of everyone on set must always be a first priority of everyone else on set. If you see a problem – anything that could hurt someone -- call it out loud. Don't be shy or quiet about safety.

During the months it has taken me to write this book a dastardly villain has attacked the whole world. COVID19 is a game changer for the entire Entertainment World, and no one yet knows how, when, and to what extent we can get back to normal. It sucks. I hate not being able to get on set and film. I hate even writing about it.

Fact is, it's a virus. As with all viruses, anti-biotics like penicillin have no effect. At this point in time, there is no vaccine (although several are being tested and there is hope). What it comes down to for now is simply this: everyone needs to do what they can to limit the spread of the disease. That is done primarily by regular hand washing and mask wearing, because both of those greatly inhibit the virus' ability to transfer to new hosts.

There is a free "Safe-Sets COVID19 Certificate" process going around on the Internet. I did it in less than 15 minutes, which shows that it is not difficult to get. It's basic information, and probably not very helpful for anyone wanting to resume filming … though it is at least a step in that direction.

To my knowledge most movie theaters, legit stage productions, music concerts and festivals, and big events like Comic-Con have shut down with as yet no announced plans to reopen. Film and television production completely shut down for months, although I've read of a handful of productions slowly getting back to work (overseas).

We already see restaurants and other companies closing for good, forced into bankruptcy by this villain. That will no doubt happen in the Entertainment World, too. In fact, it's more likely in our world because other industries can resume (at least with partial operations) where audiences of any size will probably be prohibited and/or avoided for a long time afterward.

Sheesh. Enough doom and gloom. Let's get back to dreaming and planning to make films!

Set Etiquette

Setiquette?

"Setiquette" should be a real word, or at least an industry slang word that everyone knows. It should, quite simply, be something one thinks about on every set, every production, big and small.

Film sets are full of expensive equipment, and frantic people in stressful, deadline driven situations. Gear can be broken; people can be hurt. Sometimes people are hired who should not have been. I once came very close to dying in a theatre when someone did something that they had no right to do. (By the way, the person who almost caused my death was beaten up by my friends and blackballed from working in San Diego theatres. I could never recommend that kind of action, but I admit it made me feel good.)

Well run sets are like the mechanical gears of a clock, all turning together with engineered precision. But one obstruction can stop everything.

Look, I don't want to lecture. I'm not your mama. You're an adult (or close to it, right?) and you decide for yourself what kind of person you are or want to be. None of you should need to read the following etiquette sections. But – well, shit, just about any time spent on sets reveals that a depressing number of you do need to work on this.

Cell Phones

I'm starting here because this is one of the most pernicious realities we face in modern times. It's very ironic: although cell phones are used to spread social media, they have exactly the opposite effect on creating unity – they are anti-social. Every minute we spend looking at a cell phone is a minute we are not looking at or interacting with the people around us.

On film sets, the most important thing I can stress is the combined purpose of mission. Everyone is there to get a job done. Not to play games, watch cat videos, check weather patterns, listen to podcasts, chat with distant friends, laugh or cry at blunders, follow politics, or any other distraction.

Quentin Tarantino is famous for his strict no-cell-phones policy. He means it. He fires people for bringing a cell phone to his sets!

Phones can be helpful tools. But please, keep it in your pocket and use it only if needed to help you do your job on set.

"But," you say, "There's so much down time on set. What if I'm bored?" Bored?? If you are serious about wanting to make something of yourself in this industry, there is no better place to learn than on sets. In those moments when you have nothing to do, sit quietly and observe. Learn. Figure out everything around you. Bored? Hell, no!

Good Practice

Don't think of this as a finishing school lesson. These are just good practices that will make life on set easier and more copacetic for all:

- Call time is the time you are supposed to be ready to work, not the time you pull into the parking lot or arrive with your equipment. You should arrive 20 minutes before the call time, or earlier if you have a lot of equipment or require extra prep time.

- Don't be late. Don't leave people hanging. Don't cost the production money!

- Be respectful to everyone.

- Dress appropriately.

- Have pen & paper for note taking.

- Listen carefully.

- Ask questions if you don't understand.

- Focus on what you're doing.

- Complete tasks as quickly & efficiently as possible.

- When your assigned task is completed, check in with your superior. Don't stand idle, and just as importantly, don't presume you know what to do next.

- Carry a small black marker to label your water bottles with your name or other identifying mark, so that you can find it again instead of repeatedly getting new bottles and leaving half-filled waste around you.

- Bring a camp chair to outdoor shoots, plus sun and bug protection.

- Don't steal. It's a small, tight industry and word will spread quickly if you can't be trusted. (For example, I've heard from four different sources the same story of a cameraman in my area borrowing and then pawning someone else's drone, and then offering to pay the owner only its current well-depreciated value. That kind of shit gets talked about.)

Know Your Spot on Set

On set, it is vitally important that you do what you are supposed to do, and not anything else. Yes, we are all creative types, with brains, and it's hard to accept the idea that we must be cogs in a wheel. But if the filmmaking machine is to run smoothly, every cog needs to be in place. Be mindful of how the whole machine works. For example:

- Everyone has a job to do. Don't interfere or restrict their ability to succeed at their job.

- Don't offer to help, unless (i) they ask, or (ii) you see a safety risk that clearly requires your assistance. It's nice to offer to help, right? Wrong: offering to help techies and other people who pride themselves on their abilities can come across *to them* as if you are implying they are not capable.

- Be sure you know your job well, know what is expected of you, and be able to do it.

- Speak up if you need clarification or training. We all start somewhere, and there's no shame in asking. It's far better than having to admit ignorance later.

- Don't mess with anyone's stuff, whether crew or cast. Things break easily and when you least expect. Film things are expensive; you can't afford to replace them, so you can't afford to touch them.

- Don't wander over to someone else's spot. Example: the "video city" monitor area is set up only for certain professionals to use (generally, the director, 1st AD, makeup artist, production designers – plus the producers and other money people, since they're paying for it anyway). It is not your tv lounge. Do not ever go look, no matter how bored or curious you are.

- Realize that "talent" is the least special category on set, unless you are also a "star". Get over it. You might someday be a star, but until then you are talent, and you need to stay out of everyone else's way.

- Never ever annoy a star (or even talk to them, unless invited to do so). One of my fondest memories is spending an hour on set with John Huston, but that just happened. He talked to me first, and we had an easy conversation without me once asking for an autograph. Same for meeting Robert Byrne of Talking Heads, Kevin Kline, Charles Bronson, Robert DeNiro, and Kenneth Branagh. Take your cue from the people you meet, and talk with them only if and when they feel like it. Otherwise, with a short word, they can have security run you off the set.

- Recognize how difficult it is for an actor to get into character, and give them the space and time to do so. Don't do anything to take them out of character before filming. An example of this is Quentin Tarantino's clapper woman on several of his films, a person who has become famous in her own sake for how funny she is while doing her job (Google her yourself); but I would fire her in a heartbeat, for distracting actors right at the moment when they should be ready to film. Quentin's set may be an anomaly, and/or she must be a really good friend of Quentin's. I don't recommend you try it.

Early in my career I was working for an LA film production company as "assistant assistant cameraman" (what is usually called 2nd AC) and at some point dropped a screwdriver while I was about 3 feet up on a ladder. No one was within 50 feet of me, so I hopped down, picked up the screwdriver, and got back to work. But immediately a short, red-faced guy ran up to sputter into my face things like "How dare you!" and "You're taking food out of other guy's mouths, out of their kids' mouths!" I stared at him, having no earthly idea what the f*** he was talking about. Until he sputtered out that there was a union guy on set whose job it was to pick up that screwdriver, and it was this guy's union job to make sure I did my job and not another person's job. Whatever the case may be, know how you fit in.

Drop the Drama

All kidding aside, leave your personal drama at home. Do not bring your troubles to the set. Do not burden others with your problems. We all, of course, have problems. If there are 30 people on set, imagine the time it would take if every person took time to whine, complain, vent, or cry about their personal problems. Letting just one person do so opens the door to others, until the whole set becomes toxic.

Sometimes, it's not you. You're just doing your thing, but that person next to you goes on and on about their personal life – and you don't feel you have any authority or right to tell them to stop. But you can discourage them by not listening to their drama. Don't give them an audience. Move away, change the topic, or ask them about the production. If they continue, tell them you don't have time for it. You don't.

Shut Up

Rude advice?

You don't have to say everything you're thinking. You never know when the person you're complaining about is standing right behind you, or their friend is, or you're on a camera ….

Sweet and simple advice: Know when to shut up. One quick example: I've worked with an incredibly skilled makeup artist, who has difficulty finding work because everyone knows she runs her mouth non-stop all day long. She is nice and sweet, but talks nonstop. Even professional announcers with inhuman breath control would be jealous of her. People tell her to be quiet, but I don't think she gets it. She will be quiet, until the next opportunity to speak, and then she motor mouths again. I firmly believe her career would be more successful if she ever caught on and reformed this aspect of her personality.

Speaking of makeup artists, you should shut up *for them*, too. They are part of the show, part of your production, let them focus and do their job. You want them to make you look good, don't you? Don't talk on your cell phone while they are doing their job. No chatting with others, no running dialogue lines, no drinking or eating! Just sit there, be professional and let them make you look good.

If you do give advice (and you should reconsider the urge in most cases), have the grace to say it only once. The same makeup artist noted above often gave her 2 cents worth, and then repeated it over and over, as if she could turn it into a nickel or dime. But seriously, people don't want your advice, even the first time, especially the 2nd time, and for God's sake not the 3rd time!

Honestly, your advice is not welcome. Most likely, you're saying something stupid. If you do make a good point, odds are someone there will resent you for making them look stupid. It's a lose-lose situation for you. My Momma always said, "Better to keep silent and be thought a fool, than open your mouth and remove all doubt." Someday, maybe you will be in charge. At that time, your voice will count. Until then, shut up and dream of that day.

This refers also to your cell phone, and anything else you have on you which might make a noise, even a tiny peep. Don't take that stuff on set, or at least make sure it can't make a peep. You'd be amazed how loud a tiny little beep or vibration is when "Quiet on set!" has been called and filming begun. Turn your cell phone to silent, not vibrate. Or even better, turn it off.

Pay attention to your body. On set, little things like shifting your weight or putting your hands in your pockets can cause enough noise to ruin a take. If you are one set during filming, learn to freeze during takes. Stop all movement. Literally all movement. Even your bowel movements! Yes, I mean it; if you are hungry or constipated or whatever, and your stomach is talking loudly, leave the set.

Creepy Behavior
Don't be a creep!

Seriously. Filmmaking is hard enough to break into, meet the right people, and prove your abilities. Don't sabotage yourself by thinking it is also a chance to date.

Have you seen the meme going around film groups, a guy saying, "Hey Girl! I got your number off the call sheet." (shudder) If you EVER think you should call someone for a date (boy or girl) because you found their number on a call sheet or anywhere else in connection with their professional lives ... strike that thought right out of your deluded mind! That is way too close to "stalking" for comfort, and 99 times out of 100 you will just creep them out.

You meet someone on set, and you strike up a relationship ... OK. I'm not saying we aren't human, with all the urges that go along with that condition. But be professional. That's all I'm saying.

My personal advice does go farther: don't date anyone on any active project. Hook up later, if at all. Working and dating at the same time is almost guaranteed to end badly for you and the production.

Be prepared

Strive to be that person who is always prepared, not only for what you need yourself, but also for what others might need to borrow. I always carry a slate with me. It's not always my job to have one, but I've been on many sets where no one else thought to bring one, and I get brownie points for letting them use it! I carry a pocketknife regularly, and get lots of points for having it handy to offer. This business is all about reputation and word of mouth. Be prepared, and you'll become known as someone nice to have around.

Carry on your person, generally

- Small black marker (for labeling your water bottle, mostly)
- Pen and paper to write notes on
- Cell phone (turned OFF, or at least absolutely silent – no vibration, nothing)
- Extra battery for your cell phone (a USB power bank is perfect)
- Cell phone charger cable!

On your person if you're a PA

- The above items, plus:
- Spare hot bricks (batteries) for other people's walkies
- Walkie talkie
- Copy of call sheet
- Pocketknife
- Flashlight (don't run down your cell phone)

In your car

- Change of clothing – multiple sets if you are an actor – but everyone should have a change or two, to make sure you have something to change into after somehow ruining what you have on (it happens!), or because of a drastic weather shift
- Sunscreen -- I prefer the solid stick type, since it is quick and easy to use, and less likely to spill or make a mess in your bag
- Bug spray, again I prefer solid stick
- Hat
- Snacks (like a box of granola bars that won't go bad – don't get any with chocolate or peanut butter which melt in hot cars)
- Book for when you have down time

- Headshots / resumes / business cards
- Backup items of whatever you use on set

PART VI: EQUIPMENT

I've waited until late in this book to address equipment for the simple reason that most people approach filmmaking from exactly the opposite perspective, and I think that's wrong. Talk with newbies about filming a project, and they will most likely jump immediately to talking about what camera they have, instead of what skills or what script. It's easy to get caught up in the excitement of buying new equipment (and stealing, borrowing, trading). I love the thrill of finding a great buy on Craigslist, the adrenalin rush of the final eBay seconds, the warm satisfaction of opening a box, and the confidence of a well-outfitted studio. Our capitalistic society wants us to focus on material items. But just because you bought it, doesn't mean you know how to use it!

Don't get me wrong: good equipment is crucial. For every job, there is the correct tool. The biggest difference between the home DIY person and a real professional is the knowledge of what tools to use in any given situation. A pro comes in and, using the right tool, finishes a job in 20 minutes that takes an amateur three days. So true, too, in the indie film world. Pros who know what they're doing get the right equipment, even if they have to invest their first born to do so. But the rest of us think we can film Hollywood blockbuster style films with our smartphones.

The thing about equipment is this: it's over-rated. Good filming and television was being done in the 1950's, when they used candles in front of shoeboxes (I'm exaggerating). Supposedly the computers NASA used to send men to the moon were bigger than a car, and could do less than your average smartphone can now. And yet, they got the job done! So become a pro, and lavish your inner geek with the latest super gadget – but until then, make good shit with what you can afford.

The following is all good, even the "cheapish" items. I'll let you decide what you can afford. Then later, in Section VII, I'll offer some really cheap tricks for those of you with a DIY mentality and budget.

Rent or buy?

Are you the kind of person that must own things, rather than rent? I feel strongly about having my own stuff. But there are really good arguments for rent filmmaking equipment.

Technology changes so fast. In recent years new cameras have come out so quickly that the older models don't hold their value. Everyone wants the latest and greatest. If you hope to sell your camera, this is a problem. On the other hand if you are like me and hang on to things that work, then who cares about resale value?

Renting has its risks. You may not be able to get what you need and want. You may end up with equipment that you are not comfortable using. You may pay a lot if you need the equipment for any length of time. If you break it, you need to satisfy the rental company (hopefully, insurance covers the loss). There may be creative situations which call for you to alter or modify your equipment in ways that you can't, if its owned by someone else.

Arguments for renting: You get to try new equipment before you decide to buy. The equipment you own is not something you can bill to your clients, but a rental cost can be passed through. Perhaps you care less about damage to a rental.

And here is the best reason, I think, for renting if you're a filmmaker. Most rentals have a weekly rate, and it makes sense to rent for a week rather than, say, 5 days. So if you have a client and a planned 5-day shoot, you can rent equipment for a week, do the shoot, AND then use the equipment for two more days on your own pet projects!

Equipment inventory

Keep an updated list of everything you own, so that you know what you have available to use. You can share such list with your DP and others, so that you can all collaborate on the kinds of shots you plan. Having an inventory list helps you prepare for shoots, as you can easily run down the list to remind yourself what to take along. It is also a good way to keep track of your stuff, so it doesn't disappear.

Here is one way to list your stuff. I recommend you do this in Excel, so that you can easily create new columns as you grow and wish to add new information. Make your list inclusive, even small stuff. Having a detailed inventory will help you prepare for gigs, so you can be confident nothing gets forgotten behind.

- Camera, with accessories specific to each camera (batteries, memory cards, card readers, chargers, rig pieces, power supply cables, rails, lens adapters, etc.)
- Lenses (including filters, matte boxes, and the like that fit certain lenses)
- Camera support (tripods, sliders, gimbal, baseplates, shoulder mount, Steadicam, etc.)
- Camera accessories (misc., such as monitor, follow-focus, gaff tape, lens cleaner)
- Lights
- Grip (light stands, c-stands, stingers, clamps, flags, reflectors, etc.)
- Audio (mics, cables, recorder, boom, etc.)
- Computer (portable hard drives, card readers, cables, printer, ink, etc.)
- Props / Set

In addition to equipment you own, keep track of stuff that your friends own! You never know when you might want to involve someone in a project. For example, you may own a Blackmagic Pocket Cinema camera and you have a client who needs four such cameras – call up your friends with the same camera and work together. Or borrow their gear.

You may want to add a column for rental rates. What you would charge for anyone to use your equipment. Not to say that you necessarily plan to loan out your prized possessions, but with the rate in there, you can more easily put together a bid for your services. An investment earns returns, right? Treat you gear like investments. Charge for it. When you up your game with next-level equipment, increase your day rate. Treat yourself like a business! So long as you are digging into your pocket, or putting profits straight back into gear, then you have a hobby or a passion, not a business.

Visual

Format / "High Definition" Quality

First, some definitions and concepts. You should understand the technical aspects of recording, storing, and editing images and sound, even if you are not actually in charge of technical stuff. Some of these concepts are a bit difficult to understand, at first, but they become old hat to veterans. (You vets, don't slam me; I will discuss these technical aspects at a basic level, because that's how people learn. I fully recognize there are many fine points you could add!)

This technical discussion is further complicated by the fact that the ways we describe data capture and storage are different than describing how data is broadcast or projected. Look at a photograph under a magnifying glass, and you'll see the image is comprised of tiny dots, and some printed pictures (as with inkjet technologies and the printing used for newspaper photographs) likewise look like dots, when magnified. This is why a measurement of print quality is "dots per inch" (DPI), where more dots results in a sharper picture. But look at a digital picture, and instead of dots, you'll see "pixels" – little squares – and the more "pixels per inch" (PPI), the sharper the picture.

The "Resolution" is the sharpness, the amount of detail in each picture. It's determined at different stages by how much information is first gathered through the lens and stored, then by how much information is retained in the editing process, and finally by how much information the display device (tv, projector, etc.) is able to present back.

A digital image is scanned *super-fast*, but not all at once. The scanner inside the camera starts at the bottom and scans up (or from the top down, whatever). It goes line by line. The resolution numbers we typically throw around are the number of lines scanned vertically. For example, a "resolution of 720" means the image is scanned in 720 horizontal lines. That's 720 pixels high. Frame size is typically 1,280 pixels wide x 720 pixels high, which means the image is stored in a total of 921,600 pixels. By comparison, "1080 resolution" means the image is made up of 1,920 x 1,080 pixels, for a total of 2,073,600 pixels. If each pixel tells us something about color and light, clearly a picture with 2,073,600 pixels contains much more information that does one containing only 921,600.

Public marketing (of tv's, computer monitors, and camera, especially) is obsessed with image resolution, probably because it is an easily quantified way to justify selling new equipment to consumers. This all started with the invention of television. Prior to that point, people went to movie theaters. Television display sets had to be better and better, and cheaper, to lure people to buy the latest model. Video cameras started becoming cheap enough, and good enough, for widespread home use – somewhere in the 80's and 90's – then quality was improved with the advent of digital processing and storage. Digital recording of images was, at first, nowhere near as sharp and detailed as film, and purists (like myself) shunned digital cameras for some time, because film had superior resolution. Manufacturers had to overcome this defect. And they did. They designed sharper and sharper recording and display devices. "High Definition" is a marketing term which was a real selling point – you'll still find old motel signs proudly advertising High Definition tv's. It was shortened to High Def and then HD, as we all became used to the idea. You may laugh now, but 720 was once considered "high definition." 720 was HD, only for the simple reason that it was a higher resolution than the prior standard (which was approximately 440 lines). Then 1080 became the accepted and desired standard. After that, 4K (which you can think of as roughly 4 times 1080, or a bit more than 4,000 dpi – I'm saying "a bit more" because there are numerous so-called 4K standards that all vary slightly, thanks to the different manufacture's marketing departments). As I write this in 2020, there are 8K – 12K cameras on the market. Where oh where does this stop?

Let's stop the marketing merry-go-round for a second to think about a few things:

- First, something filmed at 4K (or 8K or 10K …) will only look as good as the resolution of the screen on which it is shown, so a 4K film shown on a 1080 monitor looks like … you got it, 1080.

  In the early 2000's, a digital conversion swept across the world's movie theaters, with many discarding their old film projectors and investing in new digital projectors – an investment, by the way, costing theaters about $100,000 per projector! By the end of 2017, most theaters had converted. Early digital projectors were 1280 x 1024 resolution, but by now most theaters have installed 2K projectors (3840 x 2160), and 4K projectors are rare. With upgraded equipment so expensive, the majority of films are shown today on 2K projectors – so, again, any resolution in the film above that standard will not be seen. Most tv's are 720 or 1080. The highest resolution on Netflix is 2K, and 720 on Hulu and Amazon Video. Until projectors, display screens and broadcasters upgrade, filming at a higher resolution does not give you a sharper end result that anyone will see.

- Can you look at a screen and say whether it's 4K or 1080? Most people can't unless the screens are side by side. 1080 is a fine picture!

- If 1080 isn't good enough, I suspect the problem is not the resolution but instead the story. A good enough story will catch and hold the viewers' attention, without giving them even a moment to ponder about the resolution.

- One reason given for shooting in 4K is that with the higher resolution the editor can zoom into a portion of the frame and still end up with a good enough picture (a 1080 result, in other words). Imagine a single frame, with the option to divide it into 4 quarters that are each good enough. That means the editor can pan from one side of the frame to the other, or zoom in, then zoom out. It's all good, I suppose. Except for the idea (the way I see it) that the framing of the shot should be thought out ahead of time, as part of the director and DP's art. Shooting in 4K just so the editor has choices is lazy filmmaking. And the result is much more a product of the editor's vision and skill than the director's.

If you edit video you are well aware of how much more difficult it is to edit 4K than 1080. It takes a faster / stronger computer, much more storage space, and longer processing times, and all of this means it cost more to edit in 4K.

Camera

Often, the first question asked when one filmmaker meets another is simply, "What do you shoot on?" What is this, the filmmakers' form of penis envy? It's a challenge question, and one without a clearly correct answer. I swear, it's like the camera one owns is never good enough …. There is always another break-through revolutionary video camera available or coming out soon.

Generally, the answer to the question speaks volumes about where that person fits on the independent filmmaking spectrum. For example, they may say they shoot on an SLR, like maybe a Canon Rebel T3i (not bad), or better yet a Panasonic Lumix GH5 (mmmm), or they may tell you they shoot RAW 4k on a Red Dragon (ooooo, fancy).

This is not to say that one can't get great results on lesser equipment. You can certainly get the opposite (crappy results from expensive equipment), but a filmmaker with skill, talent and knowledge can get amazingly good results out of just about any camera. Don't use your lack of expensive camera gear as an excuse!

No matter the equipment, results speak for themselves. Ultimately, the only question that matters is whether or not the footage is *good enough* for its intended purpose.

And, seriously, just like you don't need to take the Ferrari to pick up groceries, you don't need fancy, expensive, function-loaded cameras to turn good stories into neat, watchable films. For example, everyone wanted high definition (1080p) when it was the "hot thing", and now everyone wants to shoot in 4K. But why? Why shoot in 4K when you plan to put your projects online, on YouTube perhaps, or otherwise expect your viewers to watch on monitor screens that are 720 or 1080, like most computer monitors? (I mean, do *you* have a 4K monitor? Or an 8K?! Do you expect your audience to have such?)

Good films can be made with a smart phone camera. Good video cameras have become more affordable (for example, Panasonic's G7 at just $500 brand new).

DSLR's ("digital single lens reflex cameras" made by Canon, Nikon, Sony, Panasonic) are mostly designed for still photography, to which they've added video. But don't sneer. Most indie and student filmmakers use DSLR's, and can get really great shots.

Professional Cameras – are you ready for the dream level?

Blackmagic makes a number of fantastic cameras that most people consider only "semi-professional" because they may not be truly as good as the next cameras we will discuss … but Blackmagic cameras are available so cheaply (relatively speaking!) that they are frequently used in the Indie and student film worlds by us newbies.

Oh, how proud I was to get the Blackmagic URSA camera! I felt like I had truly "made it", regardless of the fact that I didn't know how to film with the thing. I'm still learning. The URSA is a monster. It weighs about 16 pounds! Many don't like its big size, yet other cameras get just a big once rigged up with the monitors and sound equipment that is built in on the URSA. The URSA shoots what some call 4K, but others do not. It's "4K lite", and not quite full cinematic 4K.

The newest (as of 2020) Blackmagic 4K Pocket Cinema Camera is all the rage, now. I do love it. So small, and such a good picture.

Moving up, the Red and ARRI cameras. Big jump up in price, though!

People will argue "Which camera is best?" All you have to do is look at the Best Cinematography winners of recent years, and there is one camera clearly dominating that list: the ARRI Alexa. To prove my point, here are the cameras used by the winning films:

2019 1917	ARRI Alexa
2018 Roma	ARRI Alexa
2017 Blade Runner 2049	ARRI Alexa
2016 LA LA Land	(the one exception, this was shot on film)
2015 The Revenant	ARRI Alexa
2014 Birdman	ARRI Alexa
2013 Gravity	ARRI Alexa

2012 Life of Pi	ARRI Alexa
2011 Hugo	ARRI Alexa

I think big-money-Hollywood knows what they're doing. I myself have never been closer than 15 feet to an ARRI Alexa. Goals.

Why does ARRI dominate? Simply put, the look of the footage. There are YouTube videos comparing cameras, and I must agree that the ARRI colors, resolution, dynamic range, accuracy in contrast, big sensors, temperature control, 16-bit recording on two processors, signature prime lenses, and other things I barely understand make ARRI footage incredibly beautiful. "If I were a rich man …."

Shooting with Cellphones

Cameras in cellphones have become better and better. I enjoy shooting video with my (Android) Samsung Galaxy Edge S7, and there are better options out there. There are entire film festivals just for short films shot on phones. Cellphone footage has been used on TV shows, such as a March 2019 episode of NBC's *Tonight Show With Jimmy Fallon* shot entirely on a Samsung Galaxy S10+ smartphone, and in notable short films and music videos – it's just a matter of time before a major release movie gets made entirely using smartphones.

When I shoot with a smartphone, there are a few tricks I prefer to stabilize the results. Otherwise, it's hard to hold onto the small phones, and footage can look jittery. One solution is to get a rig, which is basically just some plastic handles with an attachment place for the phone (Amazon, about $15); the rig lets you hold and manipulate the phone with much greater security and confidence. The rig has the added benefit of additional attachment places, for say, a small shotgun mic and/or small cube LED light. This kind of set up is very helpful for filming interviews, especially if one is moving from person to person fairly quickly.

It is also helpful to get a powered stabilizer, which greatly minimizes the jitters and vibrations of normal handheld filming, and results in a cleaner, more cinematic look. I got a cheap one (the Hohem iSteady Mobile+ for $89 on Amazon) which I love.

TV Cameras

This book is for newbies getting into film, but let's talk television for a moment. Why are TV cameras so big, heavy, and expensive? Well, mostly because of what is required of a tv lens.

A broadcast tv lens must have a long focal length, and variable zoom, with parfocus, so that the operator can zoom in from some distance. For example, filming a football game requires the ability to get in tight from a camera position off-field, and then quickly readjust to follow the action. It must have a wide focal range, for quick adjustments. It must record in low light, so it must have a very wide aperture. It needs image stabilization. And finally, the zoom and iris controls must have high-precision motorized controls because long telephoto shots are too sensitive to vibrations for hand controls. That is a LOT to ask of a lens, and as a result tv lenses are huge complex instruments that can cost over $200,000!

A tv camera rig can weigh over 150 pounds. That then means tripods, dollies and other gear must be beefed up to accommodate the camera. The tripod's fluid head must be so smooth that no jitters are seen even when filming at great distances. Long telephoto shots can be ruined by just the pulse of your heartbeat! Equipment rugged enough, yet with such precise dampening and fluid movement capabilities, is very expensive.

The greatest difference between film and tv camera rigs is that film cameras are designed to get good results in controlled environments, where multiple takes are possible, but tv cameras are one-size-fits-all machines designed to get the shot when it happens, live, in situations where a second take is not possible.

Matte box

A matte box is the clunky thing mounted at the end of the camera's lens, usually with metal flanges that hinge and can be swung out on all sides of the lens. So, what it this thing for?

A matte box is very helpful for multiple reasons.

It's a sunscreen, for one. Just mounting it on your rig will help with the problem of glare on your lens. The barn doors can be swung in and out to cut light as needed.

Second, the box has slots for you to place filters in front of your lens.

Third, it looks cool, and helps convince clients that you are indeed a "professional." They will jump to pay you more. (I'm only half kidding with this.)

Some matte boxes mount on the rails of your camera rig. Some lighter models clamp onto the end of your lens. A heavier box may have more effective barn doors, but a lighter box may do a better job holding filters while allowing you to maneuver the camera more freely.

Stabilization

Small cameras, especially DSLR's, are subject to the "jitters." No matter how steady you are, the tiny tremors in your body (even your heartbeat) can and will transfer over to your footage when you try to handhold the camera.

There are various ways to counter this. Use a tripod, or monopod. Use a shoulder rig. Use a gimbal, or Steadicam. Some cameras / lenses have built-in stabilization, which helps to a degree.

One rule to keep in mind is simple physics: a larger mass reacts less to small movements. Heavier cameras suffer less. You'll get better results with a light camera once it is rigged out, which makes it heavier. Even a cell phone can be held steadily, in the right rig.

Variable ND

ND filters cut light, so when you place them in front of your lens the whole image gets darker. If you are filming in bright sunlight, you may need an ND filter just to get the exposure down to where it isn't horribly overexposed. But ND filters are even more helpful than just that. By using an ND filter, one can shoot with the aperture (F stop) opened up wider, which results in a shallower depth of field than can look awesome (this effect is called "Bokeh").

ND filters come in various gradients, from a slight tint to what looks like solid black to the naked eye. You can get several of these, sized to screw onto the appropriate diameter of your lens. Or you can get a "Variable ND", which is a filter that turns and becomes (magically!) darker, so you can keep one filter in your bag instead of a set.

Or you can use a matte box, and that way the size of your filters does not have to match the diameter of your lenses. This is especially handy if you use a number of lens with different diameter filter rings.

Good variable NDs can be expensive, and cheap filters tend to have problems. Either way, white balance your camera after you add a filter, because there can be slight color changes caused by all of them.

Building your camera rig

Cinematic cameras are generally "rigged out," meaning various accessories are attached to the camera so that everything can be moved around together. The rig adds stability to your camera just by adding mass, which helps reduce or eliminate micro shudders common when just holding a camera. Finally, the rig looks cool and shows everyone you are a professional (again, I'm just half kidding).

A basic rig starts with a cage around the camera. These can be constructed of modular pieces, or purchased already sized specifically for your camera. This cage provides multiple attachment points for everything else in the rig.

A baseplate that allows one to put the rig down handsfree on a flat surface is standard, and the baseplate is also, in addition, usually a quick-release plate that fits into your tripod. Common, too, is a top handle. This way you can mount the rig on a tripod, but also carry it around handheld. Many times a side handle is added, which gives one extra control in moving and supporting the camera.

Rails are added in order to serve as attachment points for a matte box and follow focus. A monitor is often added, depending upon what is already on the camera. Often a wireless transmitter is attached, in order to send a signal to a separate monitor for the director.

A nice option to add is a single battery to power everything (camera, monitor, follow focus, wireless transmitter, and anything else). Having one battery means it's quick and easy to re-power your rig. A battery mount is often attached to the rails on the back side of the camera, usually for a V-mount battery. Add a D-tap extension to provide extra power ports, and then attach appropriate cables to power each item.

Audio

Good sound has been defined by professional sound mixer Mark Perfetti as "the absence of bad sound." Much of a sound mixer's job entails listening intently for bad sound – sound which is often not recognized consciously by the rest of us. For example, the hum of an AC or refrigerator. It's a mistake to think that success is dependent solely upon using good equipment, for the best equipment will pick up that noise, too. Still, you should use good equipment. So, let's talk microphones.

Sound microphones ("mics") run from cheap ($20) to very expensive ($6,000+), and unfortunately you generally get what you pay for. Sennheiser is a well-known brand, one which impresses when used on set. I admit, I enjoy wearing my Sennheiser headphones, not because they are that good but because "SENNHEISER" is emblazoned prominently across the top headband.

As with other aspects of art, what sound you prefer depends upon what you like. Most professionals prefer recording with "neutral mics" as opposed to those with "added bass." You will find many mics with added bass, that boost the lower end frequencies, in other words, which gives vocals a warmer, deeper sound. You can use such mics and get that sound as you record. Or you can use a neutral mic, and boost the bass to wherever you want it in post – with this approach, you have more control over the finished sound, in post, which is why the professionals lean this way. But for newbie purposes, especially if you don't do much EQ balancing in post, then you may prefer a mic with added bass.

Types of Mics

Sound is carried as energy waves. When these waves strike our ear's tiny bones and eardrum (diaphragm), the vibrations create nerve signals which are interpreted by our brain. Microphones operate much the same, by converting sound waves into signals that can be recorded. There are 3 types of microphones:

"Dynamic" mics are cheaper, durable and common. They work just like a speaker, but in reverse. If you've ever taken off the cover of a speaker, you know you can see the diaphragm vibrate as recorded signals are turned back into sound waves. Really cool stuff. A dynamic mic has a movable induction coil suspended in the field of a magnet, and when sound waves cause the coil to vibrate, those vibrations create electrical signals that can be recorded.

One of the coolest stories ever, when the Beatles taped their song "Paperback Writer" they converted a big speaker into a mic to record Paul McCartney's bass!

Dynamic mics are a good choice in uncontrollable, wilder environments, such as shooting live news events. They reject far off sounds, do a good job on low - mid sound frequencies, and they are durable (in case your mic is knocked down and trampled in a crowd).

Considered about the best mic ever, the Shure SM57 has been used by pros for a long time to record electric guitars and drums – they are best used for such low - mid frequencies. Dynamic mics handle loud sounds and sudden spikes in sound very well, making them ideal for rock music.

Other recommended mics in this category are the Electronics RE20, Sennheiser MD421 and Shure SM7B.

"Ribbon" mics have a thin ribbon of electro-conductive material stretched between the poles of a magnet. They are much less durable, but prized for a warm sound. Because they reduce the harsh high-end sounds, they are best used for guitar amps, brass instruments, and drums. But rough handling and spikes in the sound can damage the ribbon. I've never used one of these mics, and they seem to be uncommon.

"Condenser" mics are the most commonly used in studios and on film sets where you can control the environment. They use a capacitor (condenser) to convert diaphragm vibrations into electrical current. Both dynamic and ribbon mics rely on the physical energy of sound waves, but condenser mics need power to operate – either in the mic itself, or supplied by the recording device (called "phantom power"). Condenser mics are more sound-sensitive than the other types, and produce a louder signal ("higher gain"). They are therefore ideal for vocals, and higher frequency instruments (acoustic guitar, cymbals, piano). Large Diaphragm Condenser (LDC) mics are common in studios, and considered the best for vocals (great example, the Rode NT1A), while the Small Diaphragm Condenser (SDC) aka "pencil condenser" mics are more commonly used by people on the go (great example, Shure SM81).

Condenser mics have selectable polar patterns. In other words, the area from which they pick up sound can be manipulated. Most mics are "omni-directional" – they pick up sounds from around them, equally in all directions. In contrast, mics with a "cardioid" polar pattern will pick up sound from in front, while actively rejecting "noise" (i.e. unwanted sound) from the sides and rear. A "supercardioid" pattern picks up from a smaller, more concentrated area, and "hypercardioid" even more so. "Shotgun" mics are designed to pick up sound more from where they are pointed than sounds from the sides or rear. Shotgun mics are inside "interference tubes", which have side slots cut to reduce off-axis noise; the slots are designed so that off-axis sound enters the slots in a way that actually cancels the amplitude of the waves. The longer the tube, the narrower the field of sound recorded.

"Lavalier" (Lav) mics are small clip-on mics, the type you see on the lapels of reporters. They are omni-directional, prone to picking up noise from the rustling of clothing, and sometimes difficult to hide; however, they do an excellent job picking up the voice of the person wearing it. It's a common approach for film crews to mic each actor with a lav, in addition to using a boom mic to pick up all of the actors together. Lav mics are available with long cables, allowing the actor some range of movement – and even better, there are wireless lav mics which enable the actor to move relatively freely.

Mic Cables

There are two common types of mic cables. Some mics (lavs and cheaper mics, generally) have a thin wire cable which terminates in a 3.5mm jack. More professional mics have wire cables which are thicker (heavier wire gauge, plus better shielding from noise-causing interference), and terminate in a clunky three-prong "XLR connector". There are other differences between these, besides just size.

3.5mm cables generally end in TRS or TRRS connections. Those letters stand for tip, ring, and sleeve. The TRRS connections have two rings, and are usually seen in cellphone and other small devices. The tip and rings carry powered signals, while the sleeve is the ground. These cables are usually used to carry stereo signals.

XLR cables, on the other hand, usually carry mono signals. They are comprised of three wires (2 signal and 1 ground) and therefore could carry a stereo signal. The reason they are usually used for a mono signal is the same reason they make better cables for professional use: in an XLR mic cable, one wire carries a signal and another wire carries the exact same signal but with its sound wave inverted. This is called a "balanced cable." At the receiving end, the proper equipment puts these two signals back together in a way that identifies and eliminates any noise interference that the cable may have picked up. Noise from interference is a bigger issue the longer the cable may be.

If buying an XLR cable, make sure you get one intended for microphone use. Many XLR cables are designed to carry guitar or other music, and are not ideal for lower power mic signals. My current favorite brand is HOSA, as their cables are well-built, with little to no interference noise, and strong connectors.

Mic Models

Top level mics come mostly from a limited number of companies:

- Shure

- Sennheiser
- Schoeps
- Blue
- AKG
- Neumann
- Audio Technica

Here are particular mics I recommend:

$1,000 or so

- Schoeps MK41
- Sennheiser 8040 or 8050
- Sennheiser 416 (used on many film sets)
- Rode NTG3 (the "poor man's Sennheiser 416")
- MKH50
- DPA 4018

$300 - $700

- Sennheiser 600 (love it!)
- Deity S-Mic 2
- Audio Technica AT4053b
- Audix SCX1HC
- AKG Blueline CK93
- Oktava MK012 HC
- Rode NTG4 and 4+

Cheap (under $100) but very usable

- Samson CO2 (good for indoor dialogue)
- Takstar SGC-598 (shotgun for outdoors)

Wireless Lav Mics

Wireless capabilities are no longer just found on professional sets. The prices have come down to very manageable levels. Of course, most of the cheap stuff is garbage. As newbies, we want cool equipment, and we want it cheap because we're always broke! But before you buy a wireless lav mic system, pay close attention to this next point.

The most important thing to understand is that wireless microphones work by sending out and receiving radio signals, and in the physical world of this universe there are only so many frequencies that can be used. Our little world has gotten crowded. As cell phones and other broadband broadcasters have needed bandwidth, the number of frequencies available for us schmucks has been shrunk.

In the US, broadcasting devices (such as wireless mics and walkie talkies) are subject to regulation by the FCC. Over a certain power level, you need a license. Fortunately, no license is needed for wireless mics under 50mW for body-worn transmitters, or 10mW for handheld mics. These low-power transmitters are fine, though distance is typically limited to 50 – 200 feet.

Only certain frequencies may be used. This is very important to focus on now, since the FCC issued new rules that prohibit the use of many frequencies previously available. <u>After July 13, 2020</u> you may no longer legally use any wireless mic that transmits in the frequency ranges of 617-652 MHz and 663-698 MHz. Just year I was using a borrowed Sennheiser G2, which broadcasts in those ranges. That G2 was owned by the Tampa Art Institute Film School. It probably cost them $800 or more when new, and I suspect they invested in many such systems for their students to check out and use on student films. However, after July 13, 2020 those G2 mics might cause problems for their students. There is a way to configure the G2 to use frequencies that are still legal, but will students be careful to do so? Or … one wonders if the school might sell them, perhaps to newbies who don't know they need to be careful?

So, what should you use?

Let's talk frequencies. The electromagnetic spectrum is made up of waves. The "frequency" is a measurement of how many waves are passing by in a given timeframe. Lower frequency means longer soundwaves, and higher frequencies mean shorter. Longer waves are able to go farther distances, through thicker materials, but are subject to more interference. There are three commercially available groups of frequencies used for wireless mics: VHF ("very high frequency"), UHF ("ultra-high frequency") and 2.4GHz (crowded by cellphone users). The frequency ranges used in these groups are as follows:

VHF   49 – 108 MHz and   169 – 216 MHz

UHF   450 – 806 MHz and 900 – 960 MHz

2.4GHz   2.400 – 2.483 GHz

Stay away from both VHF and 2.4GHz systems. VHF systems don't have as many channels as UHF and are more subject to interference that causes background noise in your recordings, and the 2.4GHz frequencies are so crowded by cellphone usage that you will be constantly fighting to find a channel clear of interference. However, VHF and 2.4GHz systems tend to be cheaper than UHF.

The recommended ideal range is UHF 470 – 599 MHz.

I've been using a cheap system by Movo, the WMIC70 that utilizes 48 channels in frequency range of 584 – 608 MHz. Movo no longer makes this system, and instead sells the WMIC80 in about the same frequency range. These systems sell for $140 which includes the transmitter, receiver and lav mic. Many people have complained about the reliability of these mics, but I've always been pleased with their operation.

For comparison, Sennheiser's current model G4 retails for $499. On a set recently, I ran both the G2 and WMIC70 on actors side by side. The end results were about the same for both mics – actually, I think the WMIC70 sounded a tad better. However, you do get what you pay for. The Movo products are more cheaply made and therefore not as likely to last as long as the Sennheiser systems.

Sound recorders

Sound is recorded by most cameras, however that internal sound is generally not good enough. First off, a microphone in the camera is closer to the camera operator than the subject, and therefore likely to pick up noise from the operator; this is why it's common in interviews to hear the voice of the interviewer so much louder than the voice of the subject. Turn up the gain high enough to get the subject, and the sound coming from nearby sources will "peak" (meaning it will exceed the recordable range, and sound horrible).

Internal sound is not without benefit. It can be helpful as "reference sound" because it is already synced to the video image. Most filmmakers, however, do not rely upon it as anything more than reference sound. They use external mics, to get closer to the subject, which then must be recorded on separate machines. The cost of such sound recorders varies from affordable to outrageous.

Common among newbies are models from Zoom and Tascom. I'll let others argue which is best, though I believe they are essentially the same; it just so happens I fell in love early on with Zoom products, and don't know much about Tascom, so I'm just going to tell you about Zoom.

The Zoom H1 (and its newer version H1n) are wonderful staples that are so handy I recommend having more than one. The H1 is an excellent stereo mic by itself, and as such can be used as an interview-style mic or to record ambient sounds. But where the H1 really shines is when an external 3.5mm lav mic is plugged into it, and the H1 dropped into an actor's pocket; this set up provides for excellent recording, wherever the actor goes. (It's a cheaper way, in other words, of getting the benefit of using a wireless mic while avoiding the risk of signal loss!) Brand new, the H1n retails for around $120, and is often on sale for less. Don't worry that it is plastic; mine has held up nicely on many sets.

Zoom makes other recorders. I love my H4n, which records from one or two XLR mics, or from one 3.5mm mic. You can also get a "break out cable" that allows recording of two separate mics on a single 3.5mm port. The H4n can be found used for $100 or a bit more, and retails brand new for about $160.

Both the H1 and H4n are small enough to use with a boom without any complicated sound bag. I started off carrying the recorder on a lanyard around my neck, so that both hands were free to hold the boom. Then I got smart and mounted the recorder directly on the handle of the boom (see DIY tips).

Newbies always want more, right? A nice step up in quality and professionalism is the Zoom F4 which allows input of 4 XLR mic signals, and records separate tracks plus a blended stereo mix, at the same time. The Zoom F4 can be found used under $500 (I got mine for $395 including a nice bag, on eBay). Speaking of which, you need a sound bag, as the F4 is considerably larger and heavier, and is indeed designed to be accessed from "top down" inside a bag. Get a chest harness and the bag won't both your shoulders (as much).

Moving up in cost and quality, and capacity, there are a number of sound mixers with which I sincerely hope to become better acquainted. For example, the Sound Devices 688 recorder / mixer that records 16 tracks from up to 12 input mics at a time! While you can get the Zoom H4n for $200 or so, the Sound Devices 688 is almost $6,000 … and probably worth it (heavy sigh). As a (relatively) affordable but less professional alternative, I am salivating over the Sound Devices Mixpre 6 II, which runs around a $1,000. Slightly more affordable is the Sound Devices Mixpre 3, which has fewer mic inputs so I recommend saving pennies toward the Mixpre 6 II. Sound Devices makes incredibly good equipment. When you get to that level, you're pretty much a "professional" for all extensive purposes.

Headphones

When you are recording sound on set, having a good pair of headphones is crucial. This is so you can listen to your recordings and identify problems in time to fix them. Ideally, you should monitor sound during each take. Often, I will hear something on my cans (slang for headphones) that no one else on set has noticed, for instance the hum of a refrigerator or air conditioner. Conversely, there are times when I'm pleased with the sound but others on set ask, "Did you hear that airplane?" and I'm happy to say, "No, the mic didn't pick it up."

Any headphones will do, while you're a newbie. The best for this purpose are "over the ear" and "closed back", which minimize the sound escaping from the headphones (which you absolutely don't want picked up by the mic) and isolate the wearer from ambient on-set noises. An industry standard for monitoring is the Sony MDR-7506, about $80. Ultimately, whatever fits you best is probably your best choice, given that you will wear them for long hours on end.

Sound Bag

Recording sound on-set requires multiple items, from mics to cables to batteries to gloves to tape…. The gear quickly adds up. It can become unmanageable quickly. How many times have you seen various XLR cables, shockmounts and batteries scattered around on a set? For a professional or newbie, getting your gear organized in a sound bag is a must.

A good bag is self-contained. Meaning, all you have to do is grab the bag and head out to the set; you're good to go. Well, grab your boom pole, too (they rarely fit in bags). Having everything in one bag means you can set that bag down and know precisely where your stuff is. Admittedly, one bag will likely not hold everything you want and need on set – it's good to have a second bag or other storage container that can be kept handy. Think of it as varsity and junior varsity; if an item is important enough, it makes it into the varsity bag you carry with you, while JV sits on the bench.

A basic sound bag holds (1) a recorder/mixer, (2) a shotgun mic, (3) your batteries or power bank, (4) a wireless lav mic system or two, (5) tape to affix a lav mic on an actor, (6) deadcats for the shotgun and lavs, (7) monitor headphones, and (8) good cables.

Professional sound techs on set will have thousands of dollars' worth of equipment with them. Included in the bag of one pro I highly respect (Mark Perfetti) is the following gear:

- Sound Devices 688 Recorder / Mixer – 12 input 16 track recorder ($5,900)
- Schoeps CMC6 shotgun microphone with Rycote Softie ($2,100)
- Sennheiser MKH 416 P48 shotgun microphone with Rycote Zeppelin system and windjammer ($1,950)
- Vandenberg Carbon Fibre Extendable Boom Pole ($900)
- 4 Lectrosonic 411A Digital Hybrid Wireless microphone systems (including transmitters to be worn on the actors, and receivers attached to the mixer ($10,000)
- 2 Sanken Lavalier microphones ($800)
- 3 Tram Lavalier microphones ($900)
- Denecke Smart Slate ($1,400)
- Comtek IFB system with 2 receivers ($1,275)
- BDS power system ($1,600)
- Tentacle Timecode Sync box ($300)
- ElectroVoice RE50 hand microphone ($350)
- Sony MDR 7506 headphones ($100)
- Misc. audio and power cables ($1,000)

Mark's gear is top of the line, what a true professional uses. Do the math; you'll see he has $28,575 in gear, just in the bag he typically takes with him to a set. (Oh, and I forgot to ask him about the bag he uses, but I know it's not a Walmart cheapie!) You can bet Mark has plenty more gear at home, and has probably over the years invested ten times as much into his equipment. However, don't let my obvious equipment envy make you think that Mark is good at what he does because of his equipment; no – Mark is one of the best, because of his experience, talent, and knowledge. When hired, it is Mark's skill that a producer pays for, not just his equipment.

Whew!

Let's get out of the professional world and back to us regular newbies. In comparison, when I'm paid to do sound on set, I take my own sound kit:

- Military surplus hardcase ($20)
- Zoom H4n recorder (used, $100)
- Zoom H1 recorder (used, $100)
- Rode windshield sound blimp with Rycote shock mount ($257)
- On-Stage MBP7000 boompole ($39.95)
- Sennheiser MKH 600 shotgun mic ($349)
- (2) MOVO wireless lav systems ($139.95 each)
- Paladou lav microphone ($17.99)
- Trex BH-1000 headphones ($30)
- Hosa 5' XLR cable ($14)
- XLR to 3.5mm adapter ($12)
- Tape for lavs (incl. KT tape and moleskin) ($30)
- AA batteries (a case of 60 for $22)
- Sm. vice grips ($8)

(I just upgraded my recorder/mixer to the Zoom F4 (used $300), so I'll swap it for the H4n. I've also recently purchased small condenser mics for use indoors, where a shotgun mic sometimes picks up sound bouncing off of walls. The mics I got are the Samson CO2 – really cheap, but amazingly good. I'll have to re-jigger my kit to fit them in. Aye, there's the rub … this is the never ending battle of purchasing and playing with new gear!)

My investment hits around $1,500. Nowhere near the money Mark has in his gear. And, as can be expected, I'm sure my results are nowhere near as refined and dependable as his. Nor are my skills up to his par. When I work, I can expect $100/day for my services; Mark works regularly, all year around, and commands thousands of dollars per day!

By the way, I also carry a second case with my "junior varsity" items. These are my back-up items, that I may or may not need on set but I always want them handy (on set or at out in my car) in case anything on my "varsity team" breaks down. Included in the second case are:

- Takstar SGC-598 3.5mm shotgun mic, with cold shoe shock mount ($25)
- Vidpro XM-55 XLR shotgun mic, with boom pole shock mount ($90)
- Rode Videomic Go 3.5mm shotgun mic ($120)

- Paladou 3.5mm TRRS lav mic, with TRS adapter ($19)
- BOYA 3.5mm TRRS lav mic ($20)
- Sony stereo TRS lav mic ($20)
- Audio-technica AT8415 shock mount ($59)
- Cables:
    - Bosa 10' XLR ($15)
    - 16" XLR patchcord ($10)
    - 12' GLS Audio XLR Pro Series balanced mic "snake cord" cable ($10)
    - 20' Strukture High Performance XLR microphone cable ($9)
    - 30' XLR cable
    - 20' 3.5mm TRS extension cable
    - 10' 3.5mm TRS extension cable (female to male)
    - 10' 3.5mm TRRS extension cable (female to male)
    - 3' 3.5mm TRS male to male patch cord
    - 12" 3.5mm TRS male to male patch cord
    - 24" 3.5mm TRS male to male patch cord
- Adapters:
    - (5) XLR to 3.5mm ($15 each)
    - 6" Y splitter XLR female to female ($10)
    - 6" Y splitter XLR male to male ($10)
    - Hosa YMM-261 6" 3.5mm "breakout cable" for splitting stereo into two mono signals ($5)
    - (2) 6" 3.5mm male to male patch cords
    - (2) TRRS female to TRS male
    - (2) TRRS female to ¼" male
    - (2) 3.5mm TRS y-splitters
- Sennheiser headphones (used, $22)
- Shotgun mic holder for boom pole
- Shotgun mic holder for cold shoe
- Hand grip for mic holder
- (2) foam windshields for shotgun mics
- Sm. deadcat for shotgun mic
- Hard case with SD cards: 2GB (micro), 4GB, 8GB and 16GB (micro), with 2 micro adapters ($50)

You're better off hiring the best sound tech you can afford, rather than trying to put all of this together yourself. But then … where's the fun in that?

Boom Kit

If you're a Boom Operator, you may be able to use the production's equipment, or that of the sound mixer. But you should have your own gear because (1) you will be comfortable with your own stuff and know how to best use it; (2) you know for sure that what you need will be there; (3) you'll be able to charge more for your services; and (4) you as the "person-with-gear" are more likely to be remembered and hired on the next gig than "that-guy-who-uses-our-stuff."

A good boom operator's kit is simple: really just a boom and headphones. A 16-20 foot boom will get you by in just about anything you do, even professional, but sometimes even pros need only a smaller 8-12 foot boom and there's no need to carry the extra weight of the larger boom if you don't need it. So, get both. Honestly, newbies are good just starting out with a 6-9 foot boom for under $50 (Amazon). You may carry cables, but most often the sound mixer will have cables and mic.

Here's advice I've gathered on what to add to a better, more complete boom kit, if you're serious about becoming a pro boom operator:

- Foul-weather bag. You may find yourself on a set where conditions have turned nasty, but the production decides to shoot anyway. A jacket for cold. A rain jacket, and rain pants. A hat. Rain boots or overshoes, which are also good when the producer decides you need to run through muddy water.

- Wireless capability. So nice to maneuver the boom without worrying about cable management, either the cable down the boom or the cable back to the sound mixer.

- C-Stand and boompole holder, so that you have the option of setting the boom up in a fixed position. This works well for interviews and long scenes where there is little to no movement of the actors, and your arm muscles will thank you for the break.

- Blimp (though often the sound mixer has this)

- Stand or cart with clips to store your boompole and mic in between takes, instead of resting it dangerously on the ground or on furniture.

Walkie Talkies (2-way radios)

Film sets rely heavily on "walkie talkies" and you can mostly just pick one up and use it. Just make sure you know how the buttons work! Be aware the U.S. Federal laws apply and the misuse of 2-way radios can come with consequences. I'm not suggesting you need to study the laws. Just use the radios sparingly, and make damn sure you don't use any foul language on air.

Speaking of laws, if you're buying new walkie talkies you will need to pay attention to the recent (2020) FCC regulatory changes regarding which frequencies can be legally used. Rather than repeat myself, check out the section above on wireless lav mic frequencies.

Tips for using a walkie:

- You need a waistband, so don't wear sweats or dresses to work on a set. Some people prefer to clip a walkie to their chest; if that's you, make sure you have a good vest or jacket rugged enough to hold the thing securely.

- You may want to purchase your own "surveillance" earphone / mic because (1) they're fairly cheap (about $30 on Amazon), (2) they are often hard to find on sets, where they tend to break or go missing, (3) it's a matter of individual fit and comfort, and (4) some people aren't wild about putting things into their ears that others have previously worn and sweated upon.

- Test with "Walkie Check", and someone should respond with "Good Check". One response is all that is needed.

- To get someone's attention call, "Brent for Cathy" to which Cathy should respond, "Go for Cathy". If Cathy is busy, she should say, "Standby" until she can say, "Go for Cathy."

- Productions may vary, but generally there will be a channel where everyone should "park" (i.e. stay on by default). When someone calls you, after you respond they will say "Go to channel ___" for any long or detailed talk. Don't chat in the general channel, because that is for quickly connecting team members, or general announcements. When finished with your chat, say "Back to ___"

- Here is a common channel assignment:

  - Ch 1   Production generally (park here)

  - Ch 2   open for private conversation

  - Ch 3   Transportation

  - Ch 4   open for private conversation

  - Ch 5   open for private conversation

  - Ch 6   Camera

  - Ch 7   Electric

- Ch 8   Grip

- "Keying" or "Hot Mic'ing" or "Breather!" all mean that someone has inadvertently left their microphone on, disrupting conversation. Big No No. Do this too often and you will get your walkie taken away, because it's horribly annoying to everyone forced to listen to your exhalations.

- Wait a beat after pressing the talk button before talking, or else your voice may get clipped and you'll have to repeat yourself – in addition to annoying the hell out of everyone else.

- Speak clearly and in short, concise, easily understood language. On air is not the place to wax poetical or recite full chapters of your life.

- Nor is it the place for anything private or confidential, even if you've moved to a "private" channel. Nothing broadcast over public airways is private.

Using walkies is fun. We all played with them as kids, right? But learn to control yourself and be professional. They are valuable tools on set, not toys.

Slate

Literally, a slate (or clapper board) can be as simple as clapping your hands, or writing on any piece of paper of cardboard and snapping your fingers. But you can get a good dry erase slate for less than $20 on Amazon, so why not at least move up to that level? I recommend a brand called Tycka. As you probably know, dry erase boards come in good/better/best levels of quality, and damn near only the top level actually erases as well as you want. I've tried – and *screamed* at – other slates that "ghosted" and became a mess when they wouldn't erase cleanly and easily. Finally, I found the Tycka. You're welcome.

When you're ready, move up to a digital slate. They are soooo cool. But also so expensive. Like $1,000 or more. That's a big jump from a $20 board to $1,000 – one I have not made yet, and perhaps never will.

So, presuming you got a dry erase slate, let me tell you how to trick it out. Get some 1" Velcro with the sticky back. Put a piece of Velcro on the front of the slate, on the lower part of the clapper arm perhaps, and put the matching piece of Velcro wrapped around the dry erase marker. That way your marker is never lost. Put an end to the constant Keystone Cop routine you'll see commonly on all sets: "Where's the marker? Who's got the marker? Come on, it was just here! Where'd it go?"

Put some more Velcro on the back of the slate, and there you can keep various things like a ball point pen, or maybe a small pouch to hold shot lists.

Another thing you will want to do, very likely, no matter what dry erase board you get is fix the bolt that holds the rocker arm. Every slate I've seen suffers from the same design defect, even the Tycka board I love so much. The board comes with a little bolt, and a single nut. As you use the board that nut loosens and before you know it, the nut drops off into a hidden wormhole, never to be found again. And even if not lost, as that nut loosens the arm flops around. To fix this, go to Home Depot and get a locking washer. That way you can tighten the nut to the right tension and it will stay there. By the way, the right tension for me is stiff enough that the arm does not flop open or close by itself, but I can snap it shut easily one-handed.

Another lifesaver: get some eraser caps that go on the end of the dry erase marker. That way you are never looking for (or losing) the eraser.

Finally, I prefer to alter the information on my slates. Most some printed for "Roll", "Scene" and "Take". Well, not many people shoot with actual rolls of film anymore, certainly not me, so I change that to "Card" for the SD card being used. I also add a box for "Shot" because very often you have something like "Scene 5, Shot A, Take 1". You can write "5A" in the scene box, but that gets confusing when you come across a script that has inserted scenes which are typically denoted by alphabetic characters. In other words, your script may have a Scene 5A, and then its confused with Scene 5 Shot A. (Software like Final Draft automatically numbers a new scene this way, so until a better way is found, I avoid confusion by providing a separate box for "Shot" on the slate.)

Hard cases

They appear to be built ruggedly, and many can take plenty of abuse. But! Those cases are meant for containing valuable and fragile equipment. And the cases themselves are expensive. So don't drag or throw them around. Don't be a gorilla.

Carry them up and down stairs – never drag or wheel them. Show some care, and at the same time you won't look like a lazy bum.

On set, no one should touch your gear. But … sometimes people do, especially working around other newbies. Never open a case and walk away, leaving it open or, worse yet, closed but not latched. Soon as you do, some "helpful soul" will pick it up to move it, and your expensive gear gets tumbled out.

Pelican brand cases are widely praised. I use surplus military cases, because they are really rugged and can be found (Craigslist or eBay) cheap.

Staging Area

When you get on set, whatever you are there to do very likely means you have gear with you. You need a place to set up and safely store your stuff. The safest place for equipment is the floor. Not on a couch or table, where it may fall or damage the furniture.

It's good practice to use a thick blanket (for example, the type found in moving vans) on the floor, to both define the equipment area and protect the floor.

Larger productions have actual departments (camera, grip, HMU, production, directors, etc.), each of which have their own trailer, truck, office or cordoned-off area.

Miscellaneous Handy Stuff

Like George Carlin said, "You need a place for your stuff." You always need more stuff, and then more places for your stuff. It's a mad devotion. Embrace the madness.

Tripods

Starting out, any tripod will do. You can do without, and just handhold your camera, but that gets very tiring and your results will be shaky. At some point, you will want to up your footage quality by using a stable tripod.

At a minimum, your tripod must be able to handle the wight of your camera rig. Thin, spindly legs will not carry a heavy camera. Cheap tripods invariably have bad connections. The release levers on legs don't hold, or hold too tightly, or are just designed poorly. The biggest design points to consider for filmmaking are:

First, you need a "Fluid Head" which is often interpreted to simply mean a head that pans and tilts fluidly. However, a true fluid head is actually built with internal pieces that are encased in fluid (oil), which allows you to increase or decrease the tension by controlling the amount of inner hydraulic pressure.

A good fluid head is pricey but worth it, and they are great investments because they last forever and hold their value. Manfrotto makes good fluid heads, at different price points. A fluid head I've heard highly recommended is the Sachtler FSB 8 (about $1,700 on Amazon).

Second, most common tripods have a center shaft that can be cranked up and down. A much better design are those with a pan or "bowl" at the top, in which sits a ball attached to the bottom of the fluid head. With this ball design, one can place the legs anywhere, and then level the camera quickly and easily by adjusting the ball joint. If you've ever tried to level your camera by adjusting the length of tripod legs, you know what an improvement this is. A good one is the Flowtech 75 (about $1,400). Be sure your ball size matches the bowl diameter.

Third, look for a solid baseplate that has a convenient quick release.

To test a tripod head, tighten it down to where it will just allow movement, and then pan and tilt at the same time to see how smooth the movement is. To test tripod legs, how fast and easy can you readjust the height?

C Stands

C Stands (or Century Stands) are extremely handy to have around. You can never have too many. However, they are heavy and awkward to transport, so you don't want to carry more than you need.

Most are silver colored, aluminum or steel construction. Often, they are black. Now and then you find some painted weird colors, mostly for branding purposes.

C Stands allow you to lift items into position. It's as simple as that. For example, flags and diffusers get lifted up between light sources and actors. Sound blankets get hung. Lighting instruments get placed up high. The typical C Stand telescopes up 8 -- 12 feet.

You'll see what you think are super-sized C Stands, extending 20' or higher. These are most likely "combo stands", which are beefed-up C Stands with tripod legs, instead of turtle legs.

"Grip heads" (aka "knuckles" and "gobos") are the joints where you can attach and tighten down on baby pins or extension rods. A "grip arm" generally means an extension rod with a grip head attached.

When you place a C Stand for use, point it's largest leg in the direction of the largest load. That's toward the set, if for example you are mounting a light on an arm extended toward the set. Think about how tippy the stand is, and which direction it would likely tip, and point the largest leg that way. Then put a sandbag on the largest leg; for particularly tippy stands, put sandbag(s) on the other legs, too.

It is important that you learn how to position and tighten the grip heads. Think about the pressure exerted by the weight of whatever is being hung, and make sure that the knuckle turns *toward* the weight, so that if it slips at all it will only be tightening itself.

Flags, reflectors, and diffusers

Another category you can't have too many of. Flags are used to block light, reflectors bounce light to where you want it, and diffusers let light through but alter it.

C Stands got their name because they were designed to hold "Centuries", which are large metal frames with stretched fabric, measuring 100" by 100" (hence the name). You'll see even larger diffusers on big productions.

Drones

I don't have much experience to pass on for drones, though like millions of newbies I think they are totally cool!

From videos and talking to people, and from my own failed attempts, I believe this is truly a "get what you pay for" item. Cheap drones are not worth any amount of money. They are essentially toys that break very quickly, and not at all the kind of reliable filmmaking tool you need.

Mavic Pro is highly recommended. The Spark, perhaps.

Setting up a home photography studio

It's very handy to have the ability to shoot stills or video at home, and easy enough to set up a basic studio space.

The hardest part, generally, is finding the space. You'll need at least 10' in front of a backdrop, at least. A room with 20' would be ideal. Backdrops can be anything that is not distracting. A blank wall works fine, so does a plain sheet if stretched out without wrinkles.

Natural light is wonderful, and a large window opposite your backdrop would be perfect. But more important is your ability to control the lighting. For indoors, I highly recommend LED lights which don't add heat to the room. You can get fairly cheap light kits that come with light stands and dimmers (Amazon).

Add a tripod and you're in business.

When shooting headshots, I've found a nice stereo system helps people feel at home and relax.

Setting up a home sound studio

Setting up your own home audio studio for recording is not hard, and not very expensive at a basic level. Whatever projects you're into, you'll want to be able to accomplish two things. First, you need to be able to record clean audio. And second, you need to be able to listen to the audio and hear it well enough to discern what you want to change, if anything. You want the audio you create to sound good not only on your home equipment, but also when the sound files are sent out to be listened to somewhere else. If it doesn't, you may have some "Mix Translation" issues.

Let's talk first about some principles you need to consider.

<u>Sound Isolation</u> is key. Soundproofing, in other words. Your location may not work at all, if for example you live next to a busy airport or loud 24/7 factory. You need to be able to keep external sounds out. This usually means starting with a semi-quiet location, and then beefing up your studio to make it as isolated as you can.

Windows transmit sound. Thin walls let sound pass through. Attics with thin or no insulation likewise let sound pass through. Your best bet, if external noise is a problem at your location, is an internal room without windows, preferably in your basement or otherwise with a floor overhead – and then of course no one can be walking around up there!

<u>Reverb</u> is another key factor to consider when choosing a studio room and outfitting it. This is the echo you hear as soundwaves bounce off of hard surfaces in your room. In the extreme, you hear a true echo. Usually, though, reverb causes a "hollow" sound, giving a listener a feel for the room. It distracts from your recording, and sometimes isn't even noticeable because you yourself are so used to hearing sound in that room. It interferes with your ability to really hear what your audio sounds like.

There are times when you may want to add a reverb effect into your sound project, but not always, and you need to be able to record without reverb in order to control that effect.

The problem arises from soundwaves hitting hard surfaces, like your walls, floor, ceiling, and even furniture. To minimize reverb, sound studios use soft materials, even going so far as to add soft foam tiles to the walls. Actual sound tiles are expensive, though. You can accomplish much the same thing by adding tapestries (i.e. hanging blankets) and anything else soft on your walls.

<u>Resonant Frequencies</u> is a problem similar to reverb, in that it is caused by your environment. Google what happens to bridges if the wind hits at a certain sustained frequency – it's awesome! But horrible in your studio. A buildup of frequencies occurs in every room, to a degree, based on its size and shape. You'll see this as a low-frequency build up, what you might call white noise. There's not much you can do about it, other than identify it so that you can make sure it doesn't have a bad effect on your ability to listen to audio.

Square rooms exasperate these problems, as opposed to rectangular rooms or rooms with angled walls. Soundwaves in a cube are more likely to build up upon each other as they bounce around. Professional studios built for the purpose will have non-parallel walls, slanted ceilings, padded wall panels, broken up floor plans, and the like, all designed to minimize bouncing soundwaves.

Easy Room Fixes

So, now you're worried that your home studio room isn't good enough. Fear not, there are things you can do.

Hard floors? Put down a carpet, or rugs. On set, we put sound blankets down to kill reverb. At home, you can soften the floors more permanently, and at not too much cost. A ½" thick carpet will cut down on much of the reverb, even if it doesn't cover the entire floor. If you put a rug down, add a pad underneath the rug to improve its sound absorption capacity.

Hard walls? Build some sound panels. Just like a rug, the panels need not cover every square inch of your walls. What they do is interfere with the reflection of soundwaves, so that reverb and resonant frequencies can't bounce back, or at least not build up by bouncing back and forth in your room. Soft panels absorb mid and high frequencies, and disperse low end noise. Hanging fabric on a wall helps, but to be really effective, your panels should be thicker than 2". To stop the low end bass sounds, panels 6" thick are best. There are YouTube videos on how to make sound panels. To me, it looks like many of them are essentially just like hanging a twin size mattress on your wall.

I suppose an ideal sound studio would have no hard surface at all. You should try to add sound panels toward that goal. If you can't or don't want to cover the entire wall, put the panels horizontally, with the middle of the panel at the height of your ears (as you work, whether you work sitting or standing). That way you'll be addressing the issue of sound bouncing back into your ears.

"Bass traps" are triangular foam panels built to fit into the corners of your room. They round out your space, and help stop bass energy from building up.

"Acoustic clouds" are sound absorbent panels hung from the ceiling, and are best angled to bounce whatever sound they don't absorb away from the listening (recording) location.

Speakers

Place your speakers away from walls. Many people mount speakers directly to a wall, or put them on shelves that are on a wall. Problem is, just like the body of a guitar resonates and builds up the sound of each plucked string, by placing speakers on or near walls you are essentially turning the wall into a resonating source of sound. Great for your home theater, perhaps, but not good in your studio. Speakers are built to push sound out in a specific direction, but some amount of sound emanates out from their sides and back; with your speakers against a wall, the sound going out the back causes reverb. Consider adding sound panels behind your speakers, to absorb that unwanted sound.

For your monitoring speakers, you want something that doesn't boost any particular frequency range more than others. Your speakers need to be as neutral as possible. You don't want to use speakers that flatter your work, only to find later that your work doesn't sound good when taken out to others.

There are three important points about Mix Translation, besides buying neutral speakers.

First, to hear what your audio sounds like you need to "push air." Using headphones does not give you a good understanding of what your audio sounds like when it is played over speakers (pushing air). You need to listen to speakers, not headphones. Even cheap speakers will give you a better sense than headphones.

Second, headphones are very helpful when you are putting your dialogue together. They will reveal problems that you would not otherwise hear.

Third, know how your system translates. Know the strengths and weaknesses of your speakers.

Often recommended are Genelec 8030 speakers (Amazon), but they are costly.

PART VII: TROUBLESHOOTING

Mistakes newbies frequently make

This book is designed to identify and help you avoid mistakes, and so you will find detail on these subjects in other sections, but let's run through mistakes newbies commonly make.

Framerate

Don't film at 30fps, or 50 or 60. Film at 24fps (which, technically, is 23.976fps – if your camera has options for both 23.976 and a true 24, select 23.976). This is the US cinema standard, and will give you the most cinematically beautiful look. You can film at different rates for particular effects once you learn how to get those effects.

ISO

Don't push your ISO up too high. Every camera has a base ISO rate, and you should keep it there. If you have insufficient light, adding more light is your best answer, not raising the ISO because that increases the amount of noise in the image.

Auto Settings

People get fancy DSLR cameras and then keep them set on fully automatic, mostly because they fail to learn how to use manual settings. Take the time. Learn. Autofocus on most cameras "breathes" in and out, meaning you can see the focus go in and out, as the camera readjusts. This is unacceptable for film. Use manual focus, even if you do have to film multiple takes. You'll also get the cinematic images you want only once you've learned how to adjust your aperture and lights.

Bad Exposures

Use a histogram if your camera has that option. Don't trust your eyes to tell you if the exposure is good. A histogram should fall in the middle of the graph, not peaked too far left or too far right.

Color Grading

You're missing out if you are not color grading your footage. It should be a natural step in your editing. Even the best footage will look better once it has been color graded. For best results, film in LOG, and then color grade. Alternatively, if you're not going to grade then don't film in LOG – but seriously, do film in LOG and then color grade.

Not Using Light

Take advantage of existing light. Film with natural light, or use the existing lights in your house. Too many newbies put themselves in situations where they are trying to cancel out the existing light, instead of taking advantage of it.

Bad Audio

You want your audio levels to record at approximately -12Db. Lower or higher will give you bad results. Get an external microphone, and a sound recorder so you can monitor your sound levels as your film.

Shaky Footage

Handheld cameras are subject to shaky results that come from hand tremors. Very annoying. There are many ways to stabilize your rig. Some cameras and lenses have built-in stabilization. Generally, the larger and heavier your camera rig, the less susceptible it is to the shakes.

Bad Song

Many newbies edit everything, and then choose a song for a soundtrack. Instead, you will do much better if you choose the song, and then edit to that song. Time your cuts and the movement in your takes with the song.

Forgetting your Story

Good footage is not really good, if it fails to move your story forward. Newbies get caught up in technical details, too often forgetting the story. Make your story king.

Labels

People don't mark their equipment and it goes missing. A set is an easy place to lose track of things. Put your mark on them. Some people use a label machine, others mark with a Sharpie. I prefer a paint pen (Amazon).

Not charging

Know the value of your services and charge accordingly. You've invested in equipment that someone hiring you would otherwise have to rent; ordinary course stuff might be part of your daily rate, or you might charge for particular equipment, but either way make sure you consider getting a return on your investment of both your time and equipment.

Get help

You don't have to bite off everything and chew it by yourself. Don't be afraid to get help, and to limit your services to your expertise. For example, if your client asks you to record a voiceover when that's not your thing, then recommend a friend. Or do it yourself, but subcontract out to a friend, or some company like www.fiverr.com.

Plan

Do your prebiz. Don't try to wing it without preparing. Your reputation will take a hit if you do. Make a shotlist. Make storyboards. These things help your shooting day flow well, and also help you edit.

Use contracts

The handshake deal approach works fine, until it doesn't and then you have no recourse. Contracts protect everyone involved. Insisting on contracts doesn't mean you don't trust people; on the contrary, it shows your professionalism and should inspire a greater level of trust in you. Just be sure your contracts are fair to both sides.

Don't ever compete on price

Undercutting your competitors on price does nothing but encourage them to do the same to you, and that way you all spiral down. Cutting your rate will lead you to give a less-than-wholehearted commitment to doing your best. Know your value and insist upon it. Have confidence in yourself. Charge accordingly. Show your clients that they should hire you because you are the best value, not the cheapest.

Fixing Bad Productions

The next part is intended to be a quick-reference "help me" section. Again, there are many more details on these subjects in the rest of the book, but this is a quick-fix list.

Bad Script

I'm tempted to say, there's no fix for a bad script and you should throw it away. That may be too strong, but you definitely need to address script problems long before you move forward with filming. As a writer, I think the script is the single most important item. It is possible that you can make a good movie without a good script, at least theoretically, but I wouldn't bet on that unless you and your cast are reeeeally good at improv filming. Why do so many films and tv shows fail? To me, it seems like most of them are rushed into production when they clearly needed another re-write or two.

Bad Actors

Face it, some people can act, others cannot. Don't put your friends in, unless they can act. Work with your actors – see if they can improve – with the right attitude and plenty of hard work, they should be able to. They need to break down their scenes, to understand the subtext of the dialogue and action. Help them understand how their character fits into the whole production, what they need to bring out in the character to move the story forward and help the other actors. You can usually help them best, by asking them what they are doing and why, at each beat. Keep it positive; don't berate, don't criticize, because that will make them more nervous and less likely to deliver a good performance.

Bad Director

(Are you the director? Many of us newbie filmmakers automatically put ourselves into this position just because we can. But ask yourself, honestly, is that where your strengths lie, or should you turn the reins over?)

Directors often act like kings on set. It helps, sometimes, to remind them subtly that the producer is "boss." Even if the director is king, s/he needs good people skills or the set will fall apart. Successful directors are almost always very good at pleasing people, getting extra bursts of energy out of even the most tired crew at the end of a day. Directors need to delegate. Perhaps a struggling director can benefit most with a competent 1AD.

Bad Video

In the old days, film cannisters had to be sent off for developing so no one on set even knew if the footage was recorded, let alone how good it was. Then video came along to assist film, and now most productions are entirely digital. One obvious benefit is the ability to immediately play back what was just recorded. Check your footage, make sure you like the results. It's helpful to set up a "video station", which is a monitor set up nearby where you can see exactly what the camera sees, even as it is filmed. Pay attention to framing, lighting, composition, and dead spots.

Technically, digital video cameras tend to either record as designed, or they don't work at all. But if you see flickers or bad spots, check all connections. Check your framerate and shutter speed, also, because you may be getting interference with a light or other electronic item.

"Moire" is the effect resulting from some video censors trying to pick up small repetitive patterns, like the weave of a houndstooth suit jacket. Avoid such clothing.

Some cameras are better in low light than others. Test yours. If you don't like the results, avoid those shooting situations.

Bad Sound

There are many technical reasons you may be getting bad sound. Bad mic, bad sound recorder, bad boom handling, bad sound practice, or bad cables (broken or just loose connections).

- Mic – to some degree, you get what you pay for; although I recommend the TAKSTAR SGC-598 that costs less than $25. On a quiet day at home, test multiple mics in the same situation, and see if your problem exists with all or only some. Search the name of your mic on YouTube, to see what others say about problems. Make sure your mic is "on" with a battery if required, or that you have phantom power.

- Sound Recorder – I love the Zoom recorders, lots of people like Tascam. Test at home. Most drain battery power faster than you'd imagine, so test with new batteries.

- Boom Handling – on most sets, the boom is entrusted to a junior person who likely has little to no experience. Test your boom set up – you will probably note that all sorts of rustling sounds and even big sharp bangs get recorded from movement or contact with the boom. Shifting your hands on the boom can cause bad sound; some booms have a rubber or foam hand guard to handling sounds, and some boom operators wear smooth cotton gloves. Of course, hitting the boom or mic into anything also results in loud noise. The shotgun mic should be held as close to the actor's forehead as the frame allows, if booming from above, and the operator needs to keep it pointed at the subject. Even movement of the boom through air causes noise – if that's your issue, get a good deadcat or blimp and tell your boom op to move slower and more smoothly.

- Bad Sound Practice – Too many times, sound is an afterthought. Getting good sound doesn't get as much attention as it deserves. Productions grab just anybody handy, and tell them they are doing sound. A good sound person is well worth courting. Think about sound at all times, listen actively to surrounding sounds (like airplanes), which it is easy for the cast and crew to not even notice. Turn off nearby noise-makers, like ceiling fans, the kitchen fridge, the AC, etc.

- <u>Bad Cables</u> – proper audio cables have internal shielding which is designed to reduce interference from atmospheric radio waves and other sources that create static. Good cables are worth the price charged. Read reviews carefully. If your problem is just loose connections, you're lucky; you can usually fix those yourself. Learn how to correctly coil audio cables, so that you don't introduce internal twists that ruin the shielding. Take care of your cables – don't let people step on them!

- <u>Recording Super Loud Sounds</u> – sometimes you can turn your gain down, and turn on whatever limiters and filters you have, but the sound of, say, an explosion or a rocket engine is just too loud and your sound gets clipped. If you do this a lot, there are "inline pad" attenuators you can buy. But if you do this rarely, or on the spot need a fix, here's a work-around. Instead of "mic" use the "line" input. Your recorder's preamps will expect a much hotter signal coming from the line input, which will give you a greater amount of headroom before the sound clips.

Or your sound could be technically fine, but still sound bad because the script dialogue is flat and boring, or stupid, or your actor has delivered the lines poorly.

If you have bad sound in a piece you've already filmed, there are some things you can do to clean up the sound, using programs like Adobe Audition. You can, hopefully, remove some background noise, static, hiss, and the like. But if the sound is really bad, you may need to either (1) refilm, or (2) record ADR (alternate dialogue replacement), which is the process of re-recording your actors in a sound studio as they do their best to match the visual footage. You can also Foley it: add sound effects for incidental sound sources, like footsteps or a car driving by.

Bad Money

HA! As if there is such a thing, right? What I mean, actually, is no money, or not enough. Which is a problem we all have. Best advice I've heard, film within your means. Don't set out to film a blockbuster that you know will cost millions if you have only pennies. My good friend, actor and musician Keoki Trask, would disagree; he has many examples of succeeding despite bad odds, and would tell you to follow your dreams, "Damn the torpedoes!" Okay … but maybe hedge your bets, too.

Crowdfunding has become a possible source of funds. Try it; can't hurt. The successful campaigns seem to be those with a heartfelt video, introducing yourself and your project, and explaining why you feel the production should be done. Pull at heartstrings.

Some people max out credit cards and mortgage homes. Yikes. Please don't. If you can't convince other people to invest in you, then you might not be ready. Start smaller, build up, until you have a few strong pieces that impress people enough to loosen up their purse strings.

Bad Audience

You like your film … but the audience reaction was less than stellar? There are bad audiences. Don't freak out, right away. Screen your film for others. But also pay attention to reactions, good and bad – make mental notes, and you may consider changing your film. Hollywood routinely screens films in advance of release, and may require even major changes (or not release at all).

Bad Marketing

Marketing is a luxury long denied to indie filmmakers, because only major studios could pump out the millions needed to air commercials, publish newspaper ads, or put up billboards. Then the Internet happened! You can now market your film for very little, even free. The trade-off, however, is that desktop publishing is often lame. Are you creating this stuff yourself? You may have to acknowledge that others can do it better. Making the most of Facebook or Instagram is an art in itself, practically a fulltime job – find someone good at it to help you.

Bad Trailer

A trailer for a film (or commercial for a tv show) is like a short film, and you should spend the time necessary to make it good. Please don't pull the best footage out of your project and show that! Don't tell the story. We've all seen too many trailers that leave us asking, "Why should I go see that, since it seems like I just saw the whole story?" Or we feel disappointed sitting in the theater, realizing that the best scenes were in the trailer.

Your trailer should have people excited about seeing more. Tease them. Trust that you can start simple, and merely hint at what is to come.

Bad Poster

Got name actors? Okay, put them on the poster and market the hell out of the fact that you got them. Otherwise, create a poster that evokes the emotion of your film. It should draw people in. Think about hinting at your theme.

Bad Food

I often think there's too much focus on food when making a movie. The mission is the film, not eating. You can't expect people to work all day long without food and drink, but personally I set the standards pretty low. For myself, and for my productions. When I'm an actor on set and the food is something very nice, I can appreciate it, but I don't expect that, either. Cheap pizza is fine. If your cast and crew are complaining, find different people to work with, people who aren't so difficult to please.

Afterall, most jobs don't include food. 99% of people eat breakfast before work, then take a break to go buy lunch, and then eat dinner at home. I understand that film shooting schedules often don't match up to regular 9-to-5 working hours, and on long days I totally agree with the need to stop for refreshments. But let's all focus on the real mission: making a great film.

Doughnuts, coffee, and some yogurts makes for a fine breakfast. Cold cut sandwiches for lunch. Cheap pizza for dinner. Nothing wrong with this menu. Affordable, easy to obtain and set out, easy to clean up.

PART VIII: DO IT YOURSELF

There is much to be said about the wisdom of buying good gear, since you are then buying the research and development done by others. However, many of us newbies are forced by budgetary concerns to make do with what we have.

The following are suggestions for how you can save some bucks. No one likes spending money unnecessarily, right? Also, by trying the DIY approach, you can often learn more than if you had just purchased the proper item. And … you'll have a better appreciation for the proper item when you do finally get it!

Fake Blood

Making and using fake blood is easy, on the one hand, in that there are various DIY recipes and pre-made solutions you can buy, but on the other hand sometimes very tough to get looking just right. You might accept fake-looking blood in a comedy, in fact it might heighten the comedy, but if you want realism the wrong color or texture of the blood can take your audience out of the scene.

If filming in black and white, you can get away with using chocolate syrup. Yes, this is actually how they did it on old tv shows. Chocolate syrup has good consistency, good tone, and it splatters convincingly. It's readily available, cheap, it will wash out of clothing, and your actors won't complain about getting it all over them. Even if you're filming in color, you may consider using chocolate, and either show the bloody scene in a B&W insert for effect, or else add a dramatic color overlay on top of the scene in post.

Many places (Amazon and elsewhere) will sell you ready-made blood solutions. Most are made with red food coloring, so heed this warning: the marketed blood products will likely stain clothing, hands, carpets, walls, you name it. Even those that say they are fabric safe! When I use such blood products, I do so outdoors, and I just expect to throw the clothing away.

You'll find most blood is very thin, very runny. For some uses, thin is perfect – for example, if you are running it through a pump and hose lines, to squirt into the air, or to show it quickly spreading on clothing, or the classic expanding puddle under a body on the street. But sometimes you want to show a bloody wound, as if the blood has congealed. You can thicken fake blood with corn syrup, corn starch, or even flour. For small amounts, try fudge topping, which also darkens the blood in a way I really like. You can buy thick blood "gel" that is good for applying to makeup where you want the look of a deep cut, without the blood running.

There are several recipes for DIY blood:

- In a pinch, just use red food coloring.

- Tomato juice is good when you need a large volume. Darken it with chocolate syrup or blue food coloring.

- Ketchup (catsup) is good, and again, darken it if you want. You can thin it with water.

- For a really neat bleeding effect, purchase a bottle of potassium thiocyanate, and a bottle of iron chloride (III). Both are powders. Mix small amounts of the powder with water in separate containers. Rub the potassium thiocyanate solution on your skin; it's colorless, and barely noticeable. Then put your fake knife (or whatever you're using) into the iron chloride solution and get the blade wet. When you slide that wet blade over your skin, as the two solutions mix a chemical oxidation reaction occurs – totally painless! – that makes it look as if you are cut and bleeding. People will swear the knife is slicing the skin, it's that convincing. For you chemists, the reaction is $FeCl_3 + 3KSCN \rightarrow Fe(SCN)_3 + 3KCl$. Both compounds can be purchased on Amazon, for around $30 each. (These compounds are nice adds to your makeup kit, since you can mix them together with some corn syrup for just about any use.) Keep this stuff away from your eyes!

Shotgun Microphone

Some microphones pick up sounds from all around ("equidistant" or "omnidirectional"), while shotgun mics are meant to be aimed at the intended source. To some degree, shotgun mics avoid picking up sound from other angles. The better (more expensive) shotgun mics also take in sounds from the side and actively reduce that noise.

Sennheiser is considered one of the top brands. Super expensive. Deity and Rode are highly recommended as cheaper brands, although you should still expect to pay hundreds of dollars.

My tip? You won't believe how good a super cheap mic can be until you test the TAKSTAR SGC-598. I bought in on Amazon for $21.97 simply because I was curious about claims I'd heard and the online reviews. What a delightful find. I've compared it to Rode products, and while I suppose there are audio experts out there that can be more discerning, to my ears the Takstar did an excellent job. I've used it three times now on short film projects, even once preferring it to a proffered Sennheiser!

Lavalier Microphone

A "lav" mic (or "lavalier") is the little thing you frequently see clipped to someone's collar, very often used for interviews. They are omnidirectional, and notorious for picking up all sorts of extraneous sounds that you don't want, whether other people talking or just the rustling of clothing. You can put mini deadcats on them, which will help with the sound but tend to be very visible then. Another way to minimize noise is to use gaffer's tape to secure the mic (to skin or clothing) so that it can't move around.

Cheap but good brands include Movo and Boya. You can get them for $20 or so.

Wireless lav mics are a wonderful convenience, and there are many super cheap options on Amazon as low as $50. However, most of the cheapies are probably not worth the risk of getting bad sound from interference problems.

Make your own "lav blimp" for windy outdoors by cutting off the foam tip on a makeup swab, wrap in gauze, and then cover in the cut-off fingertip of a knit glove.

Sound recorder

A cheaper way to go wireless with your sound, or at least allow your actor to move around without being under a boom mic or tied to a long audio cable, is to use a small recorder (such as the Zoom H1) with a lav mic. You just drop the recorder into the pocket of your talent. You can get the H1 used for under $100 on eBay or Craigslist, and they're not much more brand new.

Boom

A boom is any pole used to hold a microphone out toward or above the actor. It allows a microphone to be held just out of the frame but as close to the actor as possible (whether above, below, or adjacent to the actor).

The boom usually telescopes, though not always. I began with a fishing pole as a boom, and it worked sufficiently. Since you can now buy relatively cheap booms, I suggest you do so rather than suffer the laughs I got using a fishing pole.

I have a friend who uses a $2,000 carbon fibre boom, and WOW! It is so light and easy to wield! But I do fine, thank you, with a $50 RODE boompole (Amazon).

Most booms are about 8 feet long, which is a manageable length for shooting most scenes.

Boompole Holder

Most times, a boom is Hollywooded (held in the hands), but there are times when it is nice to set the boom up on a stand. For this, you need a boompole holder. Amazon has a perfect one for only $20: brand name ATian.

Use a C Stand (century stand) or a heavy duty light stand, and add a sandbag for stability. You'll also need to rig some means of attaching the boompole holder to the stand. I've seen (and I've invented) some goofy looking contraptions. To do it right, get a swivel head adapter (about $30 on Amazon) either in plastic, or even better, aluminum.

DIY boompole attachment for recorder

On small / indie film sets, the sound engineer is often also the boom operator. Holding the sound recorder and the boom at the same time is challenging.

I first tried wearing the Zoom H1 recorder or its bigger cousin, the Zoom H4n, on a lanyard around my neck while filming with a shotgun mic on a boom. That way I could start the recorder, and then use both hands to hold the boom. This works. But the lanyard is awkward, interferes with wearing headphones, and it's difficult to see the recorder to check sound levels during recording.

So I decided to attach the recorder to the boom. I bought a Small Rig 7" Magic Arm on Amazon for about $20. That works, but it adds weight on the boom and although it looked cool, I found no real advantage to being able to reposition the angle of the recorder. Also, the clamp would sometimes slip, and it didn't take long before the round black knob in the center broke (plastic!) and I had to rebuild it with a metal finger nut from Home Depot.

So I ditched the Magic Arm and instead came up with a simple DIY solution that I've been very happy with since.

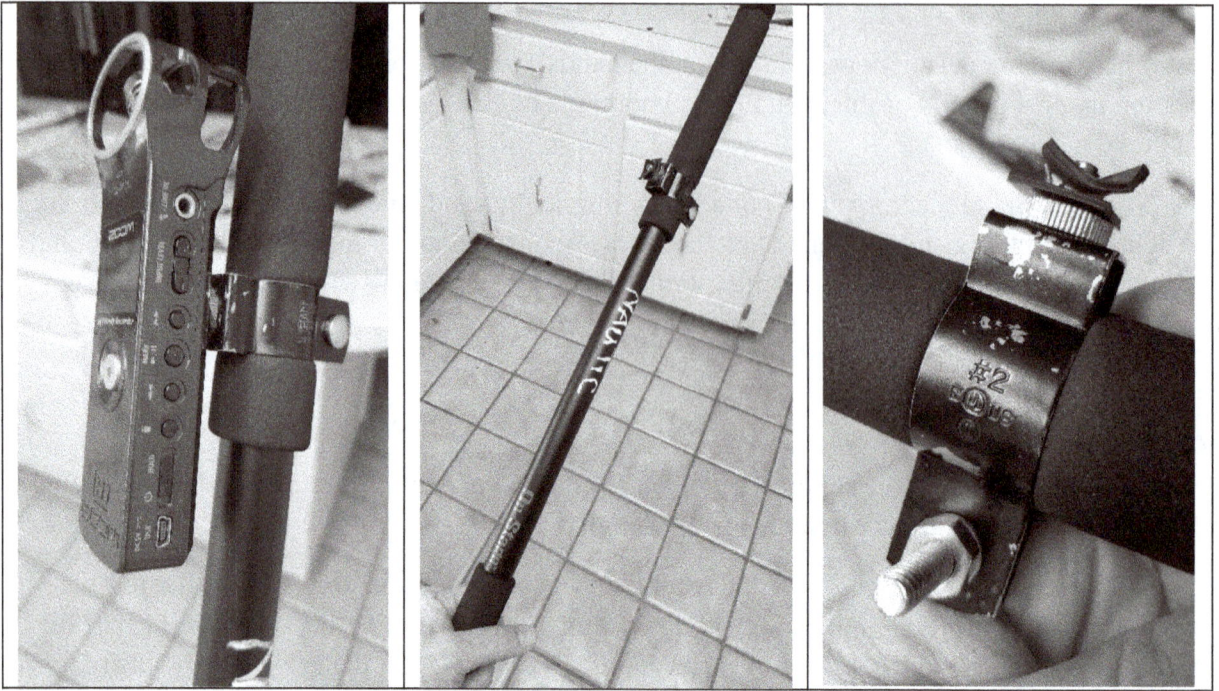

Buy

- Home Depot #2 conduit hanger (in electrical section) only 80 cents

- ¼" lock washer
- 3/8" lock washer
- 3/8" to ¼" adapter
- Black spray paint (optional)
- ½" square rubber sheet (cut from a freebie event bracelet)

I first spray painted the conduit hanger black, for no reason other than I wanted the end result to look less like a Home Depot DIY project and more like "professional" gear. I let it dry and then baked it for a few minutes at 200 degrees in the oven just to be sure.

It comes with a ¼" bolt and nut. I added a ¼" lock nut washer so that I could finger-tighten the nut and hope it stayed in place. (I later replaced the nut with a finger nut, so I can tighten without tools – but actually, since I clamped this over the foam grip already on the boom, the whole thing can be adjusted by rotating the foam grip instead of loosening this nut.)

The conduit hanger already has a hole in its end, perfectly placed for our use. I found the hole was a bit small for the 3/8" adapter I already owned, so I drilled the hole out to make it fit. You can use several things to attach your recorder, and in fact after I drilled mine I realized I had a ¼" to ¼" adapter that would have fit fine without drilling. You may also want to consider mounting with a cold shoe of some sort. Whatever. Anything that ends up with a ¼" bolt sticking up from the conduit hanger.

Because I did not use a cold shoe with locking washer, I added a small piece of rubber as a homemade washer. I just cut a ½" piece from a rubber bracelet and punched a hole in the center with my pocketknife. This bit of rubber allows me to screw the recorder down firmly and line it up with the boom pole, too.

Since I already had a can of paint, and the 3/8" adapter, and a rubber bracelet, this whole build cost me less than $2 in materials from Home Depot.

I've used it on several sets, and remain pleased. The clamp holds firmly in place, doesn't rattle or cause any noise, and the whole thing is easy to rotate on the boom when I want to adjust the angle of the recorder.

Best $2 project ever.

Clapboard

You can make or use almost anything as a clapboard. Some people, caught without a board, just clap their hands – that works, though not ideal. Dry-erase boards are cheap, so get one (or two).

Beware, though: cheap boards are often made of poor material that doesn't erase well. It "ghosts" (shows the prior marks) and smears. So frustrating on set! If you buy a cheap board and it doesn't work well, give it to your niece for her puppet shows and get a better board. I've tried a few and the cheap one I'd recommend is made by TYCKA, available on Amazon for $15.99. It erases well. It also has a built-in magnet on the arm, which helps create a crisp snapping sound when slating. And it's hardware is easily adjusted.

Many boards (including the TYCKA) are designed so that the part you write upon can be pulled apart from the clap arm, to facilitate left or right-handed clapping. I hate this (perhaps because I'm a righty and have no sympathy for lefties?) and therefore I glued the board into the bottom part of the clap arm (of course, the arm still swings). Also, the bolt holding the swing arm very often fails on these cheap boards; opening and closing repeatedly works the nut loose, and before you realize it, the nut gets lost. The solution to that is easy: add a locking washer (10 cents at Home Depot), and you might even want to hit the nut with a drop of glue.

Another wonderful improvement is to stick a piece of Velcro on the board, matched to a strip around your dry-erase marker. This allows you to keep the marker with the board at all times, and minimizes the frantic searching on set for the damn thing.

Likewise, get an eraser cap for the marker, so that you're never searching for an eraser. Only $6.30 (set of 6) on Amazon.

Brooklyn Reflector

Reflectors are, literally, anything that reflects light. You can use anything. Here's a cheap but effective idea.

All you need is white foam board (1/4" thick), spray adhesive (3M 77 is good), tin foil, and a credit card or other squeegee.

Spray the glue lightly on the dull side of the foil. Also spray the board. Flip the foil over and drop a corner onto a corner of the board, then squeegee to get the rest of the foil as flat as possible. Then trim the edges, and you're done. (I also put gaffer's tape around the edges, for looks primarily, and that addition adds a bit of professionalism.)

This gives you a reflector with both a white side and a metallic silver side. Something handy when you need it, works great, light weight and easy to store, and best of all you can beat it up and easily replace.

These boards are also great for branding! Put your logo, company name, or film name on them and then watch as they get held up everywhere.

Cell Phone Cameras

Most cell phones these days have a very good camera built in, with good video recording capabilities ready at your fingertips. Even professional photographers say, "The best camera is the one you have with you when you need it" … and often what you have handy is your cell phone.

You can easily research the best cell phone cameras. I am an Android fan, but I'm not going to get into particular phone models – for the simple reason that new phones are coming out onto the market constantly.

I won't argue that iPhones suck or Android is better – far be it from me to get into that fray! – but let me point out one extreme advantage of Android where (to date) iPhones have failed miserably: the ability to record directly onto a separate SD card. Apple forces iPhone users to purchase the phone with a certain amount of internal memory – they make more money that way. But my Android lets me add cards. I carry multiple micro SD cards to use with my Android, which means (1) I can film almost unlimited video (well, about 10 hours with the cards I currently own, and I can't imagine needing more than that unless maybe if I was traveling), and (2) I can transfer the video files out of my phone simply by removing the SD card and uploading it directly into my computer, in a fraction of the time it takes other phone users to upload into a cloud or through some awkward intermediary device. Believe me, you will see how important this point is, the first time you are on a trip and realize your memory if full but you don't have Wi-Fi.

Not all phone cameras are good for video. Add the "FILMIC PRO" app. It costs a bit ($14.99 when I last got it), but the controls and options this app adds to the video you can record on most phones is totally worth it.

Holding your cell phone can be difficult as you film. Get a rig. I'm very happy with the $10.99 Zeadio rig I got on Amazon. It's just a plastic handle, but it allows you to video with your phone in a more controlled manner, that eliminates much of the jerky movement and awkwardness. The rig also provides a convenient place to mount light(s), a small shotgun mic, and even the H1 sound recorder.

Memory

Computer memory has in recent years become cheaper and cheaper, while at the same time faster and faster. This is a great thing for photographers and videographers!

Micro SD cards have become so cheap, you should carry extras. Most recently, I bought Samsung 64GB 100MB/s (U3) micro SD cards on Amazon for only $11.99 each. Be sure to check your device specs, to see what size cards are compatible; some older devices won't use a card larger than 32 or 64GB.

Regular-sized SD cards are also affordable, enough so that you should carry a large number with you. Filming on my G7, I almost always use a 32GB card which allows for 2 – 3 hours of video (depending on resolution and frame rate settings). I carry several more cards in a hard case (many of which are available on Amazon for $12 or so), and I've never had to stop filming for lack of memory.

SD cards are becoming a standard media for video, but there are cameras that require other cards. For example, my Blackmagic URSA (which I love!) records onto C-Fast cards. While coming down in price, C-Fast cards are still quite costly – at last check, a name-brand 128GB card is $400! C-Fast cards are so expensive, that I've rigged my camera (as have many others) to record directly onto an external hard drive, which I can purchase for half the cost, or less.

Batteries

I've also never had to stop filming on set for lack of camera batteries, although I have unfortunately been on many sets where that was a problem. Carrying extra camera batteries is a must. For example, I have 8 batteries for my G7! So many is overkill for a single day's filming, since I can count on a couple hours from each battery, but I'd rather have the comfort of being over prepared than under. Batteries for the G7 are $20 each, or so, which makes a collection of them not such a horrible investment.

Fill Lights

Small lights can help, and they're cheap. For recording with cell phones or DSLRs, I recommend the Ulanzi LED 49 Dimmable, available on Amazon for just $12.95. They run a long time on AA batteries.

Using Practicals

It's great to have practicals (lights existing in your set), but often they need adapting. If too bright, switch to a lower wattage bulb. Change the look of the light, if you want, by getting a different bulb. For example, swap an incandescent with a day-light LED.

It's very handy to carry dimmers with you.

If you have no dimmer, and a light is too bright, try these ideas:

- Diffuse with paper. Any paper may work, though be careful it doesn't burn.
- Tin foil will allow you to shape and control the light coming off of a bulb.
- Window screen can be cut to shape and makes a nice scrim.
- Cut both bottom and top off of a tin can, and you can put it over the bulb.
- Clamp gel around the bulb (with C-47s)

Dimmers

Make your own dimmers with Home Depot / Lowes' products. Easy enough project, although attempt this only if you have some skill in wiring electronics.

Barndoors

Cardboard and gaff tape are all you need to make your own barndoors. However, cardboard will burn, so this will only work with LED lights that don't heat up.

Get yourself some black foil. It can be arranged around a light, and will not burn. It's also reusable. Unfortunately, it's a bit expensive. If you and some friends purchase a roll together, you'll get a great deal since you can share a roll; you really don't need to carry much with you.

Pelican Cases

Nothing beats having good, strong, dependable hard cases to protect your gear. And they come in handy for things to sit on, too.

True Pelican cases are expensive. Look instead for military surplus cases. I got six cases for $100 from someone on Facebook Marketplace. Those cases have been life savers, both in storing my equipment and – even more helpful – carrying my stuff around, like the filmmaker's version of a corporate lawyer's briefcase.

Gaffer's Tape

Duct tape is the world's answer to almost any situation. Just witness the multiple episodes about duct tape on *MythBusters*! But on set, please don't use duct tape. It leaves a horribly sticky residue behind that is miserable to remove. It will also, very likely, strip paint and cause other problems.

Use real gaffer's tape, which is designed to hold well and also release well, without gummy residue or pulling off paint (in most situations). You can also write on gaffer's tape; it's a cloth tape, perfectly suited for labels. White and black are most common, though it comes in many colors.

Finding gaffer's tape can be hard since it isn't carried at Home Depot or other common stores. And it is expensive compared to the cost of common duct tape. Some sources charge as much as $30 for a single roll, plus you may pay extra for shipping. But whatever the cost, using real gaffer's tape is worth it.

Luckily for you, I can tell you where to buy real gaffer's tape at a great price. So good, in fact, that this single tip alone more than repays you for buying this book. Amazon, of course: the tape I love is called "Gaffer Power" and it's only $13.88 / roll.

Greenscreen

You can find fairly cheap greenscreen fabric on Amazon. Typically, a 10x20 foot cloth with run $20 - $30. You can get rolls of paper, also, and it's not that expensive. Both cloth and paper have their own challenges; paper gives you a smoother, more uniform screen, without the wrinkles that are hard to stretch out in the fabric; however, paper is harder to move around without creasing it, and once creased then it stays creased. (Both wrinkles and creases create shadow points that can interfere with the chromakey process.)

If you want to cover a large space with greenscreen, perhaps even your entire set, you should use paint. Don't buy special greenscreen paint. Just go to your local paint store and have them mix the paint for you, like they would any other color. Any green can be selected in the editing process for removal, but you'll get the best results using the actual chromakey color, which is Pantone 354 C.

For small projects, get green poster board at Walgreens, or hobby stores like Michael's.

Greenscreen full body morph suits are available on Amazon for around $30. They tend to run small, so get a size larger than you typically wear. If you wear a smaller morph suit, the fabric gets stretched so much that the weave opens up, which allows colors to come out from underneath. Better to have a larger suit, even if that does result in less-than-ideal wrinkles.

Stinger

A "Stinger" is what most people would call an extension cord. However, there are all sorts of cords that extend power and/or signals on set, so we say "stinger" to be clear, and to sound cool.

Your usual extension cord from home, or from Home Depot, is good enough for many. But, not safe in all situations, because such cords are almost always 14/3 wire. That wire is not big enough to carry the voltage you need. It could actually start a fire. Film equipment (especially large lights) can draw more power than normal household-use cords are rated for.

A stinger should be made of 12/3 SJOOW wire. That's 12 gauge, 3-stranded (hot, neutral and ground) wire that's rated S (service) J (junior, meaning it can handle up to 300 volts) OO (oil resistant) and W (water resistant). A cable marked SOOW can carry up to 600 volts.

Stingers on set are usually 25', 50' or 100' long. You lose 5 volts over the length of each 100' cord – something to keep in mind.

You can buy stingers, or make them. If you choose to make them, you'll need the 12/3 SJOOW wire, and a male and female plug for the ends (Leviton is a good brand, so is Hubbell).

Free & Paid Resources:
(free at the time this book was put together, anyway)

- ActorTrade app for cell phones. A free way for actors around the world to connect and help each other learn their lines.

- Actors Access (www.actorsaccess.com) allows actors to post their profile and search casting notices for free. (The paid version, by the way, is well worth the $68/year because you are able to post more, and download sides for free.)

- IMDb (www.IMDb.com) provides invaluable information on actors and films, all for free. There are reasons why the paid IMDb PRO version (www.pro.imdb,com) is worth it, too, but start with the free and be thankful for such a font of information.

- Celtx (www.celtx.com) is often available free to students. There is a paid version, too. Celtx is software that helps with writing screenplays, in the correct formats, and also helps schedule and organize a production to get ready for filming.

- Final Draft (www.finaldraft.com) is my favorite screenwriting software. As of the time this book was written, I am using Final Draft Version 11 for my own writing, and Celtx for a script doctor job I am collaborating on; I much prefer the layout and ease of use of Final Draft. It is, to me, well worth the money.

- Looking to edit video? Davinci Resolve is a FREE download from www.blackmagicdesign.com and it's quickly becoming an industry standard for professionals and amateurs alike. There is a paid version, but it seems that the free version is essentially everything you need, even to edit full Hollywood-style feature films.

- Headshots in Florida: me! Check out my portfolio on www.nauticproductions.com.

- Headshots in New York or Los Angeles: Peter Hurley. See his work on www.peterhurley.com.

- Mass printing of headshots: the best I've found is www.printheadshots.com.

- Loads of free information for actors (like resume samples, monologues, and acting tips) at www.ace-your-audition.com)!

- www.zoetrope.com is a great site for getting other writers to review and comment, for free, on your writings. It's also fun.

Sources Used in Researching this Book:

The author acknowledges the following references used in preparation of this text.

Many of these sources were found online, and I cannot assure you that the following links will still function. Where I thought to do some digging, I tried to supply references to published materials. But let's be reasonable and think about this for a moment: this book is not a PhD thesis, it isn't likely to go down in history as an example of great American literature, nor are you, the reader, likely to be much interested in any of the following citations. I've been around enough to know the listing of sources below is most likely of value only to students who hope to convince their teachers that they actually did some research. To you students, I say, "You're welcome."

- Michael Caine Teaches Acting in Film (BBC 1987)
  https://www.youtube.com/watch?v=bZPLVDwEr7Y&feature=youtu.be&fbclid=IwAR0BJh6Xn8U84c7pNGGd8jgpBA6SrsEf6hif57gta6jUtNr3LirRsYIX8eQ

- Stella Adler: Awake and Dream! From PBS "American Masters" Season 4, Episode 2
  https://www.youtube.com/watch?v=4Yo4BLH87YY

- Uta Hagen's Acting Class (HB Studio) https://www.youtube.com/watch?v=RLSkEL3T6JI

- *Directing Feature Films, the Creative Collaboration between Director, Writers and Actors* by Mark W. Travis (Michael Wiese Productions 2002) ISBN-13: 978-0941188432; and interview of Mark W. Travis (Film Courage)
  https://www.youtube.com/watch?v=0OX44gvnjWE

- Wendy Alane Wright https://www.youtube.com/watch?v=T6ScZ5UnnFs

- Quentin Tarantino Writing Masterclass
  https://www.youtube.com/watch?v=fFWODEPd2wg

- *Set Etiquette; An Actor's Guide to Hitting Your Mark* by DL Phelps (Firehorse Entertainment 2017) ISBN-13: 978-1548672539

- Darious Britt vlogging on YouTube as D4Darious, with such titles as "How to Shoot a No-Budget Film" http://www.imdb.com/name/nm3950093/?ref_=fn_al_nm_1

- Emmy Nominated Actors Teach You How to Make it in Hollywood (Vanity Fair)
  https://www.youtube.com/watch?v=tSckE656BdQ

- "Actors Nix Union Merger" David K. Li (New York Post)
  https://nypost.com/2003/07/02/actors-nix-union-merger/

- Law Offices of Akua Boyenne Blog, October 4, 2015
  http://www.boyennelaw.com/blog/2015/10/4/why-did-sag-and-aftra-merge

- www.sagaftra.org

- www.blackmagicdesign.com

- www.pro.imdb.com

- *The Headshot – The Secrets to Creating Amazing Headshot Portraits* by Peter Hurley (2016)

- Quentin Tarantino's clapper woman https://www.pajiba.com/videos/tarantinos-foulmouthed-slate-operator-is-todays-funniest-woman.php

- Woody Allen quote https://quoteinvestigator.com/2013/06/10/showing-up/

- Charles Bukowski quote https://goinswriter.com/how-to-overcome-writers-block/

- *Setiquette 101: How to Behave on Set* https://www.youtube.com/watch?v=V9INet83fhA

- *Production Tips: Walkie Talkie Codes & Etiquette on Set* by Caleb Stephens https://www.premiumbeat.com/blog/walkie-talkie-filmmaking-codes-etiquette/

- *Walkie Talkie Lingo Everyone on Set Should Know* by AJ Unitas (2017) https://www.studiobinder.com/blog/walkie-talkie-lingo-everyone-on-set-should-know/

- *Film Set Etiquette You Should Know* https://www.youtube.com/watch?v=LxWFNb6hWzE

- Matthew Luhn's twitter feed Story Circle for Incredibles https://twitter.com/matthewluhn/status/1030106519763701760

- Scott Myers' blog *Go into the Story* "Dan Harmon, The Hero's Journey, and the Circle Theory of Story" (May 10, 2018) https://gointothestory.blcklst.com/dan-harmon-the-heros-journey-and-the-circle-theory-of-story-b64bb77d6976

- *Of course Shakespeare stole from others: Week in Books column* Independent (February 4, 2016) https://www.independent.co.uk/arts-entertainment/of-course-shakespeare-stole-from-others-week-in-books-column-a6852976.html

- *Write Screenplays that Sell: the Ackerman Way, 15th Anniversary Edition* by Hal Ackerman (Tallfellow Press 2017) ISBN: 978-1-931290-65-4

- *This is How 99% of Writers Tell a Story - Jill Chamberlain* (Film Courage July 22, 2019) https://www.youtube.com/watch?v=8aprQXvWRXU

- *On Film Directing* by David Mamet

- *How Quentin Tarantino Keeps You Hooked – Directing Styles Explained* video posted on YouTube (StudionBinder July 22, 2019) https://www.youtube.com/watch?v=NFiy-1DxJqs

- *Why is David Fincher a Genius? – Directing Styles Explained* video posted on YouTube (StudioBinder July 8, 2019) https://www.youtube.com/watch?v=F3ZSX3D1dUI

- *Al Pacino Breaks Down How He Became Jimmy Hoffa in the Irishman* posted on YouTube (Variety October 1, 2019) https://www.youtube.com/watch?v=O2KgrVf_1zQ&fbclid=IwAR2SphT-IDcR-fXwQgLvs4HZ_7_GUYLNfL81-_8NViHW0MvMrFBm6hURRS8

- *Speak for Success: 10 Fast & Effective Ways to Overcome Stage Fright* by Gary Genard (the Genard Method blog, June 19, 2016) https://www.genardmethod.com/blog/10-fast-and-effective-ways-to-overcome-stage-fright

- Website for the Producers Guild of America: www.producersguild.org

- *What Does a Producer Do: the Various Types of Producers in Film & TV* (Studio Binder, March 7, 2019) https://www.studiobinder.com/blog/what-does-a-producer-do/

- *Strengths Finder 2.0* by Tom Rath (Gallup Press 2007) ISBN: 978-59562-015-6

- *A Near-Complete History of Movies and TV Shows Shot on Smartphones* by Daniel Bean (Observer March 29, 2019) https://observer.com/2019/03/smartphone-filmmaking-movies-tv-music-videos-shot-camera-phones/

- *How Much Everyone Working on a $200 Million Movie Earns* (Vanity Fair June 7, 2016) https://www.youtube.com/watch?v=cnTF3guz7EQ

- *Feature Film Budget Breakdown* (Parlay Studios February 23, 2017) https://parlaystudios.com/blog/feature-film-budget-breakdown/

- *Job Descriptions on Media Match* (MediaMatch, US Media Industry Magazine October 20, 2019) https://www.media-match.com/usa/media/jobtypes/job-descriptions.php

- *Movies and Film: the Job Descriptions* (Infoplease, online October 20, 2019) https://www.infoplease.com/features/movies-tv-and-music/movies-and-film-job-descriptions

- *15 Essential Camera Shots, Angles and Movements in Filmmaking* (Wolfcrow September 12, 2017) https://www.youtube.com/watch?v=7y0ouVBcogU

- *Microphone Types: How to Choose the Right Mic for Your Sound* (LANDR blog April 1, 2019) https://blog.landr.com/microphone-types/

- *10 Reasons Not to Go to Film School and Is Film School Worth It?* By Ryan Koo (No Film School August 5, 2015) https://nofilmschool.com/2014/11/10-reasons-not-to-go-film-school-practical-guide-impractical-decision-jason-b-kohl

- *3 of the Best Quotes About Filmmaking* (Film Crux January 7, 2019) https://www.filmcrux.com/blog/best-filmmaking-quotes

- *Film School: A Practical Guide to an Impractical Decision* by Jason B. Kohl (Routledge July 16, 2015) ISBN-13: 978-1138804258 ISBN-10: 1138804258

- James Cameron quote (BrainyQuote) https://www.brainyquote.com/quotes/james_cameron_360513

- *Christopher McQuarrie's Advice? Stop Trying to Break In and Make Something* (No Film School October 23, 2019) https://nofilmschool.com/christopher-mcquarrie-twitter-writing-advice?fbclid=IwAR2EbUTG3_a0aIOyN7xHrT6Gnwe_EUxsAIlHJNRb1imz-xBzhF8Ig_f4jfk

- John Malkovich quote (BrainyQuote) https://www.brainyquote.com/quotes/john_malkovich_319077?src=t_producer

Recommended Reading:

- *Michael Caine – Acting in Film: An Actor's Take on Movie Making (The Applause Acting Series) Revised Expanded Edition* by Michael Caine (2000)

- *Screenplay – The Foundations of Screenwriting: A step-by-Step Guide from Concept to Finished Script, Expanded Edition* by Syd Field (1982)

- *From Agent to Actor – An Unsentimental Educations or What the Other Half Knows* by Edgar Small (1991)

- *Writing Television Sitcoms* by Evan S. Smith (1999)

- *Dealmaking in the Film & Television Industry – From Negotiations to Final Contracts* by Mark Litwak (1994)

- *Contracts for the Film & Television Industry* by Mark Litwak (1994)

- *275 Acting Games: Connected – A Comprehensive Workbook of Theatre Games for Developing Acting Skills* by Gavin Levy (2010)

- *Myth and the Movies – Discovering the Mythic Structure of 50 Unforgettable Films* by Stuart Voytilla (1999)

- *The Headshot – The Secrets to Creating Amazing Headshot Portraits* by Peter Hurley (2016)

Acknowledgements

My sincerest thanks to all who helped me with this book, many of whom had no idea they were doing so but offered "advice" just by doing their thing so well. I learned by watching so many people, listening carefully to every word offered. Thanks, too, to the thousands who post comments or even videos on Facebook, YouTube, and other sites – you bloggers and vloggers have moved our entire world closer to the Star Trek dystopian future of free and universal knowledge.

Specific thanks are indeed due to some very helpful industry people:

Mark Perfetti for sharing the contents of his sound bag. Mark is a true pro Sound Mixer, generally working in Florida, unless traveling on larger productions. Need a great sound guy? Email him at soundmixermark@gmail.com.

Jennifer Soulages for her insider's look at being a professional costume designer. She also proved to be a decent writer! Jennifer is LA-based, and travels the world. Best way to contact her is through IMDb.

Who is this author?

Readers may ask, What makes this author qualified to write this book? Well, that is a good question. But actually, I'm tempted to answer, Who the hell cares who wrote it? I mean, it's not offered as an example of good literature, is it? It's not going to be the subject of any university lit class. It's not like you can expect this bloke to turn a phrase worthy of Shakespeare. This isn't a gourmet meal divinely matched with a superb cabernet; it's much more of a ham-and-cheese sub and beer. What you need is good knowledge, not pretty prose.

My mom says I'm special … but I guess that's what they all say.

So why me? Well, I'm one of you. Presuming, of course, that you are one of the countless hopefuls trying to get a leg up in the world, and not already a Tom Cruise, Lilly Tomlin, Robert DeNiro, Emma Thompson, or Emily Blunt. (If you are, Well done, you! Ring me up, eh?)

Honestly, people already at the top levels of success in the Entertainment World are far too busy to bother with reading this book. They are also far too busy to write it. And if they did, they'd feel so entitled by their own success to totally forgo doing any research, and what you'd get would be just their own personal opinions, or fanciful memories from days gone by. Even if they did research, they'd feel so high on themselves that they'd constantly tell you the way they did it was best. Anyway, don't hold your breath; they did not write a helpful guide. And to my knowledge, they aren't writing.

Fortunately for you readers, this book is not just personal opinions, but instead the result of thousands of hours of research, experience, review, and analysis. Don't take my word alone for any of this stuff. This book is a collection of advice from all sorts of sources (many of which are listed in the Appendix). I encourage you to use this book as a starting point, and to research further for yourself.

For example, here is a brief summary of the types of things I've done to collect information on filmmaking:

- <u>Research</u> – 1,000s of hours went into collecting information, and then 1,000s of more hours in writing, organizing, re-organizing, editing, fact-checking ….

- <u>Education</u> – Theatre degree from UCSD, which included training under luminaries like Eric Christmas and Luther James, in Arthur Wagner's theatre department.

- <u>Volunteering</u> – multiple film festivals, student films, community theatres, friends' productions – it is NEVER a waste of time to help someone, and I can't possibly over exaggerate the value of meeting people.

- <u>Working backstage</u> – La Jolla Playhouse, Escondido Playhouse, and various others, set design and construction, lighting design, hang and focus, fly rail, light / sound board op, stage managing, directing, etc.

- <u>Working on film sets</u> – professional and amateur productions, paid and non-paid, union and non-union, as writer, as 1st AD, as script doctor, as 2nd 2nd Assistant Cameraman, as DP, as a PA, as sound engineer, as boom operator – one learns by doing!

- <u>Meetings</u> – countless, endless! Networking, Meetups, Film Societies, Writers Groups, etc. – in Los Angeles, Chicago, Orlando, Tampa … everywhere.

- <u>Writing</u> – my own films and plays, and as Script Doctor on the screenplays of others.

- <u>Acting</u> – stage and film: as a lead, as a supporting actor, as an extra, as background – take every opportunity you can find to get near, behind, or in front of a camera or audience.

- <u>Directing</u> – stage and film.

- <u>Filmmaking</u> – creating my own short films, submitting them on the film festival circuits.

- <u>Producing</u> – Executive Producer on a documentary project with potential reality series spin off hopes

I'm a provocative dick

Shakespeare wrote, "To thine own self, be true!"

I've used swear words in this book. I did that for a good reason. If you are disturbed by people swearing, then put bluntly: you are not ready for the Entertainment World. Sorry. I'm being blunt, perhaps some may say even harsh, but if you are serious about cooking, you have to be tough enough to stand the heat in the kitchen.

Ever check your personality through a standardized test? I did – but only when I was forced to do so. (I would never submit myself to psychological testing unless forced, because of the risk that I'd find out I might be as crazy as I feel some days.) Back when I had an office job as a corporate attorney, one of our HR managers came up with the idea that our entire leadership team would somehow become more efficient workers, if only we knew each other's personality ratings. Believe me, after more than 5 years seeing my coworkers every day, I already knew them, and they me, but oh well, HR said we had to do it.

On the Myers-Briggs personality assessment, I am an "ENTP" – more fully described as:

> "Inventive, clever, and enthusiastic, you are always on the lookout for new possibilities and problems to <u>stimulate and challenge</u> your inner world of ideas. You are curious in regard to everything that is new and you seldom feel at ease with the status quo. You have a great need for <u>intellectual novelty</u>, and from time to time you may even challenge people or organizations just to squeeze some new idea out of them. You tend to have a love of discussions and verbal sparring, and in a discussion, you may follow an argument to its most extreme conclusion. In such cases you may even be suspected of being <u>provocative</u> for the sake of it. When a truly new idea manages to take hold of your imagination, you are quick to see how that idea could be turned into a project in the real world. You have a great enthusiasm for such projects. The problem is that you have such a vivid imagination that you may sometimes <u>start more projects than it is humanly possible to finish</u>."

I must admit, that's a better description of me than I get from reading about my Zodiac sign (Libra), sitting for Tarot Card readings, or listening to girlfriends read the bumps on my scalp.

But who needs standardized psychology tests, when we all have real life sounding boards as handy as the people around us? For example, I recently worked as a 1st AD on a film where the production manager was a strident harpy from New Jersey. During filming, I had to pull her aside and talk to her privately about how nasty she was being to other crew members; thankfully, she agreed with me, and she was able to tone her behavior down. A few days later she and I were at dinner with the director and a number of others, when to my surprise she brought up my private counseling. When she complained that I had called her "nasty", to defuse an awkward situation I asked her what single word she thought would best describe me. She didn't hesitate. "Dick!" she screamed, in pure delight.

Well, shit. So apparently, I am a provocative dick who's constantly starting more projects than he can finish. How's that for describing a filmmaker, huh? I think I chose the right calling. True to mine own self.

Are you a dick? Are you provocative? Do you start more projects than you are likely to ever finish? You don't have to be any of these things, since (fortunately, for you) you get to find and chart your own way in this existence we call life.

About the Author:

On set of "*The Mentor*" / Photo by Anth Wareham

Brent "Nautic" Von Horn is a Florida filmmaker, bitten by the acting bug at age 16 due to a chance meeting on a San Diego movie set. Brent found himself sitting in the shade under some pine trees, having the most fascinating conversation with an old man breathing from an oxygen tank. The spirit, wit and charm of that old man made a lasting impact and helped Brent find the nerve to follow his heart and his dreams. It was many years later before he learned the old man was none other than legendary director John Huston.

Although an Iowa farm boy as a child, Brent grew up in San Diego, acting and singing in local theatre stage productions such as *Oklahoma* and *Camelot*. In college at UCSD, he helped build the professional La Jolla Playhouse theatre, and worked in several behind the stage capacities there (including light design, hang and focus, and board op; fly rail; set construction and strike; and general electrician duties), while earning a Theatre degree.

In Los Angeles, Brent worked for Paragon Arts on a film starring Cindy Williams, laying dolly track as an assistant cameraman. Brent later returned to Los Angeles as an Entertainment Attorney, with such clients as Mattel Toys (trademark licensing) and Richard Moll ("Bull" from tv's Night Court).

Nautic is indeed Brent's middle name, although few believe it. He goes by "Nautic Von Horn" on IMDb. Those who know him only as Nautic are surprised to discover his first name is Brent. Schizophrenic? Brent says, "Maybe", but Nautic says not.

Nautic is an attorney, writer, director, actor, cameraman, grip, and also a professional headshot photographer; his portfolio of photography work can be seen on his site www.nauticproductions.com.

At the time this book was begun, Nautic worked as 1st AD on a feature film in Florida, while developing 3 pilot concepts and in pre-production on another 5 films.

In his own words, Nautic says:

"Life" pulled me away from theatre. In high school and college years, I loved the theatre, everything about it. Summer stock, musicals, school plays. I ditched my med school plans and graduated with a theatre degree, worked in almost every professional and community theatre in San Diego, then moved to LA for a movie spot as "assistant assistant cameraman (which meant I laid a lot of dolly track). I turned my love of photography into a headshot business, back when actors needed black and white 8x10s. I went to law school, and returned to LA to be an entertainment attorney, breaking in with clients such as Mattel Toys and Richard Moll (you remember Bull from *Night Court*?) … but then … I let life get in the way of my dreams.

For many long years I did nothing in the Entertainment World. I was employed as a corporate attorney, married, divorced, raised my children as a single father. Then, I finally emerged from my muggle cocoon -- though whether as a butterfly or moth is questionable. I started writing again (I have always considered myself first and foremost a "writer") then built a photography studio to resurrect my headshot business, made short films that got accepted into film festivals, and began working again on feature film sets.

But most importantly, I reinvented myself by reaching out to vast networks of independent and professional filmmakers, and all those who wanted to be part of filmmaking, whether acting or technical. I realized my story isn't that different from those of others. We all go through periods of creativity and … whatever the opposite of creativity is: Depression? Sluggishness? Fear? Distraction?

I love a quote from Robin Williams, so much so that I will repeat it here: "You're only given a little spark of madness. You mustn't lose it." I lost mine, when I was taught to be sensible, but I got it back.

Comments on this book may be sent to the author via email at nauticproductions@yahoo.com No response is guaranteed, given that my mad "plate spinning" schedule could see me busy on totally different projects just about anywhere in the world, but then again I welcome your comments and may use them in the next update of this work.

www.ingramcontent.com/pod-product-compliance
Lightning Source LLC
Chambersburg PA
CBHW080606090426
42735CB00017B/3345